# Bloom's Modern Critical Interpretations

*Bloom's Modern Critical Interpretations*

Chinua Achebe's
*Things Fall Apart*
*New Edition*

*Edited and with an introduction by*
Harold Bloom
Sterling Professor of the Humanities
Yale University

BLOOM'S
LITERARY CRITICISM
*An imprint of Infobase Publishing*

**Bloom's Modern Critical Interpretations:**
**Chinua Achebe's *Things Fall Apart*—New Edition**

Copyright © 2010 by Infobase Publishing
Introduction © 2010 by Harold Bloom

Bloom's Literary Criticism
An imprint of Infobase Publishing
132 West 31st Street
New York NY 10001

**Library of Congress Cataloging-in-Publication Data**

Chinua Achebe's *Things Fall Apart* / edited and with an introduction by Harold Bloom. —New ed.
 p. cm.—(Bloom's Modern Critical Interpretations)
Includes bibliographical references and index.
ISBN 978-1-60413-581-7 ((hardcover: alk. paper): alk. paper) 1. Achebe, Chinua. *Things Fall Apart.* 2. Igbo (African people) in literature. 3. Nigeria—In literature. I. Bloom, Harold.

PR9387.9.A3T523965 2009
823'.914—dc22                    2009020349

Bloom's Literary Criticism books are available at special discounts when purchased in bulk quantities for businesses, associations, institutions, or sales promotions. Please call our Special Sales Department in New York at (212) 967-8800 or (800) 322-8755.

You can find Bloom's Literary Criticism on the World Wide Web at
http://www.chelseahouse.com.

Cover design by Ben Peterson
Composition by Bruccoli Clark Layman
Cover printed by Yurchak Printing, Landisville, Pa.
Book printed and bound by Yurchak Printing, Landisville, Pa.
Printed in the United States of America

This book is printed on acid-free paper.

All links and Web addresses were checked and verified to be correct at the time of publication. Because of the dynamic nature of the Web, some addresses and links may have changed since publication and may no longer be valid.

# Contents

Making Use of the Past in *Things Fall Apart*        115
    *Oliver Lovesey*

The Depiction of Masculinity
    in Classic Nigerian Literature        141
    *Frank Salamone*

Problematizing Polygyny in the Historical
    Novels of Chinua Achebe: The Role
    of the Western Feminist Scholar        153
    *Andrea Powell Wolfe*

The Possibilities and Pitfalls of Ethnographic Readings:
    Narrative Complexity in *Things Fall Apart*        177
    *Carey Snyder*

# Editor's Note

My introduction prophesies canonical survival for *Things Fall Apart*, since its eloquence, compassion, and loving insight surpass the "postcolonial" academic ideology that currently overvalues Achebe's best book and founds its judgments on political grounds alone. Some of the essays necessarily included here seem to me to praise *Things Fall Apart* for the wrong reasons.

Kwadwo Osei-Nyame relates the cultural significance found in the novel, after which D. N. Mkhize describes the complexity of translating *Things Fall Apart* into Zulu, and then Patrick C. Nnoromele illustrates the condition of Achebe's hero.

Ravit Reichman sees British law in Africa as an imposition and a fiction, while Joseph R. Slaughter invokes the inevitable Franz Fanon to comment on the phenomenon of silence in *Things Fall Apart*. Then Mac Fenwick sees irony as a major resource for postcolonial writing.

In a comprehensive and useful essay, Oliver Lovesey meditates upon the relation between history and fiction in Achebe, while Frank Salamone contributes an informative account of the representation of masculinity in Nigerian literature.

Andrea Powell Wolfe offers a feminist critique of Nigerian marriage customs, after which Carey Snyder refreshingly considers some of the limitations of ethnography when confronted by Achebe's mastery of narrative techniques.

# *Introduction*

## CHINUA ACHEBE'S *THINGS FALL APART*

T*hings Fall Apart* is a historical novel, set in the British colony of Nigeria at about the turn from the nineteenth into the twentieth century. Since Chinua Achebe was born in 1930, he goes back a full generation, to the Nigeria of his parents. The story's famous opening establishes a characteristic tonality: simplification through intensity (a Yeatsian formula):

> Okonkwo was well known throughout the nine villages and even beyond. His fame rested on solid personal achievements. As a young man of eighteen he had brought honor to his village by throwing Amalinze the Cat. Amalinze was the great wrestler who for seven years was unbeaten, from Umuofia to Mbaino. He was called the Cat because his back would never touch the earth. It was this man that Okonkwo threw in a fight which the old men agreed was one of the fiercest since the founder of their town engaged a spirit of the wild for seven days and seven nights.
>
> The drums beat and the flutes sang and the spectators held their breath. Amalinze was a wily craftsman, but Okonkwo was as slippery as a fish in water. Every nerve and every muscle stood out on their arms, on their backs and their thighs, and one almost heard them stretching to breaking point. In the end Okonkwo threw the Cat.

Now in early middle age, Okonkwo is an angry man, a victim of his own impatient temperament, and of his sense that he had a bad father. His quite likable father was a failure, in debt to everyone, and Okonkwo himself is enormously successful, driven by the fear that he also might fail, that he might be mistaken for his father. It would not be excessive to regard Okonkwo as a brutal person, judged pragmatically, but that would be misleading: he is not brutal by nature, but only by his compulsion *not* to repeat his father's life. I may be a little premature in ruling the critics (one or two excepted) reprinted here out of court, but I submit that Okonkwo's apparent tragedy is universal, despite its Nigerian circumstancing. It is—and this is Achebe's strength—a universal sorrow, and therefore can only be secondarily illuminated by all the ordinances of Multiculturalism, African consciousness-raising, and new-mode canonizers. This is a splendidly traditional book, Oedipal and proverbial, and owes nothing to the Four Horsemen of Resentment: Fanon, Foucault, Derrida, and Lacan. It is a timeless book: if the British Colonial regime had not driven Okonkwo to self-slaughter, then his own people would have done the job. But that, I would submit, most unfashionably, is the aesthetic value and spiritual meaning of *Things Fall Apart*. Okonkwo is an Ibo, and Achebe writes of what he knows. And yet Okonkwo could be a North American, a Spaniard, a Sicilian, an Eskimo. The end would be the same: he would kill and then take his own life.

I am aware that such a judgment would be repudiated by all of the essayists collected in this volume, but *Things Fall Apart* will survive its ideological admirers. Its firmly controlled prose, profound compassion, and loving insight into its people will not wear out. Whether the fate of Okonkwo constitutes authentic *literary* tragedy, I am uncertain. He returns, after a seven-year exile, to his own clan, and is fundamentally unchanged, but British supremacy has changed his people, particularly by conversion to Christianity. Grieved, the returning warrior mourns for his lost world, and then rejoices in the destruction of the Christian church. Humiliated by ill-treatment from the British regime's Ibo messengers, Okonkwo despairs of the clan's will to rise up against the British, and angrily beheads the most abusive of the messengers. The act is unreflecting, and inevitable, given Okonkwo's impulsive nature. Is it, or the hero's subsequent suicide, tragic?

You can argue that the Oedipus of Sophocles is also overdetermined by his nature, so that his killing of his father at the crossroads is not primarily an act of the will. And yet Oedipus earns tragic stature by his unrelenting drive for the truth, his refusal to let anything block him from full knowledge. To be victimized by a blend of temperament and circumstance is also the situation of Okonkwo. Yet what destroys him is his inability to accept change. Since the change is ignoble, the tragic argument would be that the clan must fight, though pragmatically that would mean suicide for the community. Okonkwo, as the last warrior, hangs himself because there is no way out of his dilemma. He is not an intellectual quester, like Oedipus, and there is no enigma for him to solve.

It always hurts me, rereading the book, that Achebe cannot allow Okonkwo a heroic death. But aesthetically, that is another mark of Achebe's literary tack. There is no one to fight alongside Okonkwo; he ends as isolated as Shakespeare's Coriolanus. If *Coriolanus* is a tragedy, then so is *Things Fall Apart*. Okonkwo, like the Roman hero, is essentially a solitary, and at heart a perpetual child. His tragedy stands apart from the condition of his people, even though it is generated by their pragmatic refusal of heroic death. Their refusal grants him only his final offence against the earth, and denies him an Ibo burial. This may not be tragedy, but there is heroic pathos in it, as there is in the terrible death of Coriolanus, as he cries out for the Volscians to destroy him. Achebe's motto is from Yeats, but it could also have been from Shakespeare's Volumnia, the terrible mother of Coriolanus:

Anger's my meat. I sup upon myself
And so shall starve with feeding.

KWADWO OSEI-NYAME

# Chinua Achebe Writing Culture: Representations of Gender and Tradition in Things Fall Apart

Wherever something stands,
there something else will stand.
—Igbo saying

While Achebe's early novels have been popularly received for their representation of an early African nationalist tradition that repudiates imperialist and colonialist ideology, his counter-narratives have only been narrowly discussed for their theoretical speculation on cultural and ideological production as a mode of resistance *within* the nationalist tradition that the texts so evidently celebrate. My epigraph not only recognizes that the definition of "tradition" in Achebe's work hinges upon ideological conflict, it comments also on the varying forms of consciousness that arise within discourses of self-definition within Igbo traditional culture. Moreover, it communicates the idea of complex rather than simple relationships between individuals and groups in the world of Achebe's "fictional" Igbo communities.

This essay intends an appropriation of Bakhtin's notion of "heteroglossia" and dialogism in its exploration of some concerns relevant to the question of the representation of ideology in *Things Fall Apart*. Bakhtin's notion of dialogism views narrative discourses as forms of social exchange that

*Research in African Literatures,* Volume 30, Number 2 (Summer 1999): pp. 148–164. Copyright © 1999 The Indiana University Press.

5

locate "the very basis" of individual and social "behaviour" within conflicting worldviews and "determine the very bases" of "ideological interrelations" in a manner similar to that found in Achebe's narrative. Novelistic discourse thus performs "no longer as [mere] information, directions, rules, models," but enables us to locate dialogue in its more immediate ideological and political context (342). Hayden White implies something of this immediacy of context when he suggests distinguishing between "a discourse that openly adopts a perspective that looks out on the world and reports it" and one that "make[s] the world speak itself and speak itself as a story" (2).

Writing stories that speak for themselves is central to Achebe's novelistic agenda. In a famous early essay, he wrote: "I would be quite satisfied if my novels . . . did no more than teach my readers that their past . . . was not one long night of savagery from which the first Europeans acting on God's behalf delivered them" ("Morning Yet" 45). Representing an African worldview through narratives that speak for themselves meant that Achebe would draw upon Igbo oral traditions to narrate the stories of his communities, while bearing in mind Richard Bauman's exhortations that in utilizing oral traditions to engage the "canons of elite" Western literary "traditions and texts," oral narrative must not be taken merely to be "the reflection of culture" or "the cognitive arena for sorting out the logic of cultural codes" in historical writing: instead, oral narratives must be utilized "contextually and ethnographically, in order to discover the individual, social and cultural factors that give it shape and meaning" (2).

Challenging and displacing the narratives of colonialist writers like Joyce Cary and Joseph Conrad meant for Achebe the appropriation of ethnographic modes of representation to prove that the communities of his African past were neither "primitive" nor "without history" (Clifford 10). James Clifford, borrowing from Bakhtin, argues that since culture is not "a unified corpus of symbols and meanings that can be definitively interpreted," ethnographic representation must incorporate a narratological dialogism that reveals culture's "contested, temporal, and emergent" nature (19). As George Marcus also contends, this dialogical approach to ethnographic representation must be borne in mind by both "outsiders" like Conrad and Cary writing about the Other and "insiders" like Achebe writing about themselves and their own cultures.[1] Henrietta Moore, among anthropologists welcoming the new dialogical ethnography of Clifford and others, agrees with them on the use of "new forms of writing such as those predicated on dialogue, intertextuality and heteroglossia to unmask and displace the unitary authority" of the "author" (107).

*Things Fall Apart*'s famous ending describes the District Commissioner's yearning to write the story of his colonized natives as a challenging ethnographic project in a moment of the colonial encounter in Africa. Having just witnessed the death of Okonkwo, one of the greatest men of Umuofia, the Commissioner fabricates an imperialist narrative and his colonial imagination prefigures the narration of the "interesting" (149) story

> [o]f this man who had killed a messenger and hanged himself. . . . One could almost write a whole chapter on him. Perhaps not a whole chapter but a reasonable paragraph, at any rate. There was so much else to include, and one must be firm in cutting out details. (149–150)

His story is contemplated as an extension of the civilizational enterprise of pacifying his "primitive" African "tribes" (150). However, the passion the Commissioner will devote to his account is merely a seductive desire for storytelling and a "function of [his own] desires, purposes, and constraints" (Chambers 4). His narrative is already displaced as his "interesting" story has already been anticipated by the skepticism of Achebe's "insider" narrative. For Achebe has already written back to contest the "reasonable" paragraphing of history by writers like Cary and Johnson, "outsiders" who devoted their accounts to similar ambitious projects as the Commissioner's. The Commissioner's potentially seductive story about one of the most tragic events in his administration is an almost impossible future project. His highly controversial and abrupt "reasonable paragraph" has already found adequate representation and space in the entire exchanges among Umuofians and between Umuofia and the Christian missionaries and the colonial government in Achebe's narrative.

As Chambers suggests further, since there is a direct "relationship between storytelling and the art of government," we must contextualize "storytelling as an event that *presupposes* a situation and mobilizes social relationships so as to give it a performative force" (4–5; emphasis added). Achebe, following Fanon, locates Igbo societies in the liminal space of history in which they grapple with the imperialist endeavors of colonial power by telling Bernth Lindfors in an interview that it is in "that 'zone of occult instability' where the people dwell" that their regenerative powers "are most potent" ("Achebe on Commitment" 16). The complicated occult zone of African and colonialist history and the representation of the ideologically "real" and "fictional" dimensions of that zone is encapsulated in the Commissioner's effort both to represent "reality" and to "censor" it.

This near appropriation of a totalizing narrative of culture finds another form of expression in the tradition and politics of *Things Fall Apart*. The story re-enacts phases of the precolonial and colonial traditional order of African history by featuring the beginnings of some significant moments of nationalist ideological crises in the communities of Umuofia and Mbanta.

Masculine traditions operate as forms of consciousness that act foremostly to legitimize specific ideals and values and to distribute and restrict authority within Umuofia, one of the most powerful of Igbo communities. Umuofia is not only "feared by all its neighbours," but is also "powerful in war and magic" (8). Achebe relates the reasons behind individual and communal crises in a society in which war heroes, titled and wealthy subjects, and other celebrated figures are dominantly male.

Umuofia is already weakened by internal cleavages and it is only when the processes of cultural breakdown intensify with the arrival of the white colonizers that Obierika, one of the greatest men in the society, affirms how the "clan can no longer act like one" and has "fallen apart" (127). The story of Okonkwo and Umuofia at the threshold of historical transition may be read in the first instance as the narration of an epic African masculine nationalist tradition.[2] Achebe's text links and identifies power and authority with masculinity. Umuofia's masculine traditions are heralded and celebrated and the representation of masculine ideology is progressively played out mainly through the representation of the legendary Okonkwo and his obsessive pursuit of the fulfilment of personal power and recognition within the clan. As a young man, Okonkwo "invents" himself and consolidates his position within the clan by overthrowing Amalinze the Cat. With this feat, "Okonkwo's fame had grown like a bush-fire in the harmattan" (3). Okonkwo's victorious feat in the famous wrestling match that begins the story of Umuofia is also one that "the old men" (3) agreed was one of the most laudable exploits "since the founder of their town engaged a spirit of the wild for seven days and seven nights" (3). The legitimation of male-centered traditions in Umuofia resonates in many ways with Raymond Williams's view that dominant traditions often aspire to "an active and continuous selection and reselection" and "a projected reality, with which we have to come to terms on its terms, even though those terms are always and must be the valuations, the selections and omissions" of "men" (16).

From a very early age, Okonkwo is obsessed with championing his masculinity

> [l]est he should be found to resemble his father. Even as a little boy he had resented his father's failure and weakness, and even now he still remembered how he had suffered when a playmate had told him that his father was an *agbala,* that was how Okonkwo first came to know that *agbala* was not only another name for a woman, it could also mean a man who had taken no title. And so Okonkwo was ruled by one passion—to hate everything that his father Unoka had loved. One of those things was gentleness and another was idleness. (10)

Okonkwo's masculinity becomes a defensive resource and his adherence to a masculine philosophy will thenceforth order his world. In articulating his identity and justifying his actions, he cultivates his masculinity as a defense of personal honor in the face of potentially overwhelming circumstances in an antagonistic universe. The obsession with masculinity is an essential shield marked also by the excessive indulgences expressed in Okonkwo's outrageous assertiveness and his intense repudiation of certain subjective values such as "gentleness" and "idleness." In Okonkwo's world, the ignominious predicament of his father, Unoka, simultaneously torments and propels him towards achieving his highest ambitions in life. Okonkwo is in a way led to define himself and to apprehend his world *negatively*. By constructing his identity and embedding his actions in a perverse sense in his rebelliousness against everything that his father Unoka represents, Okonkwo apprehends his world pessimistically. To a considerable degree, then, Okonkwo's "cosmos" is self-made and his identity "depends entirely on its creator [himself] for its configuration" (Olney 4).

Umuofia's acknowledgment of Okonkwo's spectacularly masculine feat exists in potential opposition to other events and achievements. However, Umuofia's selective traditions and Okonkwo's masculinist assertions converge to marginalize the women, *efulefus, osus, agbalas,* and others within the community. Umuofians have a special word for dispositions such as "gentleness" and "idleness": the Igbo word *agbala* is not only another name for women, it also refers to weak and lazy men such as Okonkwo's father, Unoka. In inventing its traditions and linking Okonkwo's feats with them, Umuofia's authoritative discourse consciously omits other representable values and ideals and Okonkwo's own exclusion from his worldview of, among other things, "gentleness" and "idleness," is a position that Umuofia's fabricated traditions sanction.

However, as Derek Wright observes regarding the social order in Umuofia: "Okonkwo's impetuous, aggressive individualism and the belief behind it—that he must wipe out his father's memory by succeeding in everything his father has failed at—are out of harmony with a society which is renowned for its talent for social compromise and which judges a man according to his worth, not that of his father" (78). Further, Wright contends that Okonkwo's "cult of virility, by mistaking the nature of courage and confusing gentleness with weakness, upsets the sexual equilibrium that maintains a delicate balance between male values and female and maternal ones" (78). We can agree with Judith Butler that "limits are always set within the terms of a hegemonic cultural discourse predicated on binary structures" that "distorts what is assumed to be true" about the formation of identity and subjectivity and restricts the "imaginable and realizable gender configurations within culture" (9).

With Williams, too, we can argue that the ideology of culture establishes a "structure of feeling" and the selective tradition of a dominant culture when we trace the modes by which Okonkwo's adherence to certain values and ideals and Umuofia's validation of these values converge to generate the masculine nationalist tradition represented by *Things Fall Apart*. Simon Gikandi has already made very strong points arguing that "ideology as process and critique, rather than product and dogma, is the key to understanding Achebe's narrative strategies" (12). It is important, however, to add that Achebe's story depicts the organization of the Umuofian community and its control of authority within the specific context of a gendered ideology and politics.[3]

Umuofia's dominant traditions exist in tension with what Williams describes as "residual" or oppositional traditions (41). *Things Fall Apart* also exposes the limitations of the system of values that the phallocentric traditions of Umuofia endorse by answering to Chambers's belief that "meaning is not inherent in discourse and its structures, but is contextual, a function of the pragmatic situation in which the discourse occurs" (3). The functioning of language in the narrative also supports Jonathan Culler's observation that "what is involved in narrative is an effect," that "a hierarchical opposition, in which one term is said to be dependent upon another conceived as prior, is in fact a rhetorical or metaphysical imposition and the hierarchy could well be reversed" (183). Language and proverbs in Achebe's narrative provide significantly adjustable orders of interpretation and underscore the view of Umuofians themselves that "[a]mong the Ibo the art of conversation is regarded very highly, and proverbs [and other forms of language] are the palm-oil with which words are eaten" (5). Achebe examines the ways in which language functions in his community and the means through which individuals articulate resistance, exposing especially the flaws within the social order that allow for an ambivalent approach to tradition and culture.

Differing sets of values expose the limits of representation and authority within Umuofia. The language of representation that orders hierarchy and authority within Umuofia initially engenders, as Barthes would argue, a kind of fixed ideological "index" for the regulation and distribution of authority within the social order. However, as Barthes also contends, "signs" and significations might be invoked in place of the restrictive "index" of language to reorder narrative and to enforce the abolition of the "limit, the origin, the basis" and "the prop" of tradition. Signs, then, provide the means to "enter into the limitless process of equivalences" and "representations that nothing will ever stop, orient, fix," or "sanction" (*S/Z* 40).

Umuofia's traditions thus sustain a different order of things and enable diverse modes of self-consciousness and a skeptical relativism that allows individuals to look beyond the rigid hierarchies of a restrictive social order and to redefine their roles and positions within culture. Achebe's essay on *chi* in Igbo cosmology reveals the flexible order of his society:

> Since Igbo people did not construct a rigid and closely argued system of thought to explain the universe . . . anyone seeking an insight into their world must seek it along their own way. ("Morning Yet" 94)

Achebe demonstrates that a selective appeal to "tradition" is wholly feasible within the Igbo worldview. This accommodating spirit of tradition enables individuals to appraise the limitations that are seen to inhere within the traditions of Umuofia, making it possible to identify in Molly Hite's formulation the fact that "in a given society and historical period, changes, emphasis and value can articulate the 'other side' of a culturally mandated story, exposing the limits it inscribes in the process of affirming dominant ideology" (4).

How might we pursue further Barthes's distinction between the stable indices and contradictory signs of narrative? In the story of Umuofia, Barthes's identification of the open-endedness of representation is played out at a level of human interaction where the contest between Williams's "dominant" and "residual" traditions is also staged. A fascinating moment in the narrative has Okoye, one of the most important men of the clan, a titled man, "also a musician" but "not a failure like Unoka" and "a great talker" (5), visit his friend, Unoka, to retrieve a debt owed him. After "skirting" around the subject "for a long time" (5), Okoye finally asks Unoka to pay back the money owed him. Unoka's response draws Okoye's attention to the visual illustration of his debts to different people:

> 'Each group there represents a debt to someone, and each stroke is one hundred cowries. . . . I owe that man a thousand cowries. But he has not come to wake me up in the morning for it. I shall pay you, but not today. Our elders say that the sun will shine on those who stand before it shines on those who kneel under it. I shall pay my big debts first.' (6)

Negotiating his survival while trapped by economic necessity, Unoka, compelled into being resourceful, is also at his most articulate. Unoka's response touches on the general issue of survival within the culture. Achebe seems concerned here with raising the question of survival. As he told Feroza Jussawalla in a recent interview, his narratives define the relationship between storytelling, storytellers, and survival: "It is important that the storyteller tells the story the way he sees it, not the way the emperor wants it to be told"

(81). Unoka's response is most significant for its manipulation of the wisdom implicit in the language of proverbs as a strategy of survival by deferring the debt he owes. Additionally, he questions the hierarchy of eminence and authority that titled men like Okoye and Okonkwo represent within Umuofia. Richard Priebe remarks in reference to the tradition of Umuofia that "proverbs encompass strategies for individual equity that are antithetical to the closed system of prenatal destiny we find in the story" (51).

Unoka operates within the flexible codes of his culture and its definition of reality to question the interpretive forms that order existence. Unoka's reinterpretation and reconstruction of the "real" and the important circumvents the signifying economy of realism of his culture and he finds a way to "invent" a conceptual universe where the redefinition and reinterpretation of reality enable him to emerge momentarily within its traditions as a figure of authority. As Wahneema Lubiano notes about the social order of Umuofia, character is "not a unified and stable identity" but an ability "to renegotiate the terms of someone else's perception of reality or of oneself" (198). The encounter between Okoye and Unoka reveals complex forms of masculinity not necessarily of the order represented by Obierika, Okonkwo, or other great men, and these forms of masculinity are also asserted. Margaret Turner argues persuasively regarding Unoka's importance within the clan as a whole that "Unoka [the musician] is a failure in material terms, but not if his stature is measured on a scale one might think is Achebe's own—ensuring the survival of the culture by recording the deeds of past greatness and lessons for continued living" (34).

Discussing the use of African literature as a mode of restoring value within his traditional society, Achebe observes that "any presence [within his culture] which is ignored, denigrated, denied acknowledgement" may become a "focus for anxiety and disruption" ("African Literature" 3). Although Umuofia's laws, customs, and the proclamations of its oracles communicate coercive impulses, individuals may also renegotiate themselves around the sacrosanct traditional values represented as incontrovertible and which are meant both to ensure the clan's survival and to consolidate its traditions. The story of Obiako, the palm tapper, illustrates further the power of disruption and resistance. Obiako's interesting story is almost self-explanatory:

'Obiako has always been a *strange* one', said Nwakibie. 'I have heard that many years ago when, when his father had not been dead very long, he had gone to consult the oracle. The Oracle said to him, "Your dead father wants you to sacrifice a goat to him." Do you know what he told the Oracle? He said, "Ask my dead father if he ever had a fowl when he was alive." Everybody laughed heartily. . . . (15; emphasis added)

Retaining a stable system of values within Umuofia's traditions is threatened by such personal accounts as Obiako's. Umuofia's consciousness of itself, which it articulates through ancestral veneration, is challenged by such "marginal" stories as Obiako's, which in their rebelliousness are not merely obstructive to the perpetuation of Umuofia's traditions, but appraise the restrictiveness of tradition in ways that men like Okonkwo and wealthy, titled men like Nwakibie cannot comprehend. Implied in Nwakibie's derisive reference to Obiako's "strange" disposition is the insinuation that Obiako's position is of little ideological significance within the respected traditions of the clan. Within the highly ideological and coercive ambience of Umuofia, however, stories like Obiako's are not merely trivially subversive but are of emancipatory significance. Characterizing the ideological crisis within his traditional society uncovers the ambivalences of ideology in narrative and reorients the meaning and import of the relationships between Achebe's "texts" and their reproduction of historical narrative.[4]

Reading the "other side" of Achebe's Igbo-African nationalist tradition means alternating the narrative viewpoint to radically transform the story and its underlying assumptions. As Hite argues, "the coherence of one line of narration rests on the suppression of any number of 'other sides.'" Further, she adds, "alternative versions . . . might give the same sequence of events an entirely different set of emphasis and values" (4). By highlighting themes and characters seen conventionally as peripheral, Achebe's story transgresses the perception of his writing as penetratingly masculinist.[5]

The personal narratives of "marginalized" individuals such as Obiako and Unoka together with those of women correlate the narrative as encapsulating a progressively consolidating framework of resistance and survival. Achebe seems interested in confirming Foucault's interesting observation that "[w]here there is power, there is resistance, and yet, or rather consequently, this resistance is never in a position of exteriority in relation to power" (*History* 95). Following Foucault's hypothesis in *The Order of Things*, Achebe sets his text within a reflexive liminal phase, or "middle region," where culture is "continuous and graduated" and "linked to [a] space constituted anew and at each time by the driving force of time" (xxi). Indeed, Achebe himself proposes an order of things not unrelated to Foucault's: "[A]rt is what I have chosen to call my Middle Passage." He adds further that if art is to be offered as a "celebration of . . . reality," it must involve the "creative potential in all of us" and a demonstration "of the need to exercise this latent energy again and again" ("African Literature" 3).

Achebe's dilemma in finding an appropriately "democratic" means of representing the Igbo nationalist tradition he narrates is reiterated in the following statement made to Raoul Granqvist: "If you look carefully, the women were never really dealing alone with issues pertaining to women, they were dealing with issues pertaining to society" (Granqvist 18). Achebe character-izes Umuofia's women in the joys and tribulations of their motherhood and selects specific moments of their lives to represent some of the most mean-ingful cultural and historical aspects of existence in Igbo communities. Some agonizing moments that members of Okonkwo's household undergo com-municate the complications of existence and reveal how the forces disruptive of life tie Umuofians to rituals and customs central to the traditions of Igbo culture. The stories of Ekwefi, Okonkwo's second wife, and her daughter Ezin-ma are vital to the narrative's enactment of the strategies of survival within Umuofia's world. Ekwefi has a special relationship with Ezinma, "an only child and the centre of her mother's world. Very often it was Ezinma who had decided what food her mother should prepare" (55). The two women partially deny Okonkwo some of the authority he seeks to wield over them by conspir-ing to ensure that Ezinma eats eggs despite Okonkwo's threat to beat Ekwefi if she continues to let Ezinma have the delicacy.

Ezinma is born an *ogbanje* (55), a child who endlessly appears in her mother's womb in a sequence of birth and death and is probably destined to have a short life. Ekwefi's previous "nine children had [all] died in infancy, usually before the age of three" (55) and Ekwefi blames "her own evil *chi* who denied her children" (57). The story links the two women to the importance of custom and ritual to direct attention to the importance of motherhood and childbirth within an Igbo-African framework of historical interpreta-tion. The epic dimensions of the story are registered symbolically but not fully explored in the temporary leadership role that Ezinma holds in the search for her *iyi-uwa* (57), which links her to the spirit world. The *iyi-uwa*, if found, will end Ezinma's *ogbanje* cycle and terminate Ekwefi's suffering.

Significantly, women and children "returning from the stream" (58) and a whole "crowd" (59) of clan members follow Ezinma who, unintimidated by Okonkwo's threatening presence, leads the community on a sort of merry-go-round in the search for her *iyi-uwa*. When Ezinma finally discloses the secret location of the *iyi-uwa*, its retrieval marks the severance of her links with the spirit world and the mutual triumph over death by Ezinma and Ekwefi makes the relationship between them even more special, for under the circumstances of evil destiny with which Ekwefi seems afflicted, mothers are denied the joys of motherhood while children are not allowed the opportunity to grow up.[6] As Grace Okereke argues in her poem on childbirth, "the war of childbirth is the gunfight / of women" (23). Achebe explores further in the *ogbanje* story of Ezinma the importance of human communal struggles within a *gendered* con-text by making the triumph of the two women an affirmation of the strength of their individual *chi*'s. Their survival where Okonkwo does not eventually survive in the clan foregrounds the unwavering dispositions that allow women control over their existential predicaments. Achebe's text, to use Dominick

LaCapra's words, reveals how "human entities" may "rework and at least partially work through . . . in critical [and] transformative fashion" their social
struggles (4). The inappropriateness of the colonial imagination of "primitive"
behavior in traditional Igbo society is exposed by the stress on ritual and custom within traditional culture and the demonstration of the power of narrative
to educate about history in order to refute the idea that traditional Igbo communities were "victims of circumstance(s)" whose politics were "very largely
one of drift" and whose actions were "not controlled by logic" (Basden 9).

An extraordinary episode in the novel has Okonkwo reclining after an
evening meal, while Ekwefi and Ezinma and Okonkwo's other wives and
their children also enjoy an evening of storytelling. Ezinma is about to relate
how "Tortoise and Cat went to wrestle Yams" (71) when Chielo, the priestess
of Agbala, interrupts Okonkwo's household with the message that Agbala,
the deity of the Oracle of the Hills and the Caves, "wanted to see his daughter," Ezinma (72). Okonkwo is severely reprimanded by Chielo for protesting
against Ezinma being taken away and for daring "to speak when a god speaks"
(72). Ekwefi has her own exchanges with Chielo, who is "possessed by the
spirit of her god" (71), while her voice "like a sharp knife cutting through the
night" (71) is "as clear as metal" (72):

'I will come with you too,' Ekwefi said firmly.
'Tufia-a!' the preistess cursed, her voice cracking like the angry
bark of thunder in the dry season.
'How dare you, woman to go before the mighty Agbala of your
own accord? Beware woman lest he strike you in his anger.' (72)

When Chielo finally takes the crying Ezinma away, "a strange and sudden
weakness" (73) descends upon Ekwefi. Ekwefi becomes "a hen whose only
chick has been carried away" (73). Defying the likelihood of retribution
from Agbala and with a curt reply to Okonkwo when he asks where she is
going, Ekwefi pursues Chielo on a circuitous journey from Umuofia to what
turns out to be "Umuachi, the farthest village in the clan" (75) on a night
described also as "full of thick darkness" (73). It is important to recall the
fear that the clan as a whole has of the night and its darkness: "Darkness
held a vague terror for these people, even the bravest among them" (7). The
extremely bold Ekwefi who follows Chielo is deterred neither by the fact
that on several occasions "her eyes were useless in the darkness" (74), nor
that she "hit her left foot against an outcropped root and terror seized her"
(74), nor even by her remembrance of "a dark night like this" (74) when,
returning with her mother from the stream, they "had seen *Ogbu-agali-odu*,
one of those evil essences loosed upon the world by the potent 'medicines'
which the tribe had made in distant past against its enemies but now had

forgotten to control" (74). Ekwefi relives "all the terrors of the night" and even remembers how on that occasion both she and her mother had expected "the sinister light" of the clan's "uncontrolled medicine" to descend on them and "kill them" (74), but she perseveres in following Chielo throughout. We are indeed reminded of the moment when Okonkwo's own wrestling feat that establishes his popularity with the clan is compared to the fight Umuofia's founding father had "with the spirits of the wild" (1).

The journey with Chielo intimates a positive and epic heroic venture in which Ekwefi's bravery accords her an important status. Throughout the whole traumatic journey, Ekwefi's life is endangered and the particular threats for her are intensified by the ever-threatening possibility of encountering the itinerant spirits of the wild and also by the possibility of very severe retribution from Agbala, who as Chielo had warned earlier could "strike" Ekwefi. Bearing in mind the sexual difference and gendered politics of the novel that are articulated especially within the overt masculinist ideological framework that contextualizes the assertions of Okonkwo and the patriarchs of Umuofian society, we must look beyond the surface interpretation of the episode as journey and attempt a theoretical reflection that extends the surface meaning of the Chielo-Ezinma-Ekwefi encounter to locate it as an alternative Igbo nationalist tradition within which we can construct a specifically female-centered paradigm of resistance.

Ekwefi's pursuit of Chielo actually disregards the masculine traditions of the clan, for Chielo is merely the messenger of Agbala, the male deity whom Ekwefi defies. Ekwefi's defiance of Agbala constitutes an important statement on her challenge of Umuofia's sacrosanct masculine traditions. Ekwefi engages in a transgression of Umuofia's traditions and represents what Barbara Babcock describes as a "symbol of negation." As Babcock argues, the transgression of tradition is attained through symbolic "negation" when "the thinking-process frees itself from the limitations of repression and enriches itself" so that its "intellectual function" obtains "a first degree of independence from the results of repression and at the same time from the sway of the pressure principle" of tradition (30).

The epic dimensions of Ekwefi's heroic venture are also best appreciated in terms of the importance of the "journey motif" in traditional African mythology. As Daniel Kunene's retelling of the journey motif in traditional mythological narratives reveals, one of the most significant thematic aspects of these journeys is the dangers courageous mothers experience in the attempt to protect their endangered children.[7] Seen also in the light of Okonkwo's own singular and spectacular defeat of Amalinze the Cat in which Okonkwo's feat is compared to the battle in which the founder of Umuofia "engaged a spirit of the wild for seven days and seven nights" (3), Ekwefi's journey through the darkness in defiance of all the wandering malevolent spirits whose destructive power she somehow evades is of loaded theoretical and ideological significance. The Chielo-Ezinma-Ekwefi encounter touches also on crucial issues of gender and the authority of narrative.

Although Okonkwo's courageous overthrow of Amalinze evokes a manner of association whereby Umuofia associates virtues like heroism and bravery with him, the Ekwefi story also creates processes of reconstruction through which we associate women with heroic values. We may ponder also some interesting questions regarding the particular details and circumstances of Ekwefi's journey. Why, for instance, does Okonkwo not follow Chielo into the "darkness" *immediately* with the same impulsiveness and defiance that mark some of his more audacious actions, but instead allows a "reasonable and manly interval to pass" before going "with his matchet to the shrine where he thought they must be" (80)? Why does Okonkwo resign himself so easily to Ekwefi's decision to follow Chielo *immediately* into the darkness, in spite of the priestess' admonition to Ekwefi that Agbala might "strike [her] . . . in anger" (72), an event that is likely to also affect Okonkwo and possibly his entire household? And why does Okonkwo only begin to feature in the whole scene when both Ekwefi and Ezinma are already out of any substantial danger? In his usual manner of concealing his real thought and feelings, Okonkwo "had felt very anxious but did not show it" (80) when "Ekwefi had followed the priestess" (80). May we not suspect that Okonkwo was less inclined to brave all the odds on this particular occasion?

Definitely one discerns, when Okonkwo finally appears with his machete in hand at the end, that his own masculinity has been both literally and symbolically violated, for he has already been on several futile trips to Chielo's shrine. As Carole Boyce Davies comments regarding the Chielo-Ezinma-Ekwefi episode, Okonkwo's "machete, the symbol of his male aggression, is of no use at all in this context" (247). We might add, though, that the very presence of the machete and the fact that Okonkwo arms himself signify the real threat of danger confronting Ekwefi as she alone braved the darkness. Further, Okonkwo's emasculation is not only foregrounded; his very impotent incursions into the night and the spirit world at the time when both Ezinma and Ekwefi are most endangered prefigure for him a loss of authority and a deeper disillusionment about his position within the clan that he is later on to experience.

Is it not of some significance to the story of Umuofia as a whole that barely a day or two after the Chielo-Ekwefi-Ezinma incident has highlighted Ekwefi's strength of character and at a time when the "spirit(s)" have again "appeared from the underworld" (87), Okonkwo is forced into exile after accidentally shooting the son of the dead Ezeudu at the latter's funeral? May we not read the story of the three women and the displaced Okonkwo with all its insistent re-orderings of significations of gender and authority as being of cardinal importance to Achebe's construction of the contested nature of power and authority within the clan? Foucault's observations on the erosion of authority and identity are instructive here. Foucault argues that in analyzing the move from wholeness to disintegration or from origination to fragmentation, it is no longer a question of establishing the place of an "originating subject" but rather one of identifying the "modes of his functioning"; in particular, it is also a question of establishing and "depriving the subject" of his "role as originator, and of analysing" him "as a variable and complex function of [the] discourse" in which he is implicated? ("Author?" 158).

In reading about the fearless Ekwefi and especially after our familiarity with her struggle with Ezinma in their mutual triumph in the "war" of childbirth, the narrative foregrounds the emasculation of Okonkwo at precisely the point where it constructs alternatively viable significations around the women. Boyce Davies makes the very important observation that "the Chielo-Ezinma episode reads like a suppressed larger story circumscribed" by the focus on "Okonkwo's/man's struggle with and for his people" (247). However, it is important to note also that in a very significant way, the Chielo-Ezinma-Ekwefi episode evidently prefigures the displacement of Okonkwo and to a large degree masculine authority within the clan as a whole.[8]

Other ideologically important questions support Ato Quayson's view of the "potential inherent in Ezinma and Ekwefi's characterization for subverting the patriarchal discourse of the text" (131). Significantly, Ezinma is about to relate to Ekwefi how Tortoise and the Cat "went on to wrestle against Yams" (71) when Chielo interrupts them. A close reading of the unfinished tale in relation to the symbolic value attached to the yam, the most "important" crop within Umuofia, reveals significations associable with Ezinma and Ekwefi and the subversive potential encoded in their characterization.

Okonkwo's attempt at a young age at "fending for his father's house" (16) is made more difficult by the fact that although his "mother and sisters worked hard enough," "they [only] grew women's crops, like coco-yams, beans and cassava" (16). Since "Yam, the king of crops, was a man's crop" (16), the narrative intimates that Okonkwo's mother and his sisters can only make a minimal contribution to their own lives, especially since, as Elizabeth Isichei argues, within the Igbo economy, yam, being of "supreme importance," was "given ritual and symbolic expression in many areas of Igbo life" (8). Women's crops, such as coco-yam, are seemingly of little importance within Umuofia's culture and in its political economy as a whole. Achebe himself, however, furnishes a different account of the importance of women in the economic domain of Igbo society and of the value of putatively *female* crops:

> Men owned the yam, 'the king of crops,' but yam was a monarch
> more visible in metaphor than in reality. In traditional Igbo menu

this crop yam was eaten only once a day, in the afternoon, morning and evening meals were supplied from women's crops, cassava and coco yam etc. ("Myth and Power" 15)

As Gayatri Spivak cautions, identifying the real relationships between "marginality" and "value" within culture is complicated since the symbolic sites of exchange of value within the "socius" of culture often involve affective relations. Spivak argues that "the socius as an *affectively* coded site of exchange and surplus" is where "'marginality'. . . a constantly changing set of representations," becomes "coded in the currency of *equivalences*" of "knowledge" (227; emphases added). In the context of the gender politics of *Things Fall Apart,* meanings become unstable and even the powerful symbolic economy within which yam is privileged is threatened with disruption.

Ezinma's uncompleted fable in which "Yams" are wrestled has the dominance of yam, the symbol of authority and power within Umuofia, already under question. In Barthes's view, the text becomes "a contradiction in terms" and "multiples . . . in its variety and its plurality" (*S/Z* 15). Ezinma's tale supplies a contrastive paradigm for questioning not only Okonkwo's authority but also the masculine traditions of the clan as a whole. Indeed, the multiple configurations of masculine ideology, the authority and supremacy of the laws of the clan, and the importance of *male* gods like Agbala, whose messenger Chielo the courageous Ekwefi pursues on that memorable night and whose authority Ekwefi actually challenges, all have the very *grounds* of their authority under question. Attention to the discourses of folklore and indeed motherlore within Umuofia open up possibilities for renegotiating reality and identity within the clan.

Achebe's folktales form part of the Igbo "ethno-text," or "discursive segments that belong to the vast corpus of African traditional oral material" (Zabus 20). As forms of the "ethno-text," fables, folktales, proverbs, myths, and other forms of indigenous wisdom provide modes of interpretation that discursively engage the order of traditional society and form part of what Foucault in *The Archaeology of Knowledge* has called discursive formations. Characters' ability to reinterpret various discourses empowers them to interpret "each discourse" beyond "something other than what it actually says" (116, 118). In the world of fables, as in the real world of Umuofia, speakers can therefore "embrace a plurality of meanings" (116, 118).

In Umuofia's world, the authoritative discourses of Okonkwo and the patriarchs of Umuofia would not therefore be unchallenged. Indigenous folk wisdom, to borrow an expression from Barthes, would "save the text (and the world) from repetition." Subsequently, as Barthes argues in yet another context, we are led into an endlessly important process of interpretation and reinterpretation where the invincible image of "closed" worlds of meaning are both contestable and transformable. All first readings either of word or of text themselves become indefinite and transgressive. We visualize in Barthes's "social utopia" a complex arena for ideological negotiation where the text provides "not the transparency of social relations" but rather "the space in which no one language has a hold over any other, in which all languages circulate freely" ("From Work" 80).

Ezinma's unfinished tale of "Tortoise and Cat" versus "Yams" encodes significant possibilities for undoing the hierarchies of power and authority within a tradition where masculine authority is supplanted by female insights and indigenous folk wisdom acquires not only subversive and residual but even dominant potential. We are back then to Williams's formulations on dominant and residual and emergent cultures and to Williams's conviction that "we have to recognize the alternative meanings and values, the alternative opinions and attitudes, even some alternative senses of the world, which can be accommodated and tolerated within a particular effective and dominant culture" (39). Achebe's narrative takes Williams's arguments beyond accommodation as it evaluates the crisis of masculine authority within traditional Igbo culture. In commenting on societal politics while masterfully contemplating the limitations of coercive masculine traditions in a society where knowledge of traditional lore and the appropriation of the "ethno-text" facilitate the continual redefinition of roles and statuses, Achebe dramatizes the internal tribulations of the clan.

## Notes

1. See Marcus for a further discussion and also acknowledgment of the limitations of the project of dialogical representation, among other issues.
2. Traore provides a brilliant exploration of the novel as epic in his "Matrical Approaches."
3. Representative studies on Achebe, such as by Innes and Lindfors; Carroll; and Innes have ignored this issue. The most probing analysis of the ideology of gender so far is Quayson's "Realism, Criticism, and the Disguises of Both." See also Jeyifo for a brief but incisive correlation of the politics of gender in *Things Fall Apart* with wider issues of gender criticism in postcolonial African literature.
4. Bennett's "Texts in History" is a fruitful polemic on the ideological determinations of texts in historical narrative.
5. Stratton makes this argument. See esp. her chapter "How Could Things Fall Apart for Whom They Were Not Together?"
6. Okereke's interesting article, "The Birth of Song," compares childbirth in Igbo society and the honor attached to it to the bringing home of human heads in war by men.
7. See Kunene. It makes little difference here that the gender-reversal in Kunene's tales makes the endangered children mostly males.
8. This relates also to the new dispensations stimulated by colonialism such as the rise of a new social class of *efulefus, agbalas, osus,* and those whom the clan has

hitherto marginalized. While the clan as a whole experiences disunity, Okonkwo's personal narrative is also thus only a subtext of the nationalist crisis in Umuofia.

## Works Cited

Achebe, Chinua. "African Literature as Restoration." Petersen and Rutherford 1–18.

———. *Morning Yet on Creation Day*. London: Heinemann, 1975.

———. "Myth and Power: The Hidden Power of Igbo Women." Granqvist 11–23.

———. *Things Fall Apart*. London: Heinemann, 1986.

Babcock, Barbara. Intro. *The Reversible World: Symbolic Inversion in Art and Society*. Ed. Barbara Babcock. Ithaca: Cornell University Press, 1984. 13–36.

Bakhtin, Mikhail. *The Dialogic Imagination: Four Essays*. Ed. Michael Holquist. Austin: University of Texas Press, 1991.

Barthes, Roland. "From Work to Text." Harari 73–81.

———. *S/Z: An Essay*. Trans. from the French by Richard Miller. London: Jonathan Cape, 1975.

Basden, G. T. *Among the Ibos of Nigeria*. London: Seeley, Service, 1921.

Bauman, Richard. *Story, Performance and Event: Contextual Studies of Oral Narrative*. Cambridge: Cambridge University Press, 1986.

Bennett, Tony. "Texts in History: The Determinations of Readings and Their Texts." *Post-Structuralism and the Question of History*. Ed. Derek Attridge, Geoff Bennington, and Robert Young. Cambridge: Cambridge University Press, 1987. 63–81.

Boyce Davies, Carole. "Motherhood in the Works of Male and Female Igbo Writers: Achebe, Emecheta, Nwapa and Nzekwu." *Ngambika: Studies of Women in African Literature*. Ed. Carole Boyce Davies and Anne Adams Graves. Trenton: Africa World, 1986.

Butler, Judith. *Gender Trouble: Feminism and the Subversion of Identity*. New York: Routledge, 1990.

Carroll, David. *Chinua Achebe*. London: Macmillan, 1980.

Chambers, Ross. *Story and Situation: Narrative Seduction and the Power of Fiction*. Minneapolis: University of Minnesota Press, 1984.

Clifford, James. "Partial Truths." *Writing Culture: The Poetics and Politics of Ethnography*. Ed. James Clifford and George Marcus. Berkeley: University of California Press, 1986. 1–26.

Culler, Jonathan. "Story and Discourse in the Analysis of Narrative." *The Pursuit of Signs: Semiotics, Literature, Deconstruction*. London: Routledge and Kegan Paul, 1981. 169–187.

Foucault, Michel. *The Archaeology of Knowledge*. Trans. from the French by A. M. Sheridan. London: Routledge, 1989.

———. *The History of Sexuality. Volume 1: An Introduction*. Trans. from the French by Robert Hurley. London: Allen Lane, 1978.

———. *The Order of Things: An Archaeology of the Human Sciences*. London: Tavistock, 1970.

———. "What Is an Author?" Harari 141–160.

Gikandi, Simon. *Reading Chinua Achebe: Language and Ideology in African Fiction*. London: James Currey, 1991.

Granqvist, Raoul. *Travelling*. Sweden: Umea, 1990.

Harari, Josue V., ed. *Textual Strategies: Perspectives in Poststructuralist Criticism*. London: Methuen, 1986.

Hite, Molly. *The Other Side of the Story: Structure and Strategies of Contemporary Feminist Narratives*. Ithaca: Cornell University Press, 1989.

Innes, C. L. *Chinua Achebe*. Cambridge: Cambridge University Press, 1990.

———— and Bernth Lindfors, ed. *Critical Perspectives on Chinua Achebe*. London: Heinemann, 1979.

Isichei, Elizabeth. *A History of the Igbo People*. London: Macmillan, 1976.

Jeyifo, Biodun. "Okonkwo and His Mother: *Things Fall Apart* and Issues of Gender in the Constitution of African Postcolonial Discourse." *Callaloo* 16.4 (1993): 847–858.

Jussawalla, Feroza, and Reed Dasenbrock. *Interviews with Writers of the Postcolonial World*. Jackson: University of Mississippi Press, 1982.

Kunene, Daniel. "Journey as Metaphor in African Literature." *The Present State/L'état présent*. Ed. Stephen Arnold. Washington: Three Continents, 1985. 189–215.

LaCapra, Dominick. *History, Politics and the Novel*. Ithaca: Cornell University Press, 1987.

Lindfors, Bernth. "Achebe on Commitment and African Writers." *Africa Report* 25.3 (1979): 16–18.

————, ed. *Approaches to Teaching Chinua Achebe's* Things Fall Apart. New York: The Modern Language Association, 1991.

Lubiano, Wahneema. "Metacommentary and Politics in a 'Simple Story.'" Lindfors 106–111.

Marcus, George. "The Redesign of Ethnography after the Critique of Its Project." *Rethinking Modernity: Reflections across the Disciplines*. Ed. Robert F. Goodman and Walter R. Fisher. Albany: State University of New York Press, 1995. 103–121.

Moore, Henrietta. *A Passion for Difference: Essays in Anthropology and Gender*. Cambridge: Polity, 1994.

Okereke, Grace E. "The Birth Song as Medium for Communicating Woman: Maternal Destiny in the Traditional Community." *Research in African Literatures* 25.3 (1994): 19–32.

Olney, James. *Metaphors of Self: The Meaning of Autobiography*. Princeton: Princeton University Press, 1972.

Petersen, Kirsten Holst, and Anna Rutherford. *Chinua Achebe: A Celebration*. Oxford and Portsmouth: Heinemann and Dangaroo, 1990.

Priebe, Richard. *Myth, Realism and the West African Writer*. Trenton: Africa World, 1988.

Quayson, Ato. "Realism, Criticism, and the Disguises of Both: A Reading of Chinua Achebe's *Things Fall Apart* with an Evaluation of the Criticism Relating to It." *Research in African Literatures* 25.4 (1994): 129–136.

Spivak, Gayatri. "Poststructuralism, Marginality, Postcoloniality and Value." *Literary Theory Today*. Ed. Peter Collier and Helga Meyer-Ryan. London: Polity, 1990. 219–244.

Stratton, Florence. *Contemporary African Literature and the Politics of Gender*. London: Routledge, 1994.

Traore, Ousseynou B. "Matrical Approach to *Things Fall Apart*." Lindfors, *Approaches* 65–73.

Turner, Margaret. "Achebe, Hegel and the New Colonialism." Petersen and Rutherford 31–40.

White, Hayden. "The Value of Narrativity in the Representation of Reality." *Critical Inquiry* 7 (1980): 5–28.

Williams, Raymond. *Problems in Materialism and Culture: Selected Essays*. London: Verso, 1980.

Wright, Derek. "Things Standing Together: A Retrospect on *Things Fall Apart*." Petersen and Rutherford 76–82.

Zabus, Chantal. "The Logos-Eaters: The Igbo Ethno-Text." Petersen and Rutherford 19–30.

D. N. MKHIZE

# The Portrayal of Igbo Culture in Zulu: A Descriptive Analysis of the Translation of Achebe's Things Fall Apart into Zulu

*T*hings Fall Apart (Achebe, 1958) is a classic in African literature written in English, and is now almost synonymous with the African Writers Series, together with the other two texts which form a trilogy, *No Longer at Ease* (1960) and *Arrow of God* (1964). This article aims at analysing the manner in which Igbo culture as reflected in administrative and religious terms in *Things Fall Apart*, the source text (ST), has been transferred to *Kwafa Gula Linamasi* (Msimang, 1995), the target text (TT). In accomplishing this, a descriptive comparative analysis is carried out in which the translator's strategies are investigated. The analysis reveals that the translator used mainly transference and cultural substitution as strategies. The conclusion drawn following this analysis is that in translating Igbo culture the translator adopted neither a source text-oriented nor a target text-oriented approach, but a compromise.

## Introduction

In this article the researcher explores the manner in which Igbo culture, specifically administrative and religious terms, has been dealt with in the TT. This is accomplished by describing and analysing strategies employed by the translator in transferring the above-mentioned cultural elements to the TT. Since the focus is on the translation of culture, it is appropriate to

*South African Journal of African Languages/Suid-Afrikaanse Tydskrif vir Afrikatale,* Volume 20, Number 2 (2000): pp. 194–204. Copyright © 2000 The University of Port Elizabeth, Department of African Languages.

start off by defining culture. The translation scholar, Newmark (1988:94), views culture 'as a way of life and its manifestations that are peculiar to a community that uses a particular language as its means of expression'.

Newmark's (1988) definition implies that culture reflects the way in which a particular cultural group perceives and interprets meaning. This implication highlights the fact that different cultural groups do not necessarily attach the same meaning to reality. Each constructs its own way of expressing its values and beliefs. Tomaselli (1985), a distinguished scholar on cultural issues in the media, agrees with this opinion. Tomaselli (1985:8) regards culture as 'the process which informs the way meanings and definitions are socially constructed by social actors themselves'. Newmark's and Tomaselli's views of culture indicate that cultural differences and similarities between different cultural groups need to be taken into account in order to attain a meaningful understanding of different groups.

In translation the recognition of different cultures is very important because it facilitates a better understanding of a translation and its original. Therefore, translation should not only be about transferring messages from one language to another, but it should also involve transferring certain cultural elements from source language (SL) to target language (TL). This is further confirmed by Bassnett and Lefevere (1990:4) who regard culture as the unit of translation, and not the word or even the text.

Mkhize (1998:5), in her study on the transference of the Igbo culture to Zulu, observes that the analysis of the ST and the TT shows that the cultural backgrounds of these texts are different. The ST, for example, is set in 1958 in Western Nigeria, and it is about Igbo people and their culture. In contrast, the TT was translated in 1995 for a Zulu readership which has its own culture. Obviously, cultural differences between the ST and the TT pose serious challenges to the translator. The translator has the task of making choices and decisions concerning various procedures and strategies to be employed in making the translation meaningful and accessible to the Zulu readership. This article therefore examines the way in which the translator met the challenge regarding the choice of strategies implemented in handling Igbo culture as reflected in administrative and religious terms.

Before we proceed with the discussion, it is important to explain that the ST is written in the Igbo idiom. In his essay 'The Africa Writer and the English Language' Achebe (1975:62) explains that

> the English language will be able to carry the weight of my African experience. But it will have to be a new English, still in full communion with its ancestral home but altered to suit its new African surroundings.

This discussion also regards English as a vehicle used to convey certain elements of Igbo culture, and in this case administrative and religious terms. Thus the question of dealing with English per se as a medium is irrelevant for the purposes of this article. Rather, our concern is to investigate the mediation of Igbo culture into the TT in so far as it is presented in non-English English. However, before the analysis is conducted, the theoretical background and framework within which the translation is carried out is briefly discussed.

## Theoretical framework

Descriptive translation theorists, like Bassnett-McGuire (1980), Toury (1980), Hermans (1985), Lambert and Van Gorp (1985) and Lefevere (1992) amongst others, suggest that the socio-cultural context in which translations take place should be considered in the study of translations. They argue that translations are never produced in a vacuum, but they are a part of a larger system and therefore should be described in terms of the target system (Lambert and Van Gorp, 1985:44). This approach is in contrast with the approach of earlier translation theorists who believed in the abstract ideal of exact equivalence between ST and TT. Catford (1965:2) illustrates this ideal concept of equivalence when he defines translation as 'the replacement of textual material in one language (SL) by equivalent textual material in another language'.

According to descriptive translation theorists, translations can never be exact equivalents of their originals because every translation involves a certain amount of manipulation for a certain purpose (Hermans, 1985:13). This view means that equivalence is not an abstract theoretical concept, but is simply seen as the existing relationship between two texts. Therefore, this approach means that studies of translations should not be prescriptive, but 'descriptive, target-oriented, functional and systematic' (Hermans, 1985:10). In other words, the description of a translation should also take into account other factors affecting it. Toury (1995:52) emphasises this wider approach towards translation in the following remarks:

> 'translatorship' amounts first and foremost to being able to play a
> social role. i.e., to fulfil a function allotted by a community . . . in
> a way which is deemed appropriate in its own terms of reference.
> The acquisition of a set of norms for manoeuvring between all
> factors which may constrain it, is therefore a prerequisite for
> becoming a translator within a cultural environment.

In order to account for this broader descriptive translation of the TT properly and systematically, Toury proposes that the translation critic establishes translational norms which he regards as guiding principles which differ from one cultural group to another. Toury (1995:54) asserts that 'the norms themselves form a graded continuum along the scale: some are stronger, and hence more rule-like, others are weaker, and hence almost idiosyncratic.'

According to Toury (1995:56–58) there are three kinds of norms in translation that can be distinguished, namely preliminary, operational and initial norms. He states that preliminary norms deal with factors that determine the selection of texts for translation as well as the overall translation strategy used. Operational norms determine the actual decisions made in the translating process itself. Such decisions may include strategies like addition, omission, substitution, etc. Regarding initial norms, Toury argues that these norms indicate the translator's choice between a source-oriented or a target-oriented approach. In the former the translator subjects himself/herself to the textual structure and norms of the ST, whereas in the latter the translator expresses the literary and cultural norms of the target readership. However, it is important to note that there is no clear-cut distinction between the two approaches; translators may decide to adopt an approach which is situated at some point between these two extremes, depending on what they want to achieve.

In this discussion, for instance, the researcher discovered that the first unanalytical reading of the TT gives the impression that the TT is source-oriented. However, close reading proves this impression wrong because it shows that the text is both source-oriented and target-oriented. The reason for the first impression is that the translator transferred a lot of Igbo words unchanged to the TT. Another reason is that the translator retained most Igbo idioms and expressions in the TT by literal translation. Despite these observations, the researcher also discovered that the TT is target-oriented as well. The target-orientation is reflected in the use of TT cultural terms and expressions in the TT. The translator accomplishes this by using mainly the cultural substitution strategy in translating certain ST cultural elements and in this article this will be shown by analysing specifically administrative and religious terms.

In the light of the discussion in the above paragraph, we can therefore say that the translator's initial norm is neither solely source-text nor solely target-text oriented since he subjects himself to linguistic and cultural norms of both the ST and the TT. Like the initial norm, the translator's operational norms i.e. the dominant use of transference and cultural substitution strategies, further confirms the translator's willingness to accommodate the systems of both the ST and the TT. Considering both systems is important because each text is embedded in its own system which imposes certain constraints upon it. Lambert and Van Gorp (1985:44) put it in this way:

The target system need not be restricted to the literary system of the target culture, since translations of literary works may also function outside literature, within a translational system. In most cases, however, the target system will be part of the literary system of the target culture, or at least overlap with it. The exact relations between the literary systems of the target and the source cultures have to be examined, which is precisely the aim of our scheme. Both source (literary) system and target (literary) system are open systems which interact with other systems.

In this article the researcher describes, compares and analyses the linguistic, literary and cultural systems of both texts. According to descriptive translation theorists such a comparative analysis should be preceded by the establishment of a tertium comparationis. Toury (1995:80) defines a tertium comparationis as an intermediary concept which serves as the invariant of the comparison. In short, this means that in carrying out a comparison the researcher needs to establish specific elements of the ST and the TT to be compared because 'an exhaustive analysis of every textual problem is not feasible' (Lambert and Van Gorp, 1985:49). This is the reason why two cultural elements namely; administrative and religious terms have been identified to serve as tertium comparationis between the ST and the TT. In the following section these terms will therefore be used to illustrate the way in which Igbo culture was handled in the translation.

## Administrative terms

Usually, administrative terms used in a country are a reflection of how a nation is administered and governed. Administrative terms may, for instance, indicate that a nation is organised in a traditional or modern way. Furthermore, they may be 'transparent' or 'opaque' (Newmark, 1988:99). By 'transparent' we mean those terms whose meaning is easily detectable. In contrast, 'opaque' terms refer to those terms whose meaning is not detectable on the surface. It is obvious therefore that if terms are not 'transparent' the translator faces a serious challenge in making terms accessible and meaningful to the target readership. Even in cases where terms seem to be 'transparent' the translator still has to make their meaning relevant and comprehensible to the target readership. A common strategy used by translators to deal with this problem is translation by cultural substitution. According to Baker (1992:31), this strategy involves replacing a culture-specific item with an item which does not have the same propositional meaning but which is likely to have a similar impact on the target reader. The main advantage of using this strategy is that it gives TT readers a familiar concept with which they can identify.

In this discussion terms which indicate the administration of the traditional Igbo society include the following: elders, titled men, egwugwu, District Commissioner and kotma. This article investigates how Msimang (1995) translated these terms. In the ST it appears that elders are the most important representatives of authority in running the Igbo society. When there are serious matters to be discussed and resolved elders take an active and indispensable part. The active participation of elders in the affairs of the Igbo community is illustrated, for example, by the settlement of a crucial dispute between the Igbos and the Mbainos (Achebe, 1958:9). Another instance which shows the active role of elders in the community lives of the Igbos is found where elders pay a fine to the District Commissioner in order to avoid war with the British (Achebe, 1958:139). In the light of these events it is obvious that elders form an inextricable part of administrative structure of the Igbo society.

In translating the word 'elders', the word indicating the socio-political structure of the Igbos, Msimang seems to prefer to use the words izingwevu (lit. people with iron-grey hair) (1995:10, 12, 40–41 and 138), abadala (lit. the old ones) (1995:40) and the phrase abanumzane asebekhulile (lit. men who have grown old) (1995:80) interchangeably. The translation of 'elders' as abanumzane asebekhulile or abadala is literal in the sense that it provides the surface meaning of the words since abadala and abanumzane asebekhulile mean 'elders' in Zulu. It is noticeable that Msimang uses the phrase abanumzane asebekhulile and the word abadala only once in the translation, otherwise he uses the word izingwevu as already indicated. The possible reason for the avoidance of the phrase and word could be that he finds them literal and thus not appealing in a literary work.

On the other hand, izingwevu, the word which seems to be the translator's favourite because of its frequency, is artistically literary because it is a hlonipha, i.e. a euphemistic word referring to old people with grey hair. Generally, a person with grey hair is symbolic of experience and maturity. Although in Zulu the word izingwevu is not used with specific reference to administration, it is, however, implied in the sense that, traditionally, men who participated in the administration of the nation were those who had gone through various stages, like fighting in wars as young men and then establishing big families as adults. Most of those men were known as izinduna (nearly literally translated as captains) and headmen (Bryant, 1967:461). Bryant (1967:461) also explains that izinduna and headmen functioned as members of the Council and executive bodies. What is of interest here is that most of those men were elders. So, by translating the ST word 'elders' as izingwevu, Msimang gives the target readership a picture of the kind of people who were responsible for the running of Igbo society. This type of cultural substitution therefore makes the text accessible to the new readership. The following extracts show the translation of the word:

> The missionaries spent their first four or five nights in the marketplace, and went into the village in the morning to preach the gospel. They asked who the king was, but the villagers told them that there was no king. 'We have men of high title and the chief priests and the elders,' they said (Achebe, 1958:105).

> Abafundisi bahlala enkundleni yasendakini kwaze kwaphela izinsuku ezine noma ezinhlanu. Kwakuthi njalo ekuseni bavukele emzini bayoshumayela ivangeli. Babefike babuze ukuthi inkosi ebusa leso sifunda ngubani. Izakhamuzi zona zaziphendula ngokuthi azinayo inkosi. 'Sineziqonga zamadoda ayizihlabani, bese kuba yizanusi, nezingwevu' (Msimang: 1995:138).

Another important administrative structure amongst the Igbos constituted titled men. According to Onuh (1992:41), title-taking in Igbo was the highest form of excellence which was acknowledged by giving titled men authority to participate actively in the governance of the community. In fact, titled men were regarded as the judiciary of the traditional Igbo community. In Zulu culture some of the men who were also members of the Council, a body responsible for the running of the affairs of the nation, wore headrings known as ongiyane or izicoco. Headring wearing, like Igbo title-taking, was regarded as the highest form of achievement in the Zulu culture. Fuze (1979:27) explains that headrings were worn by men who had gone to war and had distinguished themselves as excellent warriors. As members of the Council, it is clear that headring wearing men occupied senior positions and performed administrative duties similar to titled men in the Igbo culture. Because of the similarity of position and duty between Igbo title-taking and Zulu headring wearing, Msimang found it appropriate to translate the phrase title-taking as indoda esithunge isicoco (lit. A man who has sewn a headring) (1995:67) and Laba asebethunge ongiyane (lit. Those who have sewn a headring) (1995:80).

In addition to the above-mentioned translations, Msimang also uses the phrase amadoda ayizihlabani (lit. men who distinguish themselves) as the translation of 'titled men'. This translation may be regarded as Msimang's strategy of emphasizing distinction and excellence as prerequisites for headring wearing, like it is the case with title-taking in the Igbo culture. Cultural substitutes such as these are significant in the text because they help the Zulu readership understand the institution of Igbo title-taking better since they are

given an example from their own cultural practice. In the following extracts
we find another example in which cultural substitution was used:

> The titled men and elders sat on their stools waiting for the trial
> to begin (Achebe, 1958:62).

> Laba asebethunge ongiyane, kanye nabanumzane asebekhulile
> bona babehlezi ezihlahveni zabo, belindele ukuba ukuthethwa
> kwamacala kuqale (Msimang, 1995:80).

The administrative structure of the Igbos also consists of people known
as egwugwu. Onuh (1992:42) explains that egwugwu were part of 'The Masquerade . . . a social but secret association . . . a closed association surrounded
by mysterious beliefs and activities, with a restricted membership only to
males initiated into it.' He also points out that egwugwu, like other masquerade members, functioned 'as means of social control, compelling individuals
in the society to comply with traditional standards and way of life, as well as
guarding community property against intruders' (1992:42). From the foregoing explanation it is clear that egwugwu were working in close cooperation
with policy makers, like elders and titled men. They were in fact an extension
of the judiciary, the executive arm of Igbo law and norms. In the ST, Achebe
makes mention of egwugwu a number of times. In all instances egwugwu
are involved in some administrative function, such as the resolution of dis-
putes. For example, in Achebe (1958:64–66) the dispute between Mgbafo
and Uzowulu which is threatening the peace and unity amongst the Igbos is
settled by the egwugwu.
       Instead of translating the word egwugwu, which like 'elders' and 'titled
men' illustrates the administration of Igbos, Msimang transfers the word unchanged throughout the text. However, in ensuring that the target readership
understands the meaning of egwugwu, he supplies readers with the meaning
of the word in the glossary. Transference, according to Newmark (1988:81),
is the process of transferring an SL word to a TL text unchanged. Such a
word then becomes a loan in the TT. The following extracts illustrate how
egwugwu appears as loan word in the TT:

> 'So I have brought the matter to the fathers of the clan. My case
> is finished. I salute you.' 'Your words are good,' said the leader of
> the egwugwu. 'Let us hear Odukwe. His words may also be good'
> (Achebe, 1958:64).

> 'Yingalokho ngithi lolu daba angizolwethula kobaba besizwe.
> Udaba lwami luphelela lapho. Nina bakomkhulu!' 'Mahle amagama

akho,' sekusho umholi wawo-egwugwu. 'Ake sizwe kuOdokwe. Mhlawumbe naye unamazwi amahle' (Msimang, 1995:84).

The reason for the transference of the word egwugwu could be that the translator could not find a Zulu cultural substitution for this word since there is no institution like the Masquerade of which egwugwu is a member. It is difficult to say whether the transference obscures the understanding of the text or not. In the view of the researcher the transference of egwugwu helped the translator to present this structure to the target readership without mediation which might have brought about some confusion or change in meaning.

After the arrival of the English in Igboland the above-mentioned administrative structures were suppressed and replaced with new western ones. The major western administrative structure was headed by the District Commissioner who ruled Igboland on behalf of the queen of England. Innes and Lindfors (1978:3) explain that District Commissioners were the imposed British rulers who divided Igboland into various territories and then ruled it according to the British rule. In the ST, Achebe refers to the District Commissioner a number of times. In all instances the District Commissioner shows how the British undermined the traditional Igbo administrative structures. The French scholar, Mannoni (1956:108) ascribes this form of behaviour 'to the colonial tradition of lacking awareness of the world of others, a world in which Others have to be respected.'

In translating the term 'District Commissioner', Msimang uses the word uNdabazabantu (1995:165). This word can be considered as a cultural substitute in the sense that in South Africa, like in Igboland, the British government and other colonial governments divided South Africa into different districts and then each district had its own administrative officers who became commonly known as uNdabazabantu by the native people. The historical and political similarities between Igbo and South Africa makes the term uNdabazabantu accessible to the target readership, and the target readership easily relates to this term. The following extracts provide examples of the translation:

And so the six men went to see the District Commissioner, armed with their matchets. They did not carry guns, for that would be unseemly. They were led into the court-house where the District Commissioner sat. (Achebe, 1958:137)

Nebala amadoda ayisithupha ahamba ayobonana noNdabazabantu wesifunda, ehlome ngocelemba. Nokho ayengaziphethe izibhamu, ngoba lokho kwakungeke kwemukeleke kahle. Bangeniswa endlini yenkantolo lapho uNdabazabantu ayehlezi khona (Msimang, 1995:178).

In addition to the above-mentioned administrative structure, the British government also recruited non-Igbo African people who were known as kotma to assist them in ruling Igbo people. Kotma functioned as court messengers as well as prison warders. Achebe mentions the word kotma quite a few times. In all instances kotma served a particular administrative function on behalf of the District Commissioner. For example, they imprisoned men who had molested Christians and served as prison warders as well (Achebe, 1958:123). Such activities made them very unpopular amongst Igbo people. In the translation Msimang retains this word throughout the text as a loan word. As with egwugwu, he also provides the meaning of kotma in the glossary so as to ensure that the Zulu readership understands the word. A possible reason for the transference of kotma could be that Msimang felt that in order to preserve the negative attitude which the Igbo people had towards kotma, the word had to be retained. Another possible reason could be that Msimang thought that the use of a different word other than kotma would probably compromise the meaning by being less negative and thus fail to convey the original intended negative meaning.

The negative attitude of Igbos towards kotma is also highlighted by the nickname 'Ashy-Buttocks' (Achebe, 1958:123) which they gave to kotma. Although this nickname basically describes the ash-coloured shorts which were worn by these people, it nevertheless shows disrespect and contempt because kotma did not approve of it. Obviously, Igbos used it to humiliate them. In an attempt to capture the same spirit of the ST, Msimang translates this word as oZinqezinomlotho (lit. people with ashy buttocks) (1995:178). The intention of this literal translation appears to be that the translator wants the Zulu readership to relate to kotma in the same negative way as the ST readership. The following extracts illustrate instances where the word is used:

> These court messengers were greatly hated in Umuofia because they were foreigners and also arrogant and highhanded. They were called kotma, and because of their ash-coloured shorts they earned the additional name of Ashy-Buttocks (Achebe, 1958:123).

> Lezi zithunywa zenkantolo zazinyamanambana kubantu base-Umuofia. Phela zazithi ingani zingabantu bezizwe bese zibuye zedelela futhi zizikhukhumeza. Zazibizwa ngokuthi zingo-kotma, kanti futhi ngenxa yokugqoka izikhindi ezifana nomlotha ngokwebala, zabuye zaqanjwa igama elithi ngoZinqezinomlotha (Msimang, 1995:178).

The above discussion on the translation of terms describing administrative structures in traditional Igbo community in the ST, shows that the translator used different translation strategies to achieve different purposes. A strategy such as transference or loan words, help the translator to preserve and present traditional Igbo administrative terms as they were in the traditional Igbo community. In addition, the use of cultural substitutes facilitates the accessibility and enhances the meaningfulness of the terms. The next section investigates the translation of Igbo religious terms.

**Religious terms**

The religion of the traditional Igbo society is based on the belief of the existence of Chukwu, the Supreme Being who is responsible for the creation of the world and everything in it. According to Njoku (1978:8), traditional Igbo society believe that Chukwu 'has no equal, but he had one great enemy called "Ekwesi or Devil"'. In the ST, Achebe maintains the concept of the supremacy of Chukwu as well as the word Chukwu itself throughout the text. This could probably be regarded as a way of presenting the Igbo religion from an Igbo perspective as well as showing the world that Igbos were religious people. Like Achebe, Msimang also transfers the word Chukwu unchanged throughout the translation despite the fact that there was room to find an equivalent in Zulu cosmology, like the word Mvelinqqangi, a traditional Zulu word for God. By not changing the word Chukwu, Msimang, like Achebe, wants his readership to understand God from an Igbo religious point of view. The following extracts show both the original and the translation of the word Chukwu.

> 'We also believe in Him and call Him Chukwu. He made all the world and other gods.' 'There are no other gods,' said Mr Brown. 'Chukwu is the only God and all others are false' (Achebe, 1958:126–127).

> 'Nathi siyakholwa kulowo Nkulunkulu futhi simbiza ngokuthi nguChukwu. Wadala umhlaba wonke kanye nabanye onkulunkul.' 'Abekho abanye onkulunkulu,' kweluleka uMnu. Brown. UChukwu nguye kuphela uNkulunkulu. Laba abanye ngonkulunkulu bamanga ngothi lwabo' (Msimang, 1995:164).

In addition to Chukwu, traditional Igbos also believe in gods or deities who assist God. They believe that deities play an intermediary role and serve as divine representatives (Onuh, 1992:13). It is this belief in other gods that brought Igbos in conflict with British missionaries who did not make any 'effort to examine the traditional Igbo beliefs and relate them to Western monotheism' (Njoku, 1984:18). Some of the deities which Igbos believe in in-clude the goddess of the earth (Achebe, 1958:26), the goddess of the sky and the goddess of the thunderbolt, Amadiora (Achebe, 1958:102). According to Onuh (1992:24), the goddess of the earth is 'a giver of fertility to men, ani-mals and crops'. The religious significance of this goddess is also highlighted by the celebration of the New Yam whereby Igbos offer new yams to the god-dess of the earth and ancestral spirits (Achebe, 1958:26).

In Zulu culture, like in Igbo culture, there is also a goddess of the earth. She is known as Nomkhubulwane. Like the Igbo goddess of the earth, Nomkhubulwane is regarded as the goddess of rain and fertility. Again, like the Igbo New Yam feast, the feast of Nomkhubulwane is also characterised by the sacrifice of food to this goddess. Cultural similarities between the Igbo goddess of the earth and Nomkhubulwane, as well as the feasts explain why Msimang translated the Igbo goddess of the earth as Nomkhubulwane. In actual fact, this cultural substitute strategy can be considered as Msimang's effort to ensure that the new readership relates meaningfully to the text.

Whereas Achebe (1958) mentions the goddess of the earth more than once, he mentions the other goddesses (the goddess of the sky and the god-dess of the thunderbolt) only once in the ST. The reason for this, according to Njoku (1978:7), is that 'the most important of all the deities in religious and social life of the people is "Ala", the Earth Deity.' Obviously, the god-dess of the earth was held in higher esteem than the other goddesses. In his translation of the less significant goddesses, Msimang uses the word isithixo. Isithixo refers to a god and it is derived from Thixo, a Xhosa Christian coin-age for Qamata, a traditional Xhosa name for God. Although Xhosas do not believe in polytheism, the coinage of isithixo (lit. a god) helps to accom-modate the existence of other gods which were also worshipped. The contact between Zulus and Xhosas has resulted in the use of the word isithixo by Zulus as well. So, by translating the two goddesses as isithixo sesibhakabhaka and isithixo sezulu nokuduma respectively, Msimang (1995:135) acculturated these culturespecific items of the ST.

In illustrating the concept of deities further, Achebe also talks about the importance of the Oracle in the lives of Igbos. In the Igbo culture an oracle is understood as one of Chukwu's goddesses who plays some role in the lives of the Igbos. For example, before going to war Igbos are expected to consult with the Oracle of the Hills and the Caves as this would ensure them suc-cess (Achebe, 1958:9). The Oracle pleads to Chukwu on their behalf. In his translation Msimang (1995:10) translates the Oracle of the Hills and the Caves as uSomlomo kaMvelingqangi. USomlomo is a Zulu word used to refer to someone who speaks on behalf of someone else, for instance, a Speak-er of Parliament is also known as uSomlomo wephalamente. In contrast, uMvelingqangi, as already mentioned, is a traditional Zulu word for God. On this basis we can deduce that the phrase uSomlomo kaMvelinqgangi helps the Zulu readers to relate meaningfully to the concept of the Oracle. It is also interesting to note that the translation, uSomlomo kaMvelingqangi, is Msimang's own creation. By means of this collocation he probably wants to ensure that the Zulu readership understands that the Oracle of the Hills and the Caves was Chukwu's messenger.

The discussion of Igbo religion would be incomplete without mentioning a chi or personal spirit. Achebe (1975:93) explains a person's chi as 'his spirit being complementing his terrestrial human being: for nothing can stand alone, there must always be another thing standing beside it.' Achebe's explanation indicates that a chi is an integral part of traditional Igbo religion as Igbos perceive it as the guardian of each and every person. In fact, they believe that a person's chi is responsible for his/her fortunes as well as misfortunes (Achebe, 1958:92). The following extracts show examples in which the word chi has been used in the ST:

> At an early age he (Okonkwo) had achieved fame as the greatest wrestler in all the land. That was not luck. At the most one could say that his chi or personal god was good. But the Ibo people have a proverb that when a man says yes very strongly; so his chi says yes also. Okonkwo said yes very strongly: so his chi agreed (Achebe, 1958:19).

Clearly, his (Okonkwo's) personal god or chi was not meant for great things. A man could not rise beyond the destiny of his chi. The saying of the elders was not true—that if a man said yea his chi also affirmed. Here was a man whose chi said nay despite his own affirmation (Achebe, 1958:92).

In translating the word chi, Msimang supplies readers with a Zulu cultural substitute namely idlozi (1995:22–23). Like a chi, idlozi in the Zulu culture is believed to be 'a guardian spirit' (Doke et al., 1990:161). However, idlozi is not only a personal spirit as is the case with a chi in Igbo culture; idlozi is also collective in the sense that one spirit looks after the entire family, that is why there is a proverb which says Akudlozi lingayi ekhaya (lit. No spirit fails to go home). Despite this difference though, the target readership should find the translation of a chi as idlozi meaningful and acceptable since idlozi is a well-known concept in the Zulu religious system.

Although Msimang substitutes a chi with idlozi as already indicated, it is important to note that he retains the word chi on only one occasion. This happens when he translates the following Igbo idiom:

The saying of the elders was not true that if a man said yea his chi
also affirmed. Here was a man whose chi said nay despite his own
affirmation (Achebe, 1958:92).

Izwi labadala lalingakhulumi iqiniso nxa lithi uma umuntu ethi
yebo, nechi yakhe iyamvumela. Ingani nansi indoda okuthi lapho
ivuma kodwa ichi yayo ibe ilandula (Msimang, 1995:121).

The reason for the transference of the word chi in this instance is not clear
considering the fact that Msimang uses the word idlozi throughout the text.
However, the researcher speculates that the inconsistent translation of a chi
in this case is meant to keep the Igbo idiom intact since it embodies the
traditional Igbo religion which the translator also wants to present from an
Igbo perspective.

The examination of the religious terms discussed above illustrates clearly
that Msimang has taken the cultural contexts of both the ST and the TT
into consideration. This is shown, for instance, by the use of the original religious terms of the ST, such as Chukwu, as well as the substitution of certain religious terms with Zulu equivalents, like Nomkhubulwane and idlozi.
Furthermore, the creation of the collocation uSomlomo kaMvelinqgangi also
ensures that the new readership understands the concept of the Oracle better.
From these observations, it is obvious that Msimang tries to accommodate
both cultures.

## Conclusion

The aim of this article was to analyse the manner in which Igbo culture
as reflected in administrative and religious terms in *Things Fall Apart* was
transferred to the Zulu translation. The descriptive comparative analysis
reveals that the translator implemented a variety of strategies such as literal
translation, transference and cultural substitution. It is concluded that the
dominant use of transference and cultural substitution as strategies is an
indication that the translator wanted to accommodate both source language
and target language cultures. For example, the transference of Chukwu,
egwugwu, kotma and other Igbo words was aimed at exposing the target
readership to Igbo cultural elements without any mediation which might
change the intended original meaning. In keeping with this intention, the
translator also provided the target readership with a glossary where Igbo
words and concepts are explained. Obviously, Msimang wanted to ensure
that Zulu readers are exposed to Igbo culture as it is reflected in the ST.

In an attempt to accommodate the target language culture the translator
opted for cultural substitution. This strategy enabled him to meet the cultural
norms of the target readership, thus making the TT culturally accessible to

the Zulu readership. The substitution of terms like chi with idlozi, 'the goddess of the earth' with Nomkhubulwane, 'elders' with izingwevu and 'District Commissioner' with Ndabazabantu assists Zulu readers to relate meaningfully to the text as well as understand the text in terms of their own target language system.

The analysis of some of the above-mentioned terms also showed some inconsistency. However, it was observed that, in certain instances, inconsistency was used to achieve certain purposes. For example, the frequent use of izingwevu, a euphemistic (hlonipha) word for 'elders', as opposed to the rare use of abanumzane asebekhulile and abadala, both literal translations for 'elders', indicates that the translator wants to make the TT as artistic and appealing as possible since the text is literary. Nevertheless, there were also certain cases where it was difficult to find a valid reason for inconsistency. For instance, the translation of 'titled' man (or men) as indoda esithunge isicoco or Laba asebethunge ongiyane interchangeably does not seem to have any significance because these phrases are synonymous.

On the whole, the manner in which Msimang dealt with Igbo culture as embodied in administrative and religious terms shows that he wanted to reach a compromise between the ST and TT cultures. As a result, the translation is neither solely source text-oriented nor solely target text-oriented. Finally, the researcher recommends that a similar investigation be conducted regarding the manner in which the same terms as well as other cultural elements have been dealt with in other translations of Achebe's *Things Fall Apart*, e.g. *Dilo di Maseke* (Monyaise, 1991) a Setswana translation, *Lwadilik'udonga* (Bongela, 1993) a Xhosa translation and then the Northern Sotho *Diwele Makgolela* (Serudu, 1993). Such investigation may bring Africans together by promoting cross-cultural understanding and tolerance amongst themselves.

## Works Cited

Achebe, C. 1958. *Things Fall Apart*. London: Heinemann.

Achebe, C. 1975. 'Chi in Igbo Cosmology' in *Morning Yet on Creation Day*. London: Heinemann, 93–103.

Achebe, C. 1975. 'The African Writer and the English Language' in *Morning Yet on Creation Day*. London: Heinemann, 55–62.

Baker, M. 1992. *'In Other Words:' A Coursebook on Translation*. London: Routledge.

Bassnett-McGuire, S. 1980. *Translation Studies*. London: Meteun.

Bassnett, S. & Lefevere, A. 1990. *Translation, History, and Culture*. London and New York: Pinter Publishers.

Bongela, K.S. 1993. *Lwadilik'donga*. Houghton: Heinemann.

Bryant, A.T. 1967. *'The Zulu People' As They were before the White Man came*. Pietermaritzburg: Shuter and Shooter.

Catford, J. 1965. *A Linguistic Theory of Translation*. Oxford: Oxford University Press.

Doke, C M., Malcolm, D.M., & Sikakana, J.M.A. 1990. *English-Zulu, Zulu-English Dictionary*. Johannesburg: Witwatersrand University Press.

Fuze, M. M. 1979. *The Black People and Whence they Came*. Pietermaritzburg: University of Natal Press.

Hermans, T. (ed) 1985. *The Manipulation of Literature: Studies in Literary Translation*. London: Croom Hehn.

Innes, C. L. and Lindfors, B. 1978. *Critical Perspectives on Chinua Achebe*. Washington, D.C.: Three Continents Press.

Lambert, J. and Van Gorp, H. 1985. 'On Describing Translations'. In Hermans, T. 1985. *The Manipulation Of Literature: Studies In Literary Translation*. London: Croom Helm, 42-53.

Lefevere, A. 1992. *Translating Literature: Practice and Theory in a Comparative Literature Context*. New York: The Modern Language Association of America.

Mannoni, O. 1956. *Prospero and Caliban: The Psychology of Colonization*. London: Methuen.

Mkhize, D.N. 1998. *Cross-cultural Transference: A Descriptive Analysis of Achebe's* Things Fall Apart *into Zulu*. Unpublished MA dissertation, Johannesburg: University of the Witwatersrand.

Monyaise, D.P.S. 1991. *Dilo di masoke*. Houghton: Heinemann Publishers Southern Africa.

Msimang, C. T 1995. *Kwafa Gula Linamasi*. Johannesburg: Heinemann.

Newmark, P. 1988. *A Textbook of Translation*. London: Prentice Hall.

Newmark, P. 1991. *About Translation*. Clevedon: Multilingual Matter.

Nida, E. A. & Taber, C. 1969. *The theory and the practice of translation*. Leiden: Brill.

Njoku, J. E. E. 1978. *A Dictionary of Igbo Names, Culture and Proverbs*. Washington, D.C.: University Press of America.

Njoku, B. C. 1984. *The Four Novels of Chinua Achebe: A Critical Study*. New York: Peter Lang.

Onuh, C. O. 1992. *Christianity and the Igbo Rites of Passage*. New York: Peter Lang.

Serudu, M.S. *Di wele Makgolela*. Houghton: Heinemann-Centaur.

Tomaselli, K. 1985. *Contemporary Cultural Studies Unit*. Durban: University of Natal.

Toury, G. 1980. *In Search of a Theory of Translation*. Tel Aviv: The Porter Institute for Poetics and Semiotics, Tel Aviv University.

Toury, G. 1995. *Descriptive Translation Studies and Beyond*. Amsterdam: John Benjamins.

PATRICK C. NNOROMELE

# *The Plight of A Hero in Achebe's*
# Things Fall Apart[1]

Although *Things Fall Apart* remains the most widely read African novel, the failure of its hero continues to generate haunting questions in the minds of some of its readers, especially among those who seem to identify with the hero's tragedy. Central to this discomfort is the question: why did Achebe choose as his hero an aspiring but brutal young man who ultimately took his own life? The author himself acknowledges that he has "been asked this question in one form or another by a certain kind of reader for thirty years" (Lindfors 1991, 22).[2] According to Achebe, these readers wanted to know why he allowed a just cause to stumble and fall? Why did he let Okonkwo (the hero of the novel) fail?

Several commentators have argued that Okonkwo's failure is due to his individual character weaknesses. Many blame it on the fragmentation of the Umuofia society and the destruction of its cultural values by the co- lonial powers. Yet others stress both.[3] There is no doubt that these things played a role in the suffering mind of the hero, but to argue that they are the reason for his failure is, in my opinion, too limited. Hence, I want to argue, contrary to popular views, that Okonkwo's downfall is not necessarily due to weaknesses in character or departed African glories but rather is a func- tion of heroism in the cultural belief systems of the Igbos. As Okhamafe aptly noted, perhaps "things begin to fall apart in this nine-village Umuofia

*College Literature*, Volume 27, Number 2 (Spring 2000): pp. 146–156. Copyright © 2000 Patrick C. Nnoromele.

clan long before a European colonialist missionary culture inserts itself there" (Okhamafe 1995, 134).

*Things Fall Apart* is not a novel without a cultural context. It is a text rooted in the social customs, traditions, and cultural milieu of a people. The characters and their actions are better understood when they are examined in that light. To do otherwise not only denies the novel a full measure of appreciation, it also renders vague and imprecise the significance of certain events, actions, and actors in the story.

What we have in this novel is a vivid picture of the Igbo society at the end of the nineteenth century. Achebe described for the world the positive as well as the negative aspects of the Igbo people. He discussed the Igbos' social customs, their political structures, religions, even seasonal festivals and ceremonies. He provided the picture without any attempt to romanticize or sentimentalize it. As he said in another occasion, "the characters are normal people and their events are real human events" (Lindfors 1991, 21).[4] Achebe told the story as it is.

The fact of his account is that the Igbo clan (of which I am a member) is a group of African people with a complex, vigorous, and self-sufficient way of life. Prior to the invasion of their land and the eclipse of their culture by foreign powers, they were undisturbed by the present, and they had no nostalgia for the past. In the novel, Achebe portrayed a people who are now caught between two conflicting cultures. On the one hand, there is the traditional way of life pulling on the Umuofia people and one man's struggle to maintain that cultural integrity against an overwhelming force of the colonial imperialism. On the other hand, we have the European style which, as presented, seems to represent the future, a new community of the so-called "civilized world." It now appears this African man, Okonkwo, and the entire society of Umuofia must make a choice between the old and the new—if they have the power. The desire to become a member of European-style society has its attraction. For one, it is conveyed to the Umuofia people, including Okonkwo, as a means of enjoying the spoils of twentieth-century civilization. But Okonkwo refused to endorse the appeal. He recognized that accepting the invitation is done at the expense of the things that comprised his identity and defined his values.

So when some members of the Umuofia community unwittingly accepted the invitation and endorsed "a strange faith," things fell apart for the Igbo people in Achebe's novel. Umuofia's integrated, organic community was irreparably fractured. Their gods were blasphemed and their hero disabled. Their customs were desecrated and shattered. The people were divided or put asunder. The British District Commissioner took charge and controlled the people. So we have what seems like a total imposition of one cultural, social, and political structure upon another. The hero of the novel found himself plunged into disaster. He had to kill himself. Obierika, one of the characters in the novel, expressed it this way: "That man [Okonkwo] was one of the greatest men in Umuofia. You drove him to kill himself: and now he will be buried like a dog" (1996, 147). This was a tragic act, leading to the exacerbating question of why did Achebe let the hero fail especially among those who have experienced or confronted the harsh face of colonialism. However, Okonkwo's calamitous act was not unexpected. All that happened to him and the fact that he had to take his own life were primarily the function of the Igbo's conception of a hero and, perhaps, the rift within the clan brought about by foreign domination.

A hero, in the Igbo cultural belief system, is one with great courage and strength to work against destabilizing forces of his community, someone who affects, in a special way, the destinies of others by pursuing his own. He is a man noted for special achievements. His life is defined by ambivalence, because his actions must stand in sharp contrast to ordinary behavior. So a hero is not made in isolation; rather he is a product of the social matrix within which he operates. The person's determination to pursue his individual interest concomitantly with that of the society is a constant source of dynamic tensions because his obligations to his society can become an impediment to his individual quest for fame and reputation. However, this impediment must be overcome if he is to be a hero. Paradoxically, a hero becomes both the disrupting and integrating principles of the community. Okonkwo, the central character in *Things Fall Apart*, is the epitome of this complex concept and the personification of the cultural ambiguity of the Igbo people.

In *Things Fall Apart*, Achebe made it clear that Okonkwo's single passion was "to become one of the lords of the clan" (1996, 92). According to Achebe, it was Okonkwo's "life-spring." Okonkwo wanted to be a hero. Unfortunately, the road to heroism in the Igbo's belief system is chronically fraught with difficulties of varying degrees.

The first challenge Okonkwo was expected to overcome was his father's reputation—in this case his father had none. However, he was determined to succeed in whatever respect his father had failed, knowing full well that among his "people a man was judged according to his worth and not according to the worth of his father" (1996, 6)—a juxtaposition of opposing claims about which the narrator (quite understandably) made no attempt to reconcile.[5] His father, Unoka, enjoyed gentleness and idleness. He "was lazy and improvident and was quite incapable of thinking about tomorrow" (3). Unoka was said to rejoice in song, dance, and drinking of palm-wine as his way of avoiding responsibility. In fact, he preferred these things to tending his yam-field. He was a man without title in the village of Umuofia, and he could not endure the sight of blood (8). Biologically, he was a male, but among the Igbo, he was never a man. So people laughed at him. In order to become a hero, Okonkwo felt he must overcome this public estimation of his father. At the outset of the novel, Achebe made the following remarks about Okonkwo: "His fame rested on solid personal achievements." "He had no patience with unsuccessful men" (3). "His whole life was dominated by fear, the fear of failure and of weakness" (9). So Okonkwo hated what his father was and became the opposite.

Not only is a hero expected to overcome the reputation of his father, he is also expected to surpass the reputations of his peers. In other words, he must outperform people in his age group or those he grew up with. Among the Igbos good effort is respected, "but achievement was revered" (1996, 6). Okonkwo must achieve concrete things to be a hero and he did. Here is Achebe's account of his achievement:

> If ever a man deserved his success, that man was Okonkwo. At an early age, he had achieved fame as the greatest wrestler in all the land. That was not luck. At the most, one could say that his chi or personal god was good. But the Igbo people have a proverb that when a man says yes, his chi says yes also. Okonkwo said yes very strongly: so his chi agreed. And not only his chi, but his clan too, because it judged a man by the work of his hands. That was why Okonkwo had been chosen by the nine villages to carry a message of war to their enemies unless they agree to give up a young man and a virgin to atone for the murder of Udo's wife. (Achebe 1996, 19–20)

Okonkwo's accomplishments in Umuofia earned him the respect and honor of the elders and the people. He defeated Amalinze the Cat and was proclaimed the greatest wrestler in Umuofia and Mbaino. He demonstrated exceptional skills as a warrior of the clan by bringing home five heads during inter-tribal conflicts. Achebe portrayed him as a man with "incredible prowess" and passion to conquer and subdue his enemies (1996, 6). He was a successful farmer and married three wives—clear evidence among the Igbos of a strong and wealthy man. The ultimatum of war that he delivered to the enemy of Umuofia yielded immediate results. Achebe wrote: "When Okonkwo of Umuofia arrived at Mbaino as the proud and imperious emissary of war, he was treated with great honor and respect, and two days later he returned home with a lad of fifteen and a young virgin. The lad's name was Ikemefuna, whose sad story is still told in Umuofia unto this day" (9). Okonkwo started with nothing, but through hard work and determination he became successful.

Another barrier one is expected to overcome in the quest for heroism is the person's obligation to the society, which, of course, may adversely affect his individual quest for reputation. The nature of the dynamic tensions this can create was evident in Okonkwo's lifestyle. Perhaps this accounts for the reason some interpreters of *Things Fall Apart* think that Achebe paints "a paradoxical portrait of a protagonist who is both a typical Igbo man as well as an individual" (Lindfors 1991, 17).[6]

Among the Igbos, a person's obligation to the society calls for cooperation. It calls for submission to the counsel of elders, the precepts, and laws of the land, which are established for the good of the society. I think the most difficult aspect of it all is the subordination of one's own interest to that of the group or society. Okonkwo had a scrupulous desire to fulfill his obligation to the society, but he often realized that it only brought him to a crossroad of conflicting loyalties. A typical example of this happened on the night when the Priestess of Agbala came to take Ezinma, Okonkwo's daughter, for Agbala's blessing. In spite of his inexorable commitment to support and defend the laws of the land, Okonkwo felt the natural pull to resist established social order. He was expressively unapproving of the untimely visit by the Priestess. He perceived her arrival as an intrusion to his family's domestic life. However, his insistent but unsuccessful protestations only elicited a scream from the Priestess of Agbala, who warned: "'Beware, Okonkwo!' 'Beware of exchanging words with Agbala. Does a man speak when a god speaks? Beware!'" (Achebe 1996, 96). Albeit, the Priestess took Ezinma to the Oracle of the Hills and Caves and returned her safely to Okonkwo's family the following day. But we learned from the narrator that Okonkwo was noticeably worried, and wondered about these conflicting loyalties.

Even Obierika, who seemed to disapprove of Okonkwo's commitment to the central doctrines of his culture, observed and agonized over the lack of equilibrium between the pull of private values and public expectations. The force of this pull is succinctly captured in the following passage:

> He remembered his wife's twin children, whom he had thrown away. What crime had they committed? The Earth had decreed that they were an offense on the land and must be destroyed. And if the clan did not exact punishment for an offense against the great goddess, her wrath was loosed on all the land and not just on the offender. As the elders said, if one finger brought oil it soiled the others. (Achebe 1996, 88)

Obierika, like Okonkwo, felt the endemic tensions of conflicting cultural values—the incessant discord between public loyalty to the goddess of the clan and private loyalty to the family. But the difference between Okonkwo and Obierika was, Okonkwo was a man of few words. He allowed his actions to speak for him. However, the cumulative effects of all these things led to his eventual suicide. This is the kind of dilemma one confronts on the road to heroism and it can be overwhelming. A hero, in Okonkwo's world, must face (it seems) a constant strife between two sets of values, the societal and the personal, but he never can find the equilibrium. It is, therefore, not a surprise to see Okonkwo take his own life. I believe this was precisely what Sarr observed when he critically remarked that at times the reader of Achebe's novel is faced with contradictions. "Ibo society" he added, "is full of contradictions." "It is a male-dominated society, in which the chief goddess is female and in which proverbial wisdom maintains 'Mother is supreme'"—a sustained duality in belief systems common to much of Africa (1993, 349).[7] Central to this observation is the fact that the Igbo community is a society that is at once communal and individualistic. Such a worldview or ambiguous value system reveals, Sarr properly concluded, "the dilemma that shapes and destroys the life of Okonkwo" (349).

Although Okonkwo expressed rigidity and inflexibility in his life, Achebe told us that down in his heart Okonkwo was not a cruel man. I believe the most charitable way to understand this is by looking briefly at different manifestations of Okonkwo's esoteric life. For example, when he violated the peace week by beating his youngest wife, which was an offense to the goddess, Okonkwo agreed to make offerings as demanded by the custom of Umuofia. In fact, he offered an additional pot of palm-wine, which was a distinct indication of genuine repentance and cooperation for the good of the community. Achebe had Ezeani say to Okonkwo:

> You know as well as I do that our forefathers ordained that before we plant any crops in the earth we should observe a week in which a man does not say a harsh word to his neighbors. We live in peace with our fellows to honor our great goddess of the earth without whose blessing our crops will not grow. You have committed a great evil. [As Okonkwo heard this] He brought down his staff heavily on the floor. Your wife was at fault, but even if you came into your Obi and found her lover on top of her, you would still have committed a great evil to beat her. [As soon as Okonkwo heard this] His staff came down again. The evil you have done can ruin the whole clan. The earth goddess whom you have insulted may refuse to give us her increase, and we shall all perish. His tone now changed from anger to command. You will bring to the shrine of Am tomorrow one she-goat, one hen, a length of cloth and a hundred cowries. He rose and left the hut. (Achebe 1996, 22)

Okonkwo made the sacrifices to the earth goddess.

In another occasion, we learn that Okonkwo breathed a heavy sigh of relief when he found out that his wife Ekwefi was unharmed after he had fired at her in a fit of rage. Thus, we observe within some of these occasional flashes of cruelty a rare manifestation of tenderness. Similarly, on the night when the priestess of Agbala carried Ekwefi's daughter off to the Oracle of the Hills and Caves for the young girl to pay homage to her god, Ekwefi followed in terror for her child. Cognizant of his wife's state of terror, Okonkwo joined Ekwefi to provide re-assurance. When Ekwefi noticed Okonkwo's presence, "Tears of gratitude filled her eyes" (Achebe 1996, 106). As both of them waited outside their home in the dawn, Achebe said, Ekwefi remembered the generous love with which Okonkwo had taken her at the moment she became his wife. Perhaps Okonkwo was not a cruel man. For these occasional episodes are seemingly indications of a kind-hearted man.

Paradoxically, Okonkwo would never achieve heroism among the Igbos if he totally subordinated his interest to that of the society at large. Hence, it was incumbent on him to exhibit other qualities that might be perceived as a threat to social order. "And he did pounce on people quite often" (Achebe 1996, 3). As Achebe said, Okonkwo made people wonder whether he respected the gods of the clan. He "was popularly called the 'Roaring Flame'" (108). "Okonkwo was not the man to stop beating somebody halfway through, not even for fear of a goddess" (21). In his culture, a man who was unable to rule his own family was not considered a real man, not to mention a hero. So Okonkwo "ruled his household with a heavy hand" (9) and made people afraid of him. A hero should be impervious to emotions. The narrator told us that Okonkwo expressed no emotion, except anger. He was stoical to the harsh realities of life and appeared immune to problems. This is the life of a hero, a self-made man. Sometimes Okonkwo acted as if he was answerable to no one, and at other times he was the opposite. Obierika (Okonkwo's closest friend) pointed to this cultural ambiguity in the system when he sought (as he always did) a compromise from Okonkwo between conflicting loyalties. But Okonkwo responded impatiently, "The Earth (goddess) cannot punish me for obeying her messenger" (47). It would seem, for the Igbos, a hero must lead a life of self-contradiction; and Okonkwo was one primary example. It is, therefore, not surprising why contemporary commentators like Wasserman and Purdon contended that "Okonkwo represents a type of selfish individualism that is in essence a threat to Ibo notions of clan, and culture" (1993, 327).

In the opening lines of chapter seven, the narrator said, it seemed the elders of Umuofia had forgotten Ikemefuna (the lad who was entrusted to Okonkwo's care) but not the oracle. For three years Ikemefuna lived in Okonkwo's household. He was wholly absorbed into the family and Okonkwo became fond of him. Suddenly, the announcement came from the Oracle that Ikemefuna must be killed according to the tradition of Umuofia. The boy at this point regarded Okonkwo as a father. So, Ogbuefi Ezeudu specifically warned Okonkwo to stay at home. "The Oracle of the Hills and the Caves has pronounced it. They will take him (Ikemefuna) outside Umuofia as it is the custom, and kill him there. But I warn you to have nothing to do with it. He calls you father" (Achebe 1996, 40).

The cultural practice was that when the gods or goddesses demanded anyone for sacrifice, the family must be excluded because the Umuofia people believed that the emotional attachment the family might have for that individual would interfere with the process or the obligation to execute the demands of the Oracle. Hence, Ogbuefi Ezeudu sought for at least a passive compromise from Okonkwo. Since Okonkwo's passion was to be a hero, he felt his manliness might be called into question; therefore, he defied his friend's admonition and accompanied the procession into the forest.

What happened next would be used in the novel partly for the downfall of Okonkwo. Ikemefuna had to die. The values of the whole clan of Umuofia would be tested, if not forever, by this journey in which Ikemefuna would be killed. Achebe explained the episode in these words:

> As the man who had cleared his throat drew up and raised his machet, Okonkwo looked away. He heard the blow. The pot (of palm-wine) fell and broke in the sand. He heard Ikemefuna cry, "My father, they have killed me!" as he ran towards him. Dazed with fear, Okonkwo drew his matchet and cut him down. He was afraid of being thought *weak*. (Achebe 1996, 43; emphasis is mine).

The death of Ikemefuna invoked varying or contrasting emotional reactions from both Okonkwo and Nwoye (Okonkwo's son) which dramatizes what Okonkwo apprehended as a dichotomy between strength and gentleness. Achebe said, as "soon as his father walked in, that night, Nwoye knew that Ikemefuna [someone he had come to know and treat as a friend] had been killed, and something seemed to give way inside him, like the snapping of a tightened bow. He did not cry.... He just hung limp" (1996, 43). Nwoye would have loved to cry, but couldn't, because Okonkwo had tried to raise him up like himself. In Okonkwo's world, real men do not show effeminate emotion. Crying is not a masculine attribute.

In Chapter Eight, we are told that Okonkwo himself could not sleep. He was distraught and deeply affected by the death of Ikemefuna and his son's reaction to it. As Achebe told us, Okonkwo was not a man of many words (something traditionally viewed as a masculine quality in the Umuofia's belief system), so he bottled his feelings within his heart. For two whole days he ate nothing as he struggled to erase the memory of killing a child who called him father. It was the cumulative effects of these things, including the impact the death of Ikemefuna had on his son that paved the way to Okonkwo's eventual suicide. But the death of Ikemefuna had no immediate impact on the Umuo-fia people. It was, however, definitely an apocalyptic step towards things that were yet to come.

Later at the funeral of Ogbuefi Ezeudu, Okonkwo's gun accidentally discharged and killed the son of Ezeudu. Even though this was an accident, it was viewed as an abomination in the land, for under no circumstances would someone kill a clansman. Okonkwo and family had to flee the land before the cock crowed. They found refuge in his mother's village, Mbanta. He and his family endured seven years in exile. In the meantime, offerings were made in Okonkwo's compound, after their departure, to cleanse the land and placate the gods. Okonkwo saw this sojourn to Mbanta as a training experience in the wilderness. While he was in the village, he found out that the Mbanta clan was allowing missionaries to establish Christian churches and make con-verts especially among the untouchable. He saw how the missionaries defied the power of the local gods. His son, Nwoye, who suffered from inner turmoil as a result of the death of Ikemefuna,[8] decided to attend the mission school. He left his father's house and joined the Christian church. This was the straw that broke the camel's back. Okonkwo was furious and disappointed. He tried unsuccessfully to get the Mbanta clan to chase the missionaries out. When they couldn't get the missionaries out, Okonkwo sighed heavily and longed for his father's land, where according to him, men were men, bold, and war-like (Achebe 1996, 141).

When he finally returned to his fatherland, little did he know that the missionaries had penetrated his father's land too and made converts of differ-ent categories of Umuofia clan, ranging from the low-born and the outcast to the men of title and stature. They also established white government with a courthouse where "the District Commissioner judged cases in ignorance (Achebe 1996, 123). Obierika explained it this way: "The white man is very clever. He came quietly and peaceable with his religion. We were amused at his foolishness and allowed him to stay. Now he has put a knife on the things that held us together and we have fallen apart" (125). Fallen apart indeed! "Okonkwo's return to his native land was not as memorable as he had wished" (129). He never received the hero's welcome he dreamed of. He returned to a different Umuofia from the one he had known. In the present Umuofia, "men [have] unaccountably become soft like women" (129). He wanted to fight, but Obierika said to him: "It is already too late. . . . Our own men and our sons have joined the ranks of the strangers. They have joined his religion and they help to uphold his government. . . . How do you think we can fight when our own brothers have turned against us?" (124).

Okonkwo left and killed himself, not because of character weakness, or the departed African glories. Rather, it was the inevitable consequence of the Igbos' complex concept of a hero. As Sarma keenly pointed out:

One cannot some-how lay the blame on Okonkwo. His action at the end, hasty though it was, was quite in accordance with the traditional values. It was an act of conviction, almost religious, and the end vindicated the character of Okonkwo, who emerges as the lone representative of the Igbo value system while the entire community lay around him in a shambles. (Sarma 1993, 69)

Okonkwo, who had a resolute hunger to become a hero, was not afraid of the forces that surrounded him. However, he was so overwhelmed by the cumulative effects of his experiences on the road to heroism that he felt the only thing left to do was to commit suicide. Okonkwo had to maintain his integrity as a hero. The truth of this profound, but ambivalent, act is reflected in the Igbo proverb that says: "The thought that led a man to truncate his own existence was not conceived in a day." It was not just one single thing or event that forced Okonkwo to kill himself. His suicidal act was an ultimate expression of the compound effects of his own experiences in his unflinching desire to become a hero. Okonkwo was a hero. Hence, he had to depart from the battlefield as one. A hero would rather die than be captured and/or humiliated by the enemy. Okonkwo's death cheated his enemies, the European colonizers, of their revenge. But to the Umuofia people, it was unambiguously imprinted in their minds that there had been an irreversible break with the past. Umuofia would never again be what it was.

Contrary to the charge that the author of the novel allowed Okonkwo to stumble and fall, Achebe did not cause the hero's downfall. He was not responsible for Okonkwo's tragedy. Achebe saw his role as that of a neutral narrator. Thus, he presented, in a non-committal fashion, the tensions and conflicts between traditional values and alien culture, the "private self" and "public man" and their attendant consequences in a pre-colonial society.

## NOTES

1. Special thanks to all my colleagues and students in the Honors Program whose thoughtful questions stimulated and sustained my interest in writing this article. I am also grateful to the following reviewers, Michael H. Bright, Ronald J. Messerich, and Salome C. Nnoromele whose valuable suggestions and useful criticisms helped shaped this essay.

2. Achebe did respond to the question (without sufficient elaboration) by saying: "the concepts of success and failure as commonly used in this connection are inadequate. Did Okonkwo fail? In a certain sense, he did, obviously. But he also left behind a story strong enough to make those who hear it . . .wish devoutly that things had gone differently for him" (Achebe 1991, 22–23).

3. For this and other contemporary interpretations of the novel, see Lott and Lott (1993). This volume contains an extensive bibliographic essay on *Things Fall Apart*. See also McDougall (1986, 24–33).

4. The characters in this novel, including the gods or divinities, ancestors, and the events, are actual representations of the Igbo people and their cultural belief systems.

5. Among the Umuofia people, a hero is expected to overcome the reputation of his father. Yet the society maintains that one is not judged by the worth of one's father. This is a contradiction, an unresolved discrepancy so indicative of the Igbo traditional values. Achebe made no effort to reconcile or extract a true version from these conflicting accounts, because he was writing from the standpoint of a neutral narrator.

6. See also Devi (1993, 79–86).

7. See, for instance, Adams (1982).

8. Nwoye could not express his emotion as felt, because his father, Okonkwo, reacting to his own father's effeminacy, had taught Nwoye to believe that the expression of effeminate emotion was a sign of weakness. Thus, Nwoye tried to bottle his feelings in his heart. The unavoidable consequence of this was the despair and inner turmoil he suffered in his life.

## WORKS CITED

Achebe, Chinua. 1991. "Teaching *Things Fall Apart*." In *Approaches to Teaching Achebe's "Things Fall Apart*," ed. Bernth Lindfors. New York: The Modern Language Association of America.

———. 1996. *Things Fall Apart*. Portsmouth: Heinemann.

Adams, Monni. 1982. *Designs for Living: Symbolic Communication in African Art*. Cambridge: Harvard University, Carpenter Center for the Arts.

Devi, N. Rama. 1993. "Pre-and Post-Colonial Society in Achebe's Novels." In *Indian Response to African Writing*, ed. A. Ramakrishna Rao and C. R. Visweswara Rao. New Delhi: Prestige Books.

Lindfors, Bernth, ed. 1991. *Approaches to Teaching Achebe's "Things Fall Apart*." New York: The Modern Language Association of America.

Lott, John, and Sandra Lott. 1993. "Approaches to *Things Fall Apart*." In *Global Perspectives on Teaching Literature*, ed. Sandra Ward Lott, Maureen S. G. Hawkins, and Norman McMillan. Urbana: National Council of Teachers of English.

McDougall, Russell. 1986. "Okonkwo's Walk: The Choreography of Things Falling Apart." *World Literature Written in English*. 26.1: 24–33.

Okhamafe, Imafedia. 1995. "Genealogical Determinism in Achebe's *Things Fall Apart*." In *Genealogy and Literature*. Ed. Lee Quinby. Minneapolis: University of Minnesota Press.

Sarr, Ndiawar. 1993. "The Center Holds: The Resilience of Ibo Culture in *Things Fall Apart*." In *Global Perspectives on Teaching Literature*, ed. Sandra Ward Lott, Maureen S. G. Hawkins, and Norman McMillan. Urbana, Illinois: National Council of Teachers of English.

Sarma, S. Krishna. 1993. "Okonkwo and His Chi." In *Indian Response to African Writing*, ed. A. Ramakrishna Rao and C. R. Visweswara Rao. New Delhi: Prestige Books.

Wasserman, Julian, and Liam O. Purdon. 1993. "If the Shoe Fits: Teaching *Beowulf* with Achebe's *Things Fall Apart*." In *Global Perspectives on Teaching Literature*, ed. Sandra Ward Lott, Maureen S. G. Hawkins, and Norma McMillan. Urbana, Illinois: National Council of Teachers of English.

RAVIT REICHMAN

# Undignified Details:
## The Colonial Subject of Law

A legal world is built only to the extent that there are commitments
that place bodies on the line . . . the interpretive commitments of
officials are realized, indeed, in the flesh.

—Robert Cover "Violence and the Word" (208)

A t the end of Chinua Achebe's novel, *Things Fall Apart*, readers find the
narrative abandoned and replaced with another story. The novel tells the
story of Okonkwo, a man from the Nigerian tribe of Umuofia who, despite
a destitute upbringing, becomes one of the most powerful leaders of his clan.
Achebe's protagonist, however, is anything but an endearing hero. Haunted
by the memory of his poor and hapless father, Okonkwo becomes a proud,
short-tempered man, who beats his wives and treats those around him with a
hard-edged lack of sympathy. The novel concludes with the arrival of Christian missionaries from England, who convert members of Okonkwo's clan,
establish a church, and eventually set up a court. Following an altercation
with the priest and some of the church's converts, Okonkwo and five other
men are arrested and beaten. After their release, the clan calls a meeting,
which is interrupted by the guards who had earlier imprisoned and beaten
the men. This intrusion proves more than Okonkwo can bear: overcome
with humiliation and rage, he confronts one of the guards and kills him.

*ARIEL,* Volume 35, Numbers 1–2 (January–April 2004): pp. 81–100. Copyright © 2004
University of Calgary, Department of English.

The chapter that follows this episode shifts from Okonkwo's point of view to that of the unnamed District Commissioner, who comes to the village in search of the guard's murderer and is led by the clansmen to a tree from which Okonkwo's body hangs. The tragedy of his suicide would seem to be a natural place for Achebe's novel to end. Instead, *Things Fall Apart* concludes with the beginning of another story, which announces itself in the omniscient narrator's shift in focus from Okonkwo to the District Commissioner. Reframing Okonkwo's narrative from within the Commissioner's perspective, the narrator concludes the story from the subject position of a man who knows nothing of Okonkwo save the scant facts of the messenger's murder and the murderer's suicide. As the newly anointed protagonist leaves deep in thought about how the dead man's story might enter the wider colonial picture, Achebe's title and the novel's epigraph from Yeats' poem "The Second Coming"—"things fall apart, the center cannot hold"—acquires new force, inflected with the strained power relations of colonialism. In these moments, the man we had taken to be the novel's central figure is undone, and becomes little more than a small, anonymous part in a very different story:

> The Commissioner went away, taking three or four of the soldiers with him. In the many years in which he had toiled to bring civilization to different parts of Africa he had learned a number of things. One of them was that a District Commissioner must never attend to such undignified details as cutting a hanged man from the tree. Such attention would give the natives a poor opinion of him. In the book which he planned to write he would stress that point. As he walked back to the court he thought about that book. Every day brought him some new material. The story of this man who had killed a messenger and hanged himself would make interesting reading. One could almost write a whole chapter on him. Perhaps not a whole chapter but a reasonable paragraph, at any rate. There was so much else to include, and one must be firm in cutting details. He had already chosen the title of the book, after much thought: *The Pacification of the Primitive Tribes of the Lower Niger.* (208–208)

The heart of Achebe's novel—Okonkwo's story—turns out to be a minor narrative within a larger one, reduced to a footnote in the master colonial narrative represented by *The Pacification of the Primitive Tribes of the Lower Niger.* The tragedy that Achebe's novel records, then, is the process by which Okonkwo's narrative recedes into the background of another, becoming an "undignified detail" that those in power would do best to ignore. Okonkwo's suicide is reduced to "material" for the Commissioner's story, the scale of his life cut down to the size of a "chapter," even "a reasonable paragraph."

I begin with Achebe's novel not to make a claim about its place within the larger context of African literature. I invoke it, rather, to introduce and animate the terms of this essay's consideration of British colonial law as it was practiced in Nigeria. Viewed from the positions of both legal and literary scholarship, *Things Fall Apart* provides us with an occasion to reflect on the relationship between native and colonial law, and to do so in narratological terms. As Achebe's novel suggests, this relationship unfolds through a double-edged process of shortening and lengthening: the condensing and shrinking of one story and the simultaneous expansion of another, more epic narrative. The combined force of these transformations, I will argue, is accompanied by a dramatic shift in register, one that renders the colonized subject anonymous. Moreover, I will go on to argue that this effacement of identity lays the foundation for individual stories to do the work of documentation. In this essay, I examine the means through which colonial law transformed the stories of singular subjects within the legal framework, enlisting them, through an editorial process, in the project of documentation and the related task of elaborating a narrative of colonial justice.

Achebe's ending, to be sure, opens up a range of interpretive possibilities, positing—among other things—the indelibility of native stories, which persist in spite of colonial attempts to quash them. Along such lines, Okonkwo's suicide might be grasped as an act of defiance—an emphatic refusal to be co-opted by the Commissioner and his soldiers. My own focus here, however, begins by approaching the novel's conclusion as a depiction of how colonial texts, written by more powerful authors, replaced native stories. To suggest as much, however, is to offer only a partial view of the grounds that make possible such a replacement. For the novel's closing paragraphs relate not only what happens to Okonkwo's story, but also *where* this transformation occurs: "As he walked back to the court he thought about that book." The place where things fall apart turns out to be a location between two positions, between Okonkwo's hanged body in the village of Iguedo and the British colonial court. It is here, in the movement from one to the other—on subtle but unmistakably legal terrain—that the book that promises to incorporate Okonkwo's life in the form of "a reasonable paragraph" takes shape in the District Commissioner's imagination. There is something in the transition from village to court—a movement towards the law—that makes it possible for the District Commissioner to conceive of his book. In presenting *The Pacification of the Primitive Tribes of the Lower Niger* as the last word on Okonkwo's life, *Things Fall Apart* gestures towards the force that textualization exerts in a colonial framework, projecting its as-yet-unwritten coda not simply as narrative, but as written text. Crucially, however, this shift to writing occurs not simply through the act of inscription, but through the editorial work that precedes it. "One must be firm in cutting details," editing out minutiae that detract from the larger issues in the study of pacification.

The seemingly ethical terms in which the Commissioner justifies cutting the details of his volume are exposed as pretense when we consider a different kind of cutting that he refuses to do: namely, the act of cutting down Okonkwo's body from the tree: "a District Commissioner must never attend to such undignified details as cutting a hanged man from the tree." This literal body may well have offered an occasion for compassion, a chance for British administration to demonstrate its humane treatment of its colonized subjects. The Commissioner rejects this possibility, however, in favor of a more pedagogical aim: "Such attention would give the natives a poor opinion of him. In the book which he planned to write he would stress that point." The radically different objects of this cutting underscore the injustice in their being related at all. Simply stated, it is morally repugnant to equate the task of cutting down a hanged body with the labor of cutting the details of a life from a story that would purport to explain it. These cuttings may indeed strike an important contrast, but they are treated with equal steadfastness by the Commissioner in his determination to "stress that point" of not cutting down the dead man, as well as in his reflection that "one must be firm in cutting details."

The Commissioner's stiff resolve confirms Walter Benjamin's famous assertion in "Theses on the Philosophy of History" that there is "no document of civilization which is not at the same time a document of barbarism" (256). What emerges as especially salient here is not simply the relationship between barbarism and writing but more specifically, the brutality of documentation, the process through which a body of work, a story, an individual life must pass in order to be recognized—and recorded—as a document. It is not just the text that produces violence, in other words, but a specific kind of text: one that testifies to, documents, and establishes facts. The trajectory by which this violence exerts itself—the element that makes it violent, in other words—is another matter. It is violent, ultimately, because it effaces. The story of an individual becomes an example, a detail in a larger story of administrative success in colonial Africa.

It is important, moreover, that this transition is not one of outright elimination but of compression: the reduction of a life, and the narrative depicting that life, into a chapter or a paragraph. This process suggests the subtle complexity with which law, history and narrative were woven together in colonial Africa—a subtlety often overlooked when colonialism is imagined primarily as a system that ruled out competing indigenous legal practices. I am not suggesting here that British colonial policies did not eradicate native forms of justice; they did. I am proposing, rather, that a critical evaluation of colonialism's development demands more specificity than general descriptions of political power dynamics admit. In particular, it is this work of compression, and the redaction it enables—the ability to lift a compact story from one context and embed it in another—that is a central mechanism by which colonial law literally overwrites native law. I would like to suggest how this happens through an analysis of an exemplary opinion from colonial Nigeria, *Lewis v. Bankole*. Momentarily, I will be examining this highly significant case, which was among the first to consider the question of property rights within the context of British colonial Africa. I want first, however, to situate this case in its colonial context by setting out some basic features of the British treatment of African customary law. As I will explain, colonial law reduced and recast existing indigenous narratives and practices of law with a view to creating a more just society, one modeled upon British jurisprudence.

## I.

The application of British law in Africa was heralded as one of England's most valuable contributions to its colonies, promising to institute a legacy of reason and tolerance in a context that the British saw as utterly chaotic. Even as the colonial era waned and its critics became more numerous, the sentiment persisted that common law's influence in the colonies had been, on the whole, a positive one. As one legal scholar noted in the *Journal of African Law* at the dawn of many African nations' independence, "British administration in overseas countries has conferred no greater benefit than English law and justice" (Roberts-Wray 66). Underwriting this conviction was the long-held view of the British judge and, by extension, the system he represented, as a preserver and protector of African society. A colonial judge in Nigeria viewed his court's particular duty in this way:

> I regard this court in its equity jurisdiction as in some measure by virtue of the jurisdiction sections of the Supreme Court Ordinance 'the keeper of the conscience' of native communities in regard to the absolute enforcement of alleged native customs. (Ajayi 104)

The salutary appraisal of western jurisprudence in colonial Africa reflected the law's purported pluralism in integrating native custom with imported English law. Such integration, however, was idealistic at best: in reality, legal issues were addressed through parallel legal systems, that of English-administered courts and of the Native Courts, which were presided over by local chiefs. If a case could not be settled in a Native Court of Appeal, it was brought before a superior (Magistrates' or Supreme) Court. British officials in these courts were instructed to apply native or customary law to colonial subjects, provided that this law met the requirements of the Repugnancy Clause, which excluded practices that were anathema to "justice, equity, and good conscience" (Roberts-Wray 77). In theory, this integration was meant to tolerate and preserve existing African traditions by applying law in its local context. In practice, the confluence of these two legal systems often resulted in misreading and fragmentation, as magistrates and judges frequently misunderstood, and consequently misapplied, native law. The result was a system choked with confusion, in which British officials tended to construe indigenous practices according to their own assumptions and priorities. Not surprisingly, African customs often did not meet the repugnancy test, and those that did were frequently misunderstood by magistrates and judges, who interpreted exceptional customs as legal practices.

Ironically, the repugnancy doctrine formalized a haphazard editorial process, embedding the acceptable elements of native custom into colonial law through an irregular method of incongruent decisions. In their new imperial context, these traditions acquired a textual and political stability that reinforced the aims of empire rather than sustaining a local past. Legal scholar Peter Fitzpatrick argues:

> The potent implication of the repugnancy clause is that the native does not have a distinct and integral project since, with the repugnancy clause, a part of the resident culture can be denied here and a part there without any harm to a significant fabric of existence. Such an ultimate negation by imperialism was profoundly identified by Fanon as the fragmentation of a life once lived and the consequent rigidification of the fragments, the dynamic of which is now external to them. (110)

The difficulty of determining customary law, moreover, was compounded by the fact that this law was rooted in oral tradition; it was, quite literally, unreadable. It is with this illegibility in mind, perhaps, that British administrators instituted the practice of having native expert witnesses testify to the existence of their own laws—testimonies which subsequently would be recorded and integrated into the common law doctrine of *stare decisis*, the practice of relying on past precedents. Since *stare decisis* was not part of native law, the assumption that precedents existed and could be woven handily into the fabric of customary law changed this law beyond recognition, often turning a misinformed interpretation of custom into a binding decision. By recording decisions in this way, British legal administrators established "a body of precedent, turning local law into something akin to English case law. Precedents were invoked and debated not only in British courts, but also in indigenous ones, where actors sometimes framed their arguments against the backdrop of their understanding of how matters would be handled in colonial courts" (Mann and Roberts 14). The insistence also created, in legal practice and legal writing, a history—a juridical lineage through which the past could be traced and followed. Confounded by this complex network of intentions and circumstances—the ambiguous interface between the two legal regimes—administrators, judges, plaintiffs and defendants often missed each other in the dim light at the intersection of English and customary law.

As a way of mastering the potential uncertainty that could arise, colonial administrators drew heavily on the work of anthropologists. I will argue that the court in *Lewis v. Bankole,* in calling expert witnesses to testify to native practices, conducted itself in the manner of an investigative anthropologist. It is a well-documented fact that anthropologists were anything but foreign bodies in colonial legal policies, an involvement that resonates throughout *Things Fall Apart* in the omniscient narrator's voice, which often sounds curiously like that of a lay anthropologist. British administration of Africa had a history of drawing upon anthropological research, which was seen as objective, thorough, and unhampered by ideology. It thus became a critical and fitting ally in jurists' efforts to export British law to Africa. As one writer wistfully put it, "it is here that the work of the anthropologist is of such great value; he has the time to observe, he has no work which has to be done in a stated time, in fact he has no axe to grind except to obtain the information he desires" (Roberts 50). Such sentiment was not uncommon in the development of colonial law and administration, lending its architects an even-handed tone that was the benchmark of effective lawmaking and offering a studious, scrupulous promise of impartiality stripped of ideological underpinnings.

For their part, anthropologists were in no hurry to dismiss such praise. Even those critical of colonial practices were quick to defend their merits and overall good intentions—as did Edwin Smith, President in 1937 of the Royal Anthropological Institute. Smith writes apologetically in his introduction to a slim volume entitled *Tangled Justice,* "In throwing doubt upon the wisdom of some of the laws which have been put in force in Africa one is not impugning the motive, nor questioning the ability, of the men responsible. The ideal of justice and good government is the guiding star of British administration" (Roberts 2). Presumably part of the justice and good government to which Smith refers is not unrelated to its reliance on the findings of his own discipline, which delivered critical evaluations with the reassurance of their objectivity, lending intellectual and cultural substance to colonial legal policies.

## II.

The landmark case of *Lewis v. Bankole* was decided in the Colony of Lagos in 1909. The plaintiffs in *Lewis* claimed joint ownership rights to the property in question, an area of land referred to as Mabinuori's Compound; in order to establish these rights, they sought a declaration that the land was family property—which cannot be sold according to customary law—rather than private property, which, in accordance with English common law, can be transferred through the sale of land. With this indigenous concept of inheritance at stake, the case goes back not to the onset of the family's troubles, but to the beginning of the family itself:

> Chief Mabinuori died in 1874, leaving a family of twelve children, the eldest of whom was a daughter . . . In 1905 an action was brought by certain of Mabinuori's grandchildren . . . against certain of the occupants of the family compound who were daughters of Mabinuori and children of a deceased younger son. The claim was for a declaration (1) that the plaintiffs were entitled, as grandchildren of Mabinuori, in conjunction with the defendants, to the family compound, and (2) that the family compound was the family property of Mabinuori deceased. (*Lewis v. Bankole* 81)

In the years leading up to the decision, Mabinuori's Compound had become a source of tension between the children of Mabinuori's oldest son, Fagbemi, and Mabinuori's surviving daughters. After Fagbemi's death in 1881, his son Benjamin Dawodu took over the management of the property; after his death in 1900, his brother James Dawodu, one of the plaintiffs, succeeded as head of the family. During this time, the management of the land—and specifically, the two shops that had been built on that land—was taken over by the defendants, Mabinuori's daughters, who assumed responsibility for leasing the shops and collecting the rents. The daughters' relations with James Dawodu deteriorated, however, following his objection to his aunts' dealings with a European firm. Asserting his position as head of the family by patrilineal descent, Dawodu and several other grandchildren of Mabinuori initiated proceedings to establish legal entitlement, together with the daughters of Mabinuori, to the family compound, a block of land on the north side of Bishop Street between the Marina and Broad Street in Lagos.

*Lewis v. Bankole* was one of the first cases in which native law, and specifically the notion of family property, was the governing principle. Acting Chief Justice Speed declared in the initial proceedings in 1908 that "perhaps for the first time the Court is asked to make a definite pronouncement on the vexed question of the tenure of what is known as family property by native customary law, and the principles upon which that law should be enforced" (*Lewis v. Bankole* 82). Speed ultimately ruled for the defendants, arguing that the plaintiffs had received enough inheritance from Mabinuori to disqualify them from further rights over the family's land. Six months later, however, his decision was overturned by the Full Court, which remitted the case to the Divisional Court with two instructions: the Court was to determine which native law or custom applied in the situation, and was to reconsider the case in light of that finding.

The task of responding to the Divisional Court's request amounted to more than simply identifying the guiding principles of native property law, since colonial legal doctrine considered native law to be a question of evidence rather than law. As one judge put it in a later case, reversing the decision of a lower court: "The learned Judge appears to have referred to it as though it were a legal textbook of such authority as would warrant its citation in Court, which it certainly is not, for *native law and custom is a matter of evidence and not of law*" (*Belio Adedibu v. Gbadamosi and Sanusi* 192). To attain legal status within a colonial court, in other words, native law had to be proven, not merely presented. As I have already mentioned, the business of establishing this proof often involved authorities, such as local chiefs or individuals with expertise in native traditions, who were called as witnesses to establish the law. In keeping with this practice, the Court in *Lewis* decided to conduct a trial within a trial, consulting experts of indigenous law in order to reconstruct the case along customary lines. The story of this performance, which comes at the conclusion of several lengthy and often convoluted explanations of the case, ultimately functions as the turning point in the legal proceeding, and was viewed by the Court as the key to the legal riddle that had been troubling Mabinuori's family for years.

To establish which native law applied in *Lewis,* the Divisional Court summoned a group of Lagos chiefs to simulate a series of decisions relating to the case. The chiefs, as expert witnesses, were placed under oath and presented with a number of situations involving the vital elements of the case before the Court. The Court, in other words, did not present its expert witnesses with the case itself, but rather with a hypothetical range of scenarios, designed to extract the appropriate rule without divulging the case's actual details. For each scenario, the chiefs gave their rulings; some concurred, others differed from each other. In the end, the Court seemed to weigh only those rulings backed by consensus; the differences among the chiefs were elided, and the Court ruled that the land should be divided among the family members.

The procedure appeared reasonable enough. In order to ascertain the relevant customary law, British judges turned to native judges to see what their decision would look like in a native court, thereby gaining a sense of which precedent would operate in the case's particular circumstances. What they created, however, was an illusion of precedent, in which the Lagos chiefs delivered opinions without binding power, performing—rather than handing down—a series of decisions without force on their own terms. Their rulings could only acquire judicial power within the Divisional Court's articulation and interpretation, which proceeded as though it had uncovered the underlying precedent rather than a range of possible approaches to the case.

Given the legal reasons for relying upon expert witnesses, it is striking that what the Court in *Lewis v. Bankole* found especially praiseworthy in the chiefs' testimonies was not their impartiality or judiciousness, but their polished presentation. Writing for the Court, Chief Justice Osborne expressed his approval of the witnesses not only because their high social status promised accuracy and truth, but also because they conducted themselves appropriately. "I have no reason to doubt the correctness of the chief's [sic] pronouncement of the customs which exist in Lagos at the present day," he notes. "Moreover, I was much impressed with the fair and business-like methods which they said they would have adopted if the case had been before them for decision" (*Lewis v. Bankole* 101). Osborne responds, in other words, not only to the content, but also to the form of their testimonies, a form that suggests something other than anthropological or legal objectivity and reasserts the court's dramatic—and thus subjective—production of precedent and law. Unlike an anthropologist, what he notes is not the chiefs' cultural or legal differences, but rather a presentation that he recognizes as his own: a similarity so striking and impressive that it confers legitimacy upon the chiefs' pronouncements. Osborne's account of the chiefs' conduct leaves one with little sense of how a court in Africa looked, or of how awkward and chaotic it often was. But given how deeply he is struck by the chiefs' "fair and business-like methods," one might well imagine that something considerably different was often the case. Along such lines, one might entertain a far less orderly scenario, in which two legal worlds with little in common were forced into jarring collision, making any judge relieved to discover the unexpected similarity rather than stumbling over differences. One observer in 1937 noted the surreal nature of the performance that was colonial justice:

> The newcomer to Africa visiting the Courts of Law in different parts of the country for the first time views with astonishment the scene before him. The presiding magistrate or Judge. On special occasions in his official robes of scarlet, seated with native assessors—counsel in their robes and the prisoner in the dock— the crowd of spectators kept back by native police in uniform. A repetition of an English scene in African surroundings, often of a primitive nature. The whole atmosphere is obviously unsuited to the African mentality. As he listens to the proceedings he realises that no primitive or even partly educated native can hope to understand the workings of British justice. The Court procedure is not understood by the prisoner. If he is guilty and wished to admit it, he is often told to plead not guilty. If he desires to explain he is told he must remain silent. (Roberts 65–66)

The scene comes closer to a performance—one that appears either as drama, comedy, even mystery—than it does to a straightforward legal proceeding. The chiefs' speech acts have none of the power associated with the performative utterances of speech-act theory. In this particular colonial context, then, the seemingly performative becomes merely performance. The apparently juridical language of the chiefs is drained of its productive capacity to bring a legal world into being: their legal pronouncements exert no force in and of themselves, but instead are wholly dependent upon the larger power structures of colonial administration. By depicting the colonial courtroom as a play of costumes, stage directions, and lines spoken without knowledge or conviction, the relationship between performance and law becomes descriptive rather than normative, and estranging rather than illuminating.

The strangeness is amplified, too, by the fact that not only the presence, but also the words of those on the stand were often placed in a different context. Thus we find that the chiefs' judgments, which elsewhere would have been the law itself, become part of a story that the colonial court tells about native law—a story that is reduced and subjected to interpretation, and finally to the decision of another court. The two worlds seem out of joint with each other—an awkwardness to which the court responds by noting the chiefs' exemplary, English-like conduct.

The judge in *Lewis v. Bankole* adds a procedural concern to his impressions, however, by calling attention to a more directly legal matter in the case: the question of whether Mabinuori's land can be transferred to non-family members. Even as he accepts the chiefs' conclusion that the land can be partitioned and that power over it can reside with the family matriarch, Justice Osborne takes issue with the opinion that the land can never be sold:

> There is one other point to which I must allude, and that is whether by native customary law the family house can be let or sold. According to the Lagos chiefs, the present custom is that it can be let with the consent of all the branches of the family, but cannot be sold. The idea of alienation of land was undoubtedly foreign to native ideas in olden days, but has crept in as a result of the contact with European notions, and deeds in English form are now in common use. There is no proposal for a sale before me, so it is not necessary for me now to decide whether or no a native custom which prevents alienation is contrary to section 19 [containing the repugnancy clause] of the Supreme Court Ordinance. But I am clearly of opinion that despite the custom, this Court has power to order the sale of the family property, including the family house, in any cause where it considers that such a sale would be advantageous to the family, or the property is incapable of partition. (*Lewis v. Bankole* 104–105)

In deferring to the expert witnesses while simultaneously asserting the court's power over them, Osborne gestures towards the limits of customary law. The Lagos chiefs may be familiar with current local practices regarding land tenure, but the ultimate authority on the issue remains the colonial judge. His statement, ironically, bears a hypothetical or conditional inflection—*if* a sale were proposed, *then* the Court would order a sale—similar to that in the chiefs' testimonies. There is, however, one crucial difference: while it may not be possible for Osborne to rule on the sale of property in this particular instance, he underscores his court's binding authority to determine such issues in the future. In harnessing the power of this hypothetical mode, Osborne turns his gaze towards the future: to the court's expanded jurisdiction and with it, to the prospect of British ownership along British lines. The status of the past in *Lewis v. Bankole* is another matter, and I turn now to the Court's iteration of law and history—a relationship that I will suggest has as much to do with historical time as it does with the time it takes for the opinion to tell its litigants' stories.

## III.

The story of Mabinuori's Compound begins with the initial proceedings in 1905 and ends with the 1909 verdict. The opinion is unusually long, owing to the fact that the case was heard by a number of different courts. My citations in this essay have been drawn from the final phase of this lengthy proceeding, which embeds the opinions of lower courts in framing its decision. To be sure, the genealogy of *Lewis v. Bankole* is a complicated one, spanning several generations and a vast number of children and grandchildren. As if enacting the family repetition of successive generations, each court records its own version of events and presents them at the next appellate level, creating a confusing narrative that proceeds in fits and starts, repeating itself in spite of the fact that the story might well have been summarized more succinctly. *Lewis v. Bankole* rehearses these details a perplexing number of times and in exhaustive detail, summarizing the issues at stake and tracing their evolution again and again, as if the court suffered from a kind of narrative repetition compulsion. Enacting the very repetition that writing enables, the opinion's reiterative prose often seems to be a desperate attempt to gain mastery over a story, the complexity of which threatens to overwhelm even the steadiest hand.

The length and repetition of the story, its appeal to the distant past, lends the opinion a resonant literariness, imbued with echoes of another endless trial: Jarndyce and Jarndyce of *Bleak House* (1853). Dickens's "scarecrow of a suit" (14), without origin or endpoint, has grown to such labyrinthine proportions in the novel that "no man alive knows what it means" (14). But the resonance of this famous literary trial, in all its humor, futility, and absurdity, is framed in *Lewis v. Bankole* by a drastically different context than that of Victorian London. To read it historically is thus to politicize its rhetoric, and to understand that its length, unlike Jarndyce and Jarndyce, bespeaks not only law's futility. It also underlines the struggle to establish the legitimacy of British rule.

The process of legitimation set in motion by *Lewis v. Bankole* marks the opinion's critical difference from the twists and turns of Dickens. Rather than extending eternally into both past and future, the case worked to incorporate a pre-colonial past into the fabric of colonial law, lending the latter an appearance of having evolved naturally from the laws of the land that preceded it. Colonial legal administrators were thus able to write into existence a long-standing relationship with native law, creating a history in which British presence was an integral part. For even as colonialism's supporters often justified its law through the British integration of native customs, this justification did not make the practice legitimate. Rather, it in fact risked underscoring just how constructed and potentially illegitimate such strategies in fact were. The repetition in *Lewis v. Bankole,* like that of written opinions and printed pages more generally, thus becomes a way to create legitimacy where none had existed before. As Hannah Arendt reminds us:

> Power needs no justification, being inherent in the very existence of political communities; what it does need is legitimacy . . . Legitimacy, when challenged, bases itself on an appeal to the past, while justification relates to an end that lies in the future. (52)

The ideologies behind colonialism and colonial law had already laid the justification for the colonial legal enterprise. This justification was part of the process of imagining a future, one that would realize the Commissioner's book in *Things Fall Apart,* and that would posit a narrative—and with it, a world—in which colony and metropole balanced each other in a civilized, fruitful coexistence. What remained to be provided, however, was the legitimacy for this work, by which I mean—following Arendt's reasoning—the creation of a connection between the colonial present and the pre-colonial past.

The narrative structure of British colonial law, which offered occasions for telling old stories in their present colonial context, afforded just such an opportunity for legitimacy. It did so by suggesting, through a process that wove together colonial weft and native warp, that colonial law was part of the story from the beginning, and thus that the legal narrative had evolved through its wheels and cogs. Pierre Bourdieu, in "The Force of Law," suggests that this historical effect issues from legal language at its most fundamental. "Juridical language," he observes, "reveals with complete clarity the *appropriation effect* inscribed in the logic of the juridical field's operation. Such language combines elements taken directly from the common language and elements foreign to its system" (819).

In colonial Africa, juridical language joined forces with the particularities of English common law—most notably, its doctrine of *stare decisis*—to appropriate not only a normative universe, but also to create a sense of historical inevitability. Piyel Haldar thus remarks that by incorporating local practices into a system of precedent, colonial jurists posited English history as the regnant paradigm:

> The *legis non scripta* that forms the basis of the doctrine of *stare decisis* marks the common law system as being specifically and peculiarly English. It is for the English and, above all, it derives directly from the English since an immemorial time. . . . It is a law which, since before the beginning of legal memory, has developed with the slow accretions of 'wisdom' that evolve from the spirit of English existence. (450)

The act of asserting English history as African history, moreover, reinforced the sense that colonialism did not simply redeem native subjects, but actively constituted them. As Peter Fitzpatrick concludes, the development of colonial law meant that "[t]he colonized are relegated to a timeless past without a dynamic, to a 'stage' of progression from which they are at best remotely redeemable and only if they are brought into History by the active principle embodied in the European. It was in the application of this principle that the European created the native and the native law and custom against which its own identity and law continue to be created" (110).

Furthermore, the act of repetition itself had the effect of making something real: a story repeated often enough eventually becomes the story, the official version of events. The fact that legal decisions were no longer left to an oral tradition, but were printed and published, only accelerated this process of repetition: a decision disseminated as text generates an infinite possibility of repetition. Martin Chanock aptly notes, "Writing is the tool of administration" (303). Yet the potential mastery that a text's circulation makes possible also illuminates the possibility that this official version is, at best, precarious—and at worst, illegitimate. Writing and repetition, I am suggesting, do not "make something real," but rather produce the *effect* of this real—an illusion of permanence and with it, a sense (rather than a guarantee) that justice has been done. Each repetition thus creates the possibility—and the desire—for administrative mastery, and simultaneously subverts it with the prospect of mastery's impossibility, and of the tenuous hold of British administration.

## IV.

Robert Cover imagines law as at once structural and temporal: for him, law was a way to imagine how things might be different in the future, but not necessarily how they *might have been different* in the past. Cover writes,

> Law may be viewed as a system of tension or a bridge linking a concept of a reality to an imagined alternative—that is, a connective between two states of affairs, both of which can be represented in their significance only through the device of narrative. ("Nomos and Narrative" 101)

In the context of colonial practice, however, Cover's bridge takes on a different form, one threatening to buckle under the weight of politics and history. In colonies, law became more than a bridge to the future: it became a way to the past; it not only reduced stories to a manageable size, but tore them out of context and recast them in new, more politically and legally convenient terms. It extended this new context into a narrative that extended the reaches of colonialism well into history—and thus, into legitimacy. Seen in this light, the gaps that colonial officials perceived went beyond those questions for which, in their eyes, customary law had no answers. The gaps they perceived, and those that were filled by repetition and publication, were those of their own absence.

Colonial legal practice gave both a history to the metropole and a language: through the work of reduction and lengthy repetition, it translated customary law into the language of English law. And in the process, it ushered in a legacy, a claim to ownership, that was more creative labor than it was historical—or, for that matter, anthropological—fact. In making sense of colonial jurisprudence, then, to speak of "the story of law" would be to offer a thin description of legal practices in Africa. To describe it as such is to distort the way in which the practice of colonial law turned native law into stories precisely in order to dissolve their status as law—to interpret these stories in order to transform them into something else: to recast the disparate voices of the Lagos chiefs into a uniform body of law; or the novel *Things Fall Apart,* into the book *The Pacification of the Primitive Tribes of the Lower Niger.* To be sure, Okonkwo and the Lagos chiefs still form part of the colonial narrative—"perhaps not a whole chapter but a reasonable paragraph, at any rate." When these paragraphs were spun out into narratives, subjects of colonialism could be imagined as such not simply because they were under a British rule of law, but because this law made them subjects of much larger stories—and thus, subject *to* stories.

## Works Cited

Achebe, Chinua. *Things Fall Apart.* 1959. New York: Doubleday, 1994.

Ajayi, F. A. "The Interaction of English Law with Customary Law in Western Nigeria: II." *Journal of African Law* 4:2 (1960).

Arendt, Hannah. *On Violence.* San Diego: Harvest/Harcourt Brace, 1969.

Austin, J. L. *How To Do Things With Words.* 1962. Cambridge, MA: Harvard University Press, 1975.

*Belio Adedibu v. Gbadamosi and Sanusi* (1951), 13 W.A.C.A. 191 (West African Court of Appeal).

Benjamin, Walter. "Theses on the Philosophy of History." *Illuminations.* Trans. Harry Zohn. Ed. Hannah Arendt. New York: Schocken, 1968. 253–264.

Bourdieu, Pierre. "The Force of Law: Toward a Sociology of the Juridical Field." *Hastings Law Journal* 38 (1987): 805–853.

Butler, Judith. *Excitable Speech: A Politics of the Performative.* New York: Routledge, 1997.

Caruth, Cathy. *Unclaimed Experience: Trauma, Narrative, History.* Baltimore and London: John Hopkins University Press, 1996.

Chanock, Martin. "The Law Market: British East and Central Africa." *European Expansion and Law: The Encounter of European and Indigenous Law in 19th- and 20th-Century Africa and Asia.* Eds. W. J. Mommsen and J. A. De Moor. Oxford: Berg, 1992. 279–306.

Connolly, William, ed. *Legitimacy and the State.* New York: New York University Press, 1984.

Cover, Robert. "Violence and the Word." *Narrative, Violence, and the Law: The Essays of Robert Cover.* Eds. Martha Minow, Michael Ryan, and Austin Sarat. Ann Arbor: University of Michigan Press, 1993. 203–238.

———. "Nomos and Narrative." *Narrative, Violence, and the Law: The Essays of Robert Cover.* Eds. Martha Minow, Michael Ryan, and Austin Sarat. Ann Arbor: University of Michigan Press, 1993. 95–172.

Dickens, Charles. *Bleak House.* 1853. Oxford and New York: Oxford University Press, 1996.

Dirks, Nicholas B., ed. *Colonialism and Culture.* Ann Arbor: University of Michigan Press, 1992.

Emenyonu, Ernest N., ed. *Emerging Perspectives on Chinua Achebe, Vol. 1: Omenka: The Master Artist.* Trenton, NJ: Africa World Press, 2004.

Fitzpatrick, Peter. *The Mythology of Modern Law.* London and New York: Routledge, 1992.

Gikandi, Simon. *Reading Chinua Achebe: Language and Ideology in Fiction.* London: J. Currey, 1991.

Haldar, Piyel. "Folk Understanding: In the Shadow of the Common Law." Rev. of *In the Shadow of Marriage: Gender and Justice in an African Community,* by Anna M. O. Griffiths. *Social & Legal Studies* 9:3 (2000): 449–458.

Kymlicka, Will. *Liberalism, Community, and Culture.* Oxford: Oxford University Press, 1991.

*Lewis v. Bankole, Nigeria Law Reports,* Vol. 1 (1881–1911) (1915).

MacKinnon, Catharine. *Only Words.* Cambridge, MA: Harvard University Press, 1993.

Mann, Kristin and Richard Roberts, eds. *Law in Colonial Africa.* Portsmouth, NH: Heinemann; London: Curry, 1991.

Miller, Christopher. *Theories of Africans.* Chicago and London: University of Chicago Press, 1990.

Muoneke, Romanus Okey. *Art, Rebellion and Redemption: A Reading of the Novels of Chinua Achebe*. New York: Peter Lang, 1994.

Okechukwu, Chinwe Christiana. *Achebe the Orator: The Art of Persuasion in Chinua Achebe's Novels*. Westport, CT: Greenwood Press, 2001.

Okpewho, Isidore, ed. *Chinua Achebe's Things Fall Apart: A Casebook*. Oxford: Oxford University Press, 2003.

Pickett, Terry. *Inventing Nations: Justifications of Authority in the Modern World*. Westport, CT: Greenwood Press, 1991.

Reynolds, Thomas H. and Arturo A. Flores, eds. *Foreign Law: Current Sources of Codes and Legislation in Jurisdictions of the World. Vol. 3: Africa, Asia, and Australia*. Littleton, CO: Fred Rothman, 1993.

Roberts, C. Clifton. *Tangled Justice: Some Reasons for a Change of Policy in Africa*. London: Macmillan, 1937.

Roberts-Wray, Kenneth. "The Adaptation of Imported Law in Africa." *Journal of African Law* 4:2 (1960).

Schmidtz, David. *The Limits of Government: An Essay on the Public Goods Argument*. Boulder, CO: Westview Press, 1991.

Simmons, A. John. *Justification and Legitimacy: Essays on Rights and Obligations*. Cambridge: Cambridge University Press, 2001.

Spivak, Gayatri Chakravorty. "Can the Subaltern Speak?" *Marxism and the Interpretation of Culture*. Eds. Cary Nelson and Lawrence Grossberg. Chicago: University of Illinois Press, 1988. 271–313.

Thomas, Nicholas. *Colonialism's Culture: Anthropology, Travel and Government*. Princeton: Princeton University Press, 1994.

JOSEPH R. SLAUGHTER

# *"A Mouth with Which to Tell the Story":*
# *Silence, Violence, and Speech in Chinua Achebe's*
# Things Fall Apart

"We are not so black (in the Niger) as they have painted us," writes George Goldie, head of the British owned Royal Niger Company, in a letter dated November 13, 1897 (quoted in Flint, 105). Goldie's missive to John Holt, an economic arch-rival and a man with competing trade interests through the Liverpool based African Association, helps to close the deal for a unification of trading partners that has been the subject of semi-secret negotiations during the last few months of 1887. Taking exception to recent reports issuing from the African Association and delivered to the British Foreign Office, Goldie's letter proposes to end the bad press through an amalgamation of the various trading companies. Goldie imagines that the elimination of market competition for the resources of the Niger and the Niger Delta would benefit the companies in a number of ways: 1) with the end of provincial economic interest, the profits of the trading concerns in relation to the untapped potential of the area would increase; 2) the potentially damaging reports of the Royal Niger Company's exploitative forms of production and its unfair trading practices might be quieted; and 3) the amalgamation would postpone, if not completely stave off, discovery of the Company's failure to comply with its Royal Charter by not having established an effective system of governance and administrative infrastructure on the

*Emerging Perspectives on Chinua Achebe.* Volume 1. *Omenka the Master Artist: Critical Perspectives on Achebe's Fiction.* ed. Ernest N. Emenyonu (Trenton, N.J.: Africa World, 2004): pp. 121–148. Copyright © 2004 Joseph R. Slaughter.

Niger, which risked royal displeasure and the revocation of the Company's charter.

In his letter, Goldie addresses the subject of the Liverpool reports by explicitly challenging the representation of their substance: "They say that we have been aggressive and pushing! I do not admit 'aggression.'" (105). The ambiguity of the significance of the "aggression"—whether it refers domestically to the charges of monopolizing tendencies or to some more humanitarian notion of unfair labor practices retains its rhetorical tangle throughout his sardonic exposition: "But, if true [that we have been aggressive], so much the better for them when they become our partners, our Co-Directors, and our co-rulers.

> They will re-christen 'aggression'; they will call it 'laudable energy,' and they will emulate us in its display (105).

In his letter to the African Association, Goldie's "wit" in describing his enterprise's commercial demeanor as "not so black" suggests, beyond its obvious racist implications, that the representations of his actions are at least as important to his project as the actual "nature" of his dealings. The rest of his response proceeds to foreground clearly a seemingly pedestrian point, that a colonial/imperial dressing up of the public language can mask an identified malignancy. The capitalized stress on the commercial promotion of his future partners to "Co-Directors," while the imperial "co-rulers" remains uncapitalized, typographically suggests that the appeal of corporate amalgamation lies in its economic rather than its bureaucratic and "civilizing" aspects. This sort of rhetorical sleight of hand is, of course, not peculiar to Goldie and his prospective partners.

Tzvetan Todorov identifies this same syncretic move as part and parcel of Spain's earlier conquest of the "Indies," and thus as a paradigm for subsequent European incursions into other parts of the world. Todorov's comments on the Valladolid controversy of 1571 that precipitated the drawing up of royal ordinances directing the mode of Spanish conquest in 1573—namely, that "Discoveries are not to be called conquests," and that "preachers should ask for their [the natives'] children under the pretext of teaching them and keeping them as hostages" such that "by these and other means are the Indians to be pacified and indoctrinated"—underscore the regal directness of the text: "it is not conquests that are to be banished, but the word *conquest;* "pacification" is nothing but another word to designate the same things, but let us not suppose that this linguistic concern is a futile one. Subsequently, one is to act *under cover* of commerce, by *manifesting* love, and without *showing* greed" (his italics, 174). Todorov's argument suggests that framing differently the language of conquest affects not only a rhetorical cover for a "potentially" immoral project, but that a shift in representational perspective will also produce an imperial approach with a manifestly different appearance.

The rhetoric of the Spanish royal ordinances again finds its purpose in George Goldie's original petition on behalf of the National African Company, which was granted its Royal Charter on July 10, 1886. The language of the petition is repeated as preambular material to the actual charter: "whereas the Petition further states that the condition of the natives inhabiting the aforesaid territories would be materially improved, and the development of such territories and those contiguous thereto, and the civilization of their peoples would be greatly advanced . . ." (reprinted in Flint, 331). The material improvement and the advancement of "civilization" alluded to in the opening sections of the charter falls out of the actual articulations of rights and responsibilities royally granted to the Company in the subsequent text. However, the rhetorical pretext of economic improvement and humanitarian advancement continues to occupy a privileged place in the communications between England and the territories as the interests move from commercial to imperial. Thus, in a letter from the British Foreign Office to Major C. M. Macdonald dated April 18, 1891, the British Secretary describes the goals of the administration in the southern Oil Rivers Protectorate: "I am to observe that your object should be, by developing legitimate trade, by promoting civilization, by inducing the natives to relinquish inhuman and barbarous customs, and by gradually abolishing slavery, to pave the way for placing the territories over which Her Majesty's protection is and may be extended directly under British rule"(reprinted in Newbury, 263). It is this language—of economics, pacification, and civilization—that Achebe ironizes in 1958 at the close of *Things Fall Apart* where, after the hero Okonkwo has hung himself in despair, the British colonial officer's interior monologue occupies the novel's final words:

> In the many years in which he had toiled to bring civilization to the different parts of Africa he had learnt a number of things. One of them was that a District Commissioner must never attend to such undignified details as cutting down a hanged man from the tree. Such attention would give the natives a poor opinion of him. In the book, which he planned to write, he would stress that point. As he walked back to the court he thought about that book. Every day brought him some new material. The story of this man who had killed a messenger and hanged himself would make interesting reading. One could almost write a whole chapter on him. Perhaps not a whole chapter but a reasonable paragraph, at any rate. There was so much else to include, and one must be firm in cutting out details. He had already chosen the title of the book, after much

thought: *The Pacification of the Primitive Tribes of the Lower Niger* (147–148).

The closing scene of the novel allegorizes the production of colonial and commercial knowledge that I will examine in greater detail throughout this essay. In the District Commissioner's writings the life of the hero, whose trials, troubles, and joys have mattered for the last 147 pages, will, at best, become for colonial officers and armchair imperial fanatics a short exemplum in the Blue Books of British history.

Most of the writing about the Niger territories in the late 19th and early 20th centuries was produced by the colonial powers. Dan Izevbaye explains that "The colonial administrations accumulated such a mass of information in their intelligence reports and other field studies of the different ethnic groups that many of these documents continue to serve scholars as important historical sources" (46). One might question the simultaneous over- and under-valuing of the term *important,* given that administrative reports were, perhaps, the major British import and that they were very often confidential. Izevbaye concludes that "while these sources seemed adequate to the British administration, they did not appear to have helped the colonial administrators to a sympathetic understanding of certain 'native institutions'" (46).

As part of the corpus of private and personal correspondence that led to the protectionist amalgamation of trading interests on the Niger and in the southern oil states, Goldie's letter to Hunt candidly recasts charges of violating native institutions that had been leveled against his own company by imputing them to the threat of a British government takeover of all concerned territories. Thus, Goldie attempts to unify his competition against the unprofitable and "impracticable" possibility of a nationalized English colonialism by appealing to a sense of progress and economic pragmatism that will not want to lose precious resources to a "fictitious and premature development"(Flint 105).The threat that official imperialism seems to pose to the commercial interests of private enterprise suggests that, at least in the case of Nigeria, evolutionary and developmental rhetoric may ambiguously underpin both economic and "civilizing" endeavors.

To this point I have tabled some of the concepts that will reappear throughout this essay: notions of language (and particularly writing) as a tool in the representation and function of colonial/imperial projects, ideas of fiction and development, and in particular a relationship that recognizes the rhetoric of development, or at least "premature development," as fictitious. These, perhaps, parallel, though I want to be suggestive rather than strict about this, the postcolonial "silence, violence, and speech" in the title of this essay. As a way to link (and unlink) these tenuous relationships, I will finish setting the table by turning to comments Achebe makes in his essays that fit more comfortably with literary notions of fiction and development. In "Colonialist Criticism," Achebe directly addresses what he calls "big-brother arrogance" in much Western literary scholarship on Africa. "The latter-day colonialist critic," Achebe argues, "sees the African writer as a somewhat un-finished European who with patient guidance will grow up one day and write like every other European, but meanwhile must be humble, must learn all he can and while at it give due credit to his teachers in the form of either direct praise or, even better since praise sometimes goes bad and becomes embarrassing, manifest self-contempt" (*Hopes* 69). It is perhaps enough here to suggest the pervasiveness of these ideas by reminding the reader of an oftquoted statement, and one that Achebe himself refers to, by which the missionary and humanitarian Albert Schweitzer explained his medical work in Africa: "The African is indeed my brother, but my junior brother" (69). The apparently alluring notion of evolutionary cultural and social develop-ment, the relationship of a younger brother to an elder, is here identified by Achebe as one which has migrated into the language and theories of literary criticism. That is, the same organic theories of development that underpinned a European colonialism make an appearance in the literary critical language that still tends to locate the African novel at a stage of "immaturity" in rela-tion to writing in the "West."

What follows in this essay is an examination not of a detailed relation-ship between any particular genre of colonial writing and the production of colonial knowledge but rather a broader attempt to contextualize *Things Fall Apart* in a field of colonial discourse. I claim, in some sense, that reaction to the novel, and the various generic labels it has elicited from western critics, can best be explained by recognizing its implicit relationships to the range of writing that meant to represent the Niger region and the experiences of its inhabitants. The examples of the various types of writing produced during the commercial and colonial periods of Nigeria's history are meant, then, to be illustrative, perhaps even paradigmatic, but by no means exhaustive of the full complex of writings. Ultimately, I am arguing that when *Things Fall Apart* is read in relation to these various modes of colonial writing, the novelistic techniques and themes can be recognized as at once allegorized and explicit responses, even antidotes, to the imperial forms of textual knowing. Grouping the wide range of writings that I will look at in one essay might seem careless (and certainly each of the modes deserves its own treatment), but as David Spun explains in his book on colonialist journalism, "Colonial discourse is not a matter of a given ideological position, but rather a series of rhetorical principles that remain constant in their application to the colonial situation regardless of the particular ideology which the writer espouses" (39). This essay examines two of the rhetorical principles that seem to remain constant in writings from and about turn-of-the-century "Nigeria."

### "Nearer to his Ancestors": Organic Development and Knowledge

"Go-di-di´-go-go-di-go," announce the drums that inform the people of
Umuofia of the death of a great man, setting the scene of the funeral in
chapter thirteen of Achebe's novel. Textually the funeral provides the occasion for Okonkwo to commit his accidental killing of the dead man's son
and precipitates his removal from the village. But in a sort of reversal of a
European teleological notion of individual development, the third person
narrator takes the occasion of the ceremony to comment on the human
life cycle: "A man's life from birth to death was a series of transition rites
which brought him nearer and nearer to his ancestors" (85). What should
be stressed in this description is not so much a notion that aging brings the
individual closer to death and therefore closer to the dead but rather that
through each transitional "rite" the individual concentrates his/her relationship among ancestors. This conception of development contrasts that
invoked by colonial rhetoric in the eighteenth and nineteenth centuries.

In his essay "On Liberty" from 1859, J. S. Mill explains that "Very few
facts are able to tell their own story, without comments to bring out their
meaning" (21). One of those "facts" that turns out to require comment is his
statement in the same work that "Despotism is a legitimate mode of government" (11). Just before entering into the central argument of "On Liberty,"
Mill pauses to consider the applicability of his analysis:

> It is, perhaps, hardly necessary to say that this doctrine is meant
> to apply only to human beings in the maturity of their faculties.
> We are not speaking of children, or of young persons below the
> age, which the law may fix as that of manhood or womanhood.
> Those who are still in a state to require being taken care of
> by others must be protected against their own actions as well
> as against external injury. For the same reason, we may leave-
> out of consideration those backward states of society in which
> the race itself may be considered as in its nonage. The early
> difficulties in the way of spontaneous progress are so great, that
> there is seldom any choice or means for overcoming them; and
> a ruler full of the spirit of improvement is warranted in the use
> of any expedients that will attain an end, perhaps otherwise
> unattainable. Despotism is a legitimate mode of government *in
> dealing with barbarians,* provided the end be their improvement,
> and the means justified by actually effecting that end. Liberty, as
> a principle, has no application to any state of things anterior to the
> time when mankind have become capable of being improved by
> free and equal discussion (11) (italics mine).

Mill's reservations about the applicability of his thought on liberty reflect an evolutionary notion of development, for individuals as for nations and peoples that had gained currency in the eighteenth and nineteenth centuries. His argument provides the theoretical/philosophical warrant that backs the imperial justifications for colonialism.

Perhaps the most influential elaboration of an organic, if fostered, theory of development appears in Rousseau's 1762 treatise on natural education, *The Emile*. Rousseau's suggestion that the French peasantry have little need of the kind of education he propounds because they already exist in some proto-natural relationship to development that has been socialized out of their urban compatriots, explains his choice of hypothetical pupil. "Let us choose our scholar among the rich," writes Rousseau, explaining that "we shall at least have made another man; the poor may come to manhood without our help. For the same reason I should not be sorry if Emile came of a good family" (22–23). Too, Rousseau ponders the impact of geography and climate on development and education, arguing that "if I want my pupil to be a citizen of the world I will choose him in the temperate zone, in France for example" (22). Unlike his disposition towards a romanticized version of the poor and the peasantry of France, Rousseau's thoughts on the role of climate offer a geographical explanation for his theory of racial inferiority: "a negro cannot live in Tornea nor a Samoyed in Benin. It seems also as if the brain were less perfectly organised in the two extremes. Neither the negroes nor the Laps are as wise as Europeans" (22). For Rousseau's tutor the non-European is not only less wise than the European, but the brain is less well organized. Perhaps Rousseau only means that the brains of non-Europeans organize information differently, but given an organic/evolutionary model of development, those differences in organization (if they can be located along a vector of "civilization") would suggest a sort of primitiveness.

For Rousseau, as for Mill a century later, the acquisition of language represents an important stage in the progressive development of the individual and of civilization. Emile is, Rousseau says, "twice over; born into existence, and born into life; born a human being, and born a man" (206). The emergence from a second birth corresponds to puberty in Rousseau, but it is also the moment after which the pupil "speaks himself" (207). Mill's evolutionary conceptions of human development and civilization mean that his principles of liberty are only applicable when "mankind has become capable of being improved by free and equal discussion" (11). And, in fact, his statement invokes the classical definition of barbarian as one who misuses, or is without, language. Thus, the development of, and the dealing with, "barbarians" could never, in an etymological sense, entail free speech and discussion. For both Mill and Rousseau language is conceived of as a means and an end in the movement towards liberty and maturity. As a means, language organizes knowledge in ways that are beneficial to the development of individuals. As an end, the existence of language and the possibility of discourse become evidence of development and civilization.

The appeal and influence of these evolutionary models in the nineteenth century can be seen not only in colonial administrators' writings, but also in the work of Africans living in Europe. In 1868 James Africanus Beale Horton, a Sierra Léonean of Igbo descent trained as a medical doctor in England, published a book called *West African Countries and Peoples* in which he states that "it will be my province to prove the capability of the African for possessing a real political government and national independence" (3). Horton's polemic, however, seems to subscribe to the European rhetoric of development when he adds that "a more stable and efficient Government might yet be formed in Western Africa, under the supervision of a civilized nation" (3). The rest of the book proceeds to argue that the West Africans are capable of being "civilized." While the book employs British colonial rhetoric—for example, in his section on the Igbo he recontextualizes a stereotype that "The Egboes are considered the most imitative and emulative of people in the whole of Western Africa; place them where you will, or introduce to them any manners and customs, you will find that they very easily adapt themselves to them" (157)—it does so in a fashion that, sometimes too subtly for today's reader makes a case for the dignity and identity of the African. So, despite the fact that Horton makes a frank appeal for colonialism based on an evolutionary conception of cultures, he also explicitly recognizes dangers inherent in that call. Though Horton writes that "Nothing tends more to the civilization of a barbarous country than the immigration of civilized individuals into it. . . . It is impossible for a nation to civilize itself; civilization must come from abroad" (175), he tempers his position by warning against a commercialized colonialism and its merchant abuses: "It must be remembered that the English are considered the mildest of all civilized nations in their dealing with savage nations; but if among them we find men capable of such barbarity [a trader's inexplicable stripping and flogging of a native], what civilization must they expect from other nations, and how many centuries will it require for their civilization by merchants?" (176–177). Of course, the history of British colonialism in Nigeria eventually proved accurate Horton's assessment of the dangers of a commercialized colonialism.

In *The Order of Things*, Foucault locates a shift in modes of knowledge at the end of the eighteenth century that, in its most general formulation, structures the ways in which knowledge is collected, ordered, and disseminated. Foucault identifies *taxinomia* as the paradigm of ordering in the seventeenth and eighteenth centuries and genesis as the principle subsequently. Thus he argues that "*taxinomia* establishes the table of visible differences; genesis presupposes a progressive series; the first treats of signs in their spatial simultaneity, as a syntax; the second divides them up into an analogon of time, as a chronology" (74). Foucault's explanation of "genesis" as an ordering principle corresponds to the ideas that underpin European notions of evolutionary development, and thus might make sense of a colonialist rhetoric that argues for the savageness of the Niger natives. However, much of the writing produced under colonial regimes collects and organizes information in a taxonomic or tabular form.

Edward Said's examination of the work of early orientalists describes the product of their studies in terms that resonate with Foucault's. Said characterizes the scholarship that introduced the modern language of Orientalism in the anthropology of Silvestre de Sacy as "essentially compilatory" and in the philology of Ernest Renan as harboring "the most esoteric notions of temporality, origins, development, relationship, and human worth" (134). The two strains of knowledge ordering that Foucault identifies in his work seem to coexist and to account for the beginnings of modern Orientalism in Said's analysis. In fact, the coexistence of these two models of thought continues to support each other through the stages of British colonialism. That is, while Foucault may be correct when he identifies a general epistemological shift in European thought, the majority of colonial/commercial writing about the Niger remains committed to representing its information, or "findings," in taxonomic and tabular form. The potential paradox of this fact can be explained by recognizing the founding paradox of much European colonialism. If Foucault is right, then perhaps the reliance on tabular/taxonomic ordering in colonial writings can be accounted for by the genetic principle itself. From a colonialist perspective, the evolutionary primitive mode of ordering represented by the table might seem to suit the study of a people who the genetic theory of civilization has designated savage.

These two modes of ordering will, in the British colonial context of Nigeria, reinforce two seemingly contrary textual principles of accounting and recounting, or, in the more literary models, invoicing and voicing. Showing that one form or the other of these textual principles has a greater affinity for a commercial or an imperial colonialism would require a more thorough examination of the available writings than I undertake here. However, for convenience sake and the organization of this essay, I associate more examples of writing informed by a narrative principle of voicing with the imperial as opposed to the commercial periods of colonialism. At any account, the intimacy between the commercial enterprises and the British government makes the discrimination of distinct colonial forms difficult, if not impossible.

Returning to *Things Fall Apart*, the notion of development in the novel is also intimately linked to the acquisition and use of language, but stress is placed on the role of language in creating a social and cultural space to accommodate the announcement of the individual. It is, for instance, only when

Okonkwo's daughter, Ezinma, can speak for herself, can tell the village where her *iyi-uwa* is buried that she takes her place among the living as a person, but also as a viable social being capable of narrating her own existence: "*No ogbanje* would yield her secrets easily, and most of them never did because they died too young—before they could be asked questions" (57). A child suspected to be an *ogbanje*—a child who dies, is reborn, and dies again to plague repeatedly its parents—can only demonstrate its humanity, and, therefore, its intention to remain among the living, at the point when it comes into speech as a social function. Other parts of the novel concern the troubled relationship between Okonkwo and his eldest son, Nwoye. Okonkwo has been sorely disappointed in his son until the arrival of Ikemefuna, a boy ransomed to the people of Umuofia as settlement for the killing of one of its daughters by another village. After spending three years in Okonkwo's family, Ikemefuna seems to have had, at least in Okonkwo's mind, a good influence on Nwoye. The narrator explains that "Okonkwo was inwardly pleased at his son's development.... He wanted Nwoye to grow into a tough young man capable of ruling his father's household.... And so he was always happy when he heard him grumbling about women. That showed that in time he would be able to control his women-folk" (37). Okonkwo is, of course, deluded by Nwoye's feigning annoyance at women, but in that delusion he proceeds to encourage Nwoye's maturation.

In the novel's terms, Nwoye's development is represented by physical displacement, from the "childishness" of his mother's hut to the "manliness" of his father's *obi*. Part of the displacement and development of Nwoye's personality and masculinity entails a narrative shift as well, and Okonkwo introduces him to "stories of the land—masculine stories of violence and bloodshed.... stories about tribal wars or how he had stalked his victim, over-powered him and obtained his first human head" (37). The associative gendering of stories in the novel creates a competition between genres of speech and storytelling, and the trouble between Okonkwo and Nwoye is only aggravated by the fact that although "Nwoye knew that it was right to be masculine and to be violent," somehow "he still preferred the stories that his mother used to tell ... stories of the tortoise and his wily ways, and of the bird *en-eke-nti-oba* who challenged the whole world to a wrestling contest and was finally thrown by the cat" (37–38). The distinctiveness of story forms in the novel suggests the existence of alternative relationships to knowledge and modes of organizing that knowledge. From a European perspective, "feminine" stories take on the role of myths and "masculine" stories that of history. The "mother" stories also tend to be metaphoric while the "father" stories arrange the world metonymically; that is, Okonkwo's stories create a sort of history through inventory (of heads, yams, and titles) while the women's stories allegorize the role of speech and stories themselves in relation to both the teller and the listener. The contest between these two genres, and the mediating appeal of the "poetry of the new religion," provides the motivational force that eventually drives Nwoye out of the village and into the Christian mission, the story of which is narrated not by Okonkwo but by Nwoye's mother (104).

For the current purposes of this discussion, the importance of these stories is not their content but the fact that the novel depicts the movement from one form of narrative to another as part of the process of development in Umuofia. The novel, in fact, suggests that individual development in Igbo society entails, or at least is emblematized by, a coming into, and a facility with, language and stories. The narrator's observation that "Among the Ibo the art of conversation is regarded very highly, and proverbs are the palm-oil with which words are eaten" delimits an end of social and cultural development that values language and a narrative order of knowing (5).

### Goldie's Game: Recording Secrets in the Colonial Archive

In a July 2, 1894 letter formalizing an employment offer with the Royal Niger Company, Sir George Goldie writes to then Captain Frederick Lugard officially reminding him of the agreement they had previously entered into orally. Goldie writes that "The Company" has been engaged in "opening up tropical Africa," an endeavor "practicable," he argues, only on the condition that, "in view of the difficulties resulting from the climate, the difficulty of access to inner Africa, the barbarism of the populations and other abnormal causes, abnormal energy, persistence, patience, and above all, *discipline* should be displayed by all the officials of The Company" (Perham and Bull 52). The condition of discipline, or at least its display, on the part of officials is stressed repeatedly as a way to avoid the "two greatest dangers at home": "the apathy of public opinion . . . about western Africa" and "the excitability of public opinion, for short periods, when led astray on some popular hobby, by one sided or exaggerated reports" (53). Discipline, for Goldie, becomes a way to maintain the company's monopoly in the project of "opening up" tropical Africa, and the precise meaning of corporate discipline is elaborated in the final portions of his letter

> Every official of The Company, whether a member of the Council or a judge or an Executive officer or a soldier is very properly bound not to publish, nor to communicate to anyone likely to publish, anything connected with The Company as a Government or as a commercial society, or the Company's Territories or regions visited when in The Company's service, without the previous assent of the Governing Body of The Company.
>
> You will understand that in the difficult and complicated game which The Company is playing, every move of which has to be

calculated with the greatest care, it would be intolerable that any
individual should be allowed to be the judge of what he might
(directly or indirectly) publish or communicate to other persons
than the Council of the Company (53).

The discipline that Goldie seeks imposes a gag order meant to keep secret
any information or knowledge gathered by the Company's employees. The
rules of Goldie's game, although not completely in place until the signing of
the *General Act of The Conference of Berlin* in 1885, are dictated by international law and agreements made by the European powers for the scrambling
of Africa. The movements of the pieces, however, are only generally suggested in the articles of the Company's charter. The rules declare that "The
trade of all nations shall enjoy complete freedom" and that "All the Powers exercising sovereign rights or influence in the aforesaid territories bind
themselves to watch over the preservation of the native tribes, and to care for
the improvement of the conditions of their moral and material well-being,
and to help in suppressing slavery" *(General Act)*. While the Berlin Act
grants trade its freedom, no nation or individual with imperial/economic
interests in Africa construed the document to suggest that information
about trade obtained the same right. Thus, alluding to a sort of practical
statute of limitations on the utility of information about the Niger, Goldie
writes to Lugard that "There will be no difficulty about your publishing
books or delivering addresses after your return, *provided that all proofs are
subject to the revision of the Council*" (his stress, Perham and Bull 53).

In a personal statement appended to the official letter from the Company, Goldie explains that "it must not be imagined that The Company has
any desire to hide its actions under a bushel, but it claims and insists on its
right to state its own case" (54). Further, Goldie honors Lugard's sense of
discipline with the personal assurance that "I have no reason to doubt that
whatever you might write would pass the necessary revision in this office
with but little alteration; but it is only fair to say that there are a great number
of matters on which it would be decidedly inadvisable that anything should
as yet be published" (54). Lugard affixes his signature and remits the proper
portions of the letter to the Company, zealously pledging himself "to observe
the conditions required of me, not only during my term of service with The
Company, but for five years after its conclusion" (55).

The prohibition against publication and the disposition of secrecy serve a
pragmatic function in light of the stories that were making the rounds among
Liverpool merchants of atrocities committed by King Leopold's interests in
the Belgian Congo (Pakenham 586). It seems a safe conclusion to assume
that the information gathered under the objectives Goldie details are at least
some of what Lugard was to keep secret. Thus, beyond Lugard's attempts to

conclude diplomatically land right treaties with the natives, he is to gather survey data, to "collect general information of every kind . . . but especially to make inquires as to the existence of gold," "to obtain from natives . . . the greatest possible number of lists of itineraries," and "to note specially prevalence of Gum trees, Shea Butter trees, and rubber vines" (Perham and Bull 59). What is not suggested in Goldie's guidelines is a need to conceal relations and confrontations with the natives. A certain tendency in colonialist discourse would have made such a warning unnecessary, although Margery Perham and Mary Bull do discuss the issue of Africans in the notes on their editorial policy that preface the publication of Lugard's diaries: "Africans do not play a large part in Lugard's account, and it has not been possible to find biographical details for any of the men mentioned" (42).

The exigencies of secrecy obviously affect the manner in which information is conveyed from the colonial territories to England, but they also affect and order the ways in which individuals working for the Company relate to each other and the language in which they write their own private stories. Lugard's diaries were not published until the 1950s, and, as the introduction to them makes explicit, they were intended to be secret and to serve, in part at least, as a daily record from which he could prepare the company's reports (12). The diaries read much like other travel writings by Europeans in Africa.

Mary Louise Pratt's extensive reading of the features found in the writing of Europeans in Africa provides a thorough account of the narrative structure of those texts, and, rather than retread her ground, a quick summary of her conclusions should suffice to describe generally Lugard's diaries. A particularly poignant evaluation of John Barrow's *Account of Travels into the Interior of Southern Africa in the Years 1797 and 1798* leads Pratt to identify some of the conventional features of this explorer/travel writing: "In the main, what is narrated proves to be a descriptive sequence of sights/sites, with the travelers present chiefly as a kind of collective moving eye which registers these sights. Their presence as agents scarcely registers at all" (141). Stressing the "objective," self-effacing tendencies in another passage from Barrow's writings, Pratt shows how "the travelers' struggle to cross the river is not narrated but expressed in a much more mediated fashion, as an enumeration of the traits of the river that produced the difficulty" (142). Beyond the elision of a perceptive subject in these passages, what stands out as peculiarly distinctive about the "African landscape," and the African peoples as they are encountered, is a narrative "othering" that makes the individual, or the discrete episode, stand for an eternalized and static "history" or "truth." Thus, as Pratt explains, the 'He' that pronominalizes a particular African "is *a sui generis* configuration, often only a list of features set in a temporal order different from that of the perceiving and speaking subject" (140). This conventionalizing of description is, of course, not limited to travel and explorer writing. Rather, the invoicing and atomizing mode of much colonialist writing effaces and circumscribes the presence and voicings of individuals, both the "natives" and the "explorers," involved in actual encounters and struggles.

The features of travel narratives that Pratt identifies secret the same information that the corporate account books and reports elide, namely the existence of a native people that stands behind the text's metonymic constructive principles. In fact, the objectives that Goldie set before Lugard requested lists and taxonomies as the medium of representing to the Company both his experiences and the resource potential of the Niger. Lugard's diaries similarly take an inventory of events, places, and people encountered on his forays rather than emplotting his experience in a particular setting with individual characters.

The tendency of colonial/commercial discourse to secrecy may be best illustrated by the fate of reports that were prepared in contravention to the normal constructive principle.

In the late 1880s Major C. M. Macdonald was asked by the British Foreign Office to prepare two studies on the effectiveness and impact in the region of Goldie's Niger Company. The Foreign Office kept both reports confidential, allowing them to be seen limitedly for the first time in 1952. Macdonald found that the Company had dealt unfairly with the natives, had responded to discontent with violent reprisals from its private armed forces, and that it had failed to establish the administrative infrastructure that the charter required. Macdonald also discovered that at least some of the treaties made with local leaders had been concluded under false pretenses, hearing from one of the Company's native translators that "I made him [the 'King'] understand that he ceded his country to the Company. I made him understand that he gave his country to the Company for trading purposes . . . but I was not aware that 'ceding' meant giving over the rights of government and I dare not have made that suggestion to him" (quoted in Flint 139).

Rather than recount the findings of the reports, I want to stress the manner in which they were prepared and written. John Flint, who has studied the original confidential papers in the Foreign Office, explains that colonial reports of this type were generally prepared under the prescriptive guiding principle of "Imperial interests." Major Macdonald, however, seems to have "assumed . . . that his task was to find out the wishes of the Africans, and implement them. For him 'Imperial interests' were the interests of the Africans" (130). Thus, Macdonald conducted a "rudimentary kind of plebiscite" as he traveled around the Oil Rivers region, gathering as many different opinions and stories as he could elicit from the people: locals, administrators, and traders alike (130). The final reports, of course, could not possibly find accommodation in a colonial discourse that demanded secrecy and inventory, or perhaps secrecy through inventory, and were, therefore, relegated to the vaults in the British offices. The imposition of secrecy contractually agreed to by Lugard and imposed upon Macdonald is a clear example of the ways in which colonial discourse polices its practitioners. Literary texts tend not to be quite so crude in their configurations, examinations, and constructions of silence.

## "Where one's mouth was": Secrets and Lies and Other Oversights of Empire

"The night," writes Achebe at the beginning of Chapter Eleven of *Things Fall Apart*, "was impenetrably dark" (67). The narrative voice that opens this episode of the novel sets the environment in which the night's events take place with a Conradian epithet that at once borrows from and revises Marlow's own narrative practices in *Heart of Darkness*.

However, unlike Marlow's sweeping assignment of "impenetrable darkness" to an inhuman African nature and condition, Achebe's narrator humorously and matter-of-factly unpacks the impenetrability of that circadian darkness: "The moon had been rising later and later every night until now it was seen only at dawn. And whenever the moon forsook evening and rose at cock-crow the nights were as black as coal" (67). In Conrad, the "impenetrable darkness" has a metaphysical, if "inscrutable," cause and, therefore, meaning. Conradian darkness, in part, prompts a ruminative Marlow to entertain a "suspicion" of remote kinship with the Africans he cannot perceive, but, like other forms of colonial account keeping, it also relegates Africa and Africans to the metaphorically "dark" eras and spaces of European thought. An often-quoted example from Marlow's narrative equates impenetrability not only with prehistory and emptiness but also with silence: "Going up that river was like traveling back to the earliest beginnings of the world, when vegetation rioted on the earth and the big trees were kings. An empty stream, a great silence, an impenetrable forest" (66). The silence of impenetrability variously possesses Marlow and Kurtz and is possessed by them. However, the story Marlow tells sets up the antagonism between a voicing narrative—the kind which Kurtz cannot tell as a result of the reduction of his capacities to a state of pure, disembodied voice—and an imperial invoicing project—figured as a keeping and itemizing of accounts most explicitly represented by the station clerk and his clinical, antiseptic ledgers and lists. The contest for imperial control of the story line, of representation, and thus the contest over how to understand Kurtz in relation to the company's project, and Marlow's relation of the story becomes an implicitly thematic conflict for the characters in the novel itself. Marlow, lying on the deck of the steamship while it is under repair, overhears the manager and his nephew discussing the necessity for the upcoming journey to the inner station. Responding to a description of the complications Kurtz causes the station manager, the uncle consoles him by explaining that "The climate may do away with this difficulty for you" (63). The conversation proceeds, illustrating the constructive and representative competition between voicing and invoicing:

> "He [Kurtz] sent his assistant down the river with a note to me in these terms: 'Clear this poor devil out of the country, and don't bother sending more of that sort. I had rather be alone than have the kind of men you can dispose of with me.' It was more than a year ago. Can you imagine such impudence!" "Anything since then?" asked the other hoarsely. "Ivory," jerked the nephew; "lots of it—prime sort—lots most annoying, from him." "And with that?" questioned the heavy rumble. "Invoice," was the reply fired out, so to speak. Then silence (63).

Voicing in *Heart of Darkness* is not an uncomplicated affirmation of narrative capacity, just as invoicing is clearly not an inherently contemptible mode of discursive accounting. But Marlow's narrative is structured around the principles of invoicing and secrecy, and although he claims to detest lying, he misrepresents Kurtz's pamphlet on the civilization of the "savages" by excising the offending postscriptum in which Kurtz scrawled the infamous words "Exterminate the brutes."

Philosophically, and even theologically, Conrad uses the Jansenist trope of "impenetrable darkness" to signify the inscrutable beginnings of man. That is, Africa stands in the European imagination on the timeline of organic development as that place from which human beings emerged, and thus as a place that is ultimately unknowable. This, of course, is another way of deploying the evolutionary model of development so that Africa becomes the physical location for the staging of a European confrontation with its pre-existence. What the editors of Lugard's journals said about the role of Africans in his writings could equally be said of *Heart of Darkness*, that "they do not play a large part." The secrecy that enshrouds the figure of the African may, in fact, be dictated by the same commercial interests that quieted Lugard. Early in his narrative, after he has signed the company contract, Marlow says that "I undertook amongst other things not to disclose any trade secrets," and he affirmatively submits, "Well, I am not going to" (36). Later in the novel, after determining that the native heads displayed on spikes outside of Kurtz's hut are not "ornamental but symbolic," Marlow reiterates his commitment to secrecy: "I am not disclosing any trade secrets" (96–97). As a reader, one must wonder what precisely are the secrets Marlow keeps, but as a critic it seems compelling to ask how a principle of narrative secrecy inflects the text. These questions cannot likely be answered by looking at Conrad's text in isolation, and I believe that Achebe suggests a response in his novel.

The passage that opened this section of the essay in which Achebe debunks the impenetrability of darkness by explaining certain facts about the moon and the night continues by exploring the importance of speech and the shapes of stories that are shared in the darkness of an African night. However, rather than inf(l)ecting the narrative with secrecy, the narrator domesticates the darkness, ironizing Marlow's fixation by explaining that inside one of Okonkwo's wife's huts "A palm-oil lamp gave out a yellowish light. Without it, it would have been impossible to eat; one could not have known where one's mouth was in the darkness of that night" (67). In a direct affront to the European imagination of "impenetrable darkness," the characters in the novel are capable not only of finding their mouths for eating, but also for speaking.

This introduction to darkness establishes the scene of speech in which the most elaborate of the narrative interventions continues the polyphony of voices in the novel. Ekwefi, Okonkwo's youngest wife, and her daughter Ezinma, his favorite child, exchange stories through acts of narration that are more than mere ways to pass the time, more than idle and simple lessons in the guise of parable. Rather, the sharing of stories is itself figured as a process of development in which the daughter practices her storytelling skills as part of her matrimonial heritage. Barbara Harlow has commented on this scene and noted that an examination of the role of women in *Things Fall Apart* "would identify women as the main storytellers . . . a function that, on the one hand, affirms African women as the bearers and nurturers of African traditions but that, on the other hand, subjects that charge to a new interpretation when these very traditions are rewritten and given a vital assignment within the strategies of national liberation" (79 n.1). Harlow reads the mothertale of the Tortoise and the Birds as an anti-colonialist allegory, one which demonstrates the need for the natives of the nation (the birds) to use both force and rhetoric to overthrow a colonialist power (the tortoise). The story Ekwefi tells to her daughter through the impenetrable darkness can also, however, be read as a warning passed from mother to daughter against Okonkwo's fathertales. Ekwefi's story recounts how all the birds had been invited to a feast in the sky. The wily Tortoise soon discovered their plans and, despite their initial protestations, convinced the birds to provide him with feathers so he could accompany them to the feast. As they were all flying to the party, the birds elected Tortoise to be their spokesman. He explained it was customary that they all take new names for the event. After the birds had chosen their names, Tortoise declared that "He was to be called *All of you*" (68). When the people of the sky offered their food to all of you, Tortoise convinced the birds that it was the people's custom to feed the spokesman first. Soon there was nothing left; the birds took back their feathers and abandoned Tortoise with no way to return home. Parrot, however, agreed to deliver a message to his wife. When Parrot reached Tortoise's house, he told his wife to place all of the hard objects they owned out in front of the house. Tortoise, unable to see clearly because of the height, jumped and broke his shell on the "hoes, matchets, spears, guns and even his cannon" (70). A medicine man repaired his shell, but, according to Ezinma's story, it has not been smooth since.

While this story would likely be read from an ethnological perspective as a pseudoscientific, mythical explanation of how tortoise broke his shell, Harlow has persuasively argued that the story also illustrates an anti-colonial imperative of using the tools of both rhetoric and weaponry to unburden a colonized country (75). While I find Harlow's explication of the story provocative and convincing, I think the one-to-one mapping of the story onto a strict anti-colonialist allegory risks diminishing other insinuative aspects of the tale. The story not only illuminates generally the colonial situation, but it also provides a particular warning against the dangers of a metonymic system of political and civic representation in Igbo society. That is, the story contains significant warnings about both external and internal threats from an ambitious and universalizing individualism.

Perhaps the most illustrative example of the internal metonymic usurpation of the people's voice is reflected in the language of the Royal Niger Company's treaties. In his essays, Achebe explains that there are two general strains of myths in his home village of Ogidi that explain the absence of kings in his society (*Hopes* 163–164). And yet, the British required sovereigns to authorize the legitimacy of the treaties they concluded with the people of southeastern Nigeria. Thus, they sometimes rhetorically created kings and kingships where none had existed before. The language of the *Agreement between Onitsha and the National African Company* from 20 August *1884* and the subsequent revisions of that Agreement in the *Onitsha Protectorate Treaty* of 9 October 1884 exemplify this point. The first agreement states that "We, the undersigned King and Chiefs of Onitsha, after many years of experience, fully recognize the benefit accorded to our country and people by their intercourse with the National African Company (Limited), and in recognition of this we now cede the whole of our territory to the National African Company (Limited) and their administrators for ever" (reprinted in Newbury 107). The second agreement, concluded by the British government when questions arose about the legitimacy of private enterprise treaties under international law, reads "The King, Queen, and chiefs of Onitsha hereby engage to assist the British Consular or other officers in the execution of such duties as may be assigned to them, and further, to act upon their advice in matters relating to the administration of justice, the development of the resources of the country, the interests of commerce, or in any other matter in relation to peace, order, and good government, and the general progress of civilization" (109).

In a further tortoisy move, H. P. Anderson circulates a confidential memorandum in the British Foreign Office that asks for guidance in interpreting the treaties for the upcoming Berlin Conference. "We should have to refer in Conference to our Treaties," he worries. "The first question to be decided . . . is what interpretation we put on those Treaties. . . . They do not, like the French Treaties, mention the word 'suzerainete', but they are believed to be much on the same lines of the German Treaties. The Germans, as we know, interpret these as conferring an exclusive German Protectorate; *what view should we say* that we take of ours?" (my emphasis 186). The concern over a unified interpretative stance in relation to the treaties stresses the rhetorical use of the "agreements." In a preface to a governmental collection of British West African documents, the authors explain that none of the treaties were considered to have the force of law; rather, "The obligations they impose are of a moral, not a legal order; and if the Crown disregards them there is no redress" (Wight 8). Thus, the documentary elevation of a native individual to the status of king, to a metonymically usurped form of tortoise's "all of you," does not establish a speaking subject among the Igbo, but rather rhetorically sanctions a voice that guarantees the transfer of that capacity to the British.

The tale of the Tortoise and the Birds, however, cannot be limited to an allegorized version of these historical events. At a more general level, the breaking of Tortoise's shell foreshadows Okonkwo's self-destruction and re-confirms the danger of a metonymic, atomizing practice of representation. Both Tortoise and Okonkwo have committed the same rhetorical/narrative crime. There is some textual justification for Okonkwo's sense that he has somehow earned the right to act unilaterally on behalf of the people of Umuofia. The novel opens with a mythologizing of Okonkwo:

> His fame rested on solid personal achievements. As a young man of eighteen he had brought honor to his village by throwing Amalinze the Cat. Amalinze was the great wrestler who for seven years was unbeaten, from Umuofia to Mbaino. He was called the Cat because his back would never touch the earth. It was this man that Okonkwo threw in a fight which the old men agreed was one of the fiercest since the founder of their town engaged a spirit of the wild for seven days and seven nights. The drums beat and the flutes sang and the spectators held their breath. Amalinze was a wily craftsman, but Okonkwo was as slippery as a fish in water. Every nerve and every muscle stood out on their arms, on their backs and their thighs, and one almost heard them stretching to breaking point. In the end Okonkwo threw the Cat (3).

But, in an often-overlooked passage, Okonkwo is replaced in the symbolic order of things by a newcomer twenty years after his own match. Umuofia enshrines the young wrestler in Okonkwo's place, in the words of the new village song: "Who will wrestle for our village? Okafo will wrestle for our village. . . . Has he thrown a hundred Cats? He has thrown four hundred Cats. Then send him word to fight for us" (36). In the village of Umuofia, Okonkwo's role as a fighter, as a doer, has waned; what is left to him as expression of his influence is that which is left to all of the village elders, language and speech, demonstrations that are difficult for a stammering man. Okonkwo's undoing at the end of the novel results from his inability to speak persuasively and from his rash preference for decisive action over the culturally sanctioned discursive form of mediation.

The allegory of the Tortoise and the Birds underscores the need for balance in responding to an immediate threat. The fact that the story can be interpreted as both a lesson in colonial resistance and a warning against the sort of isolated hotheaded response of the individual dramatically illustrates the subtlety of the African *griot*. Examining a Hausa tale, Achebe emphasizes the inherent subversive power in its structure, a power which will surface, he says, in "a revolutionary time, and when it comes you don't need another story. It is the same story that will stand ready to be used; and this to me is the excellence of the griot in creating laughter and hiding what you might call the glint of steel." (Rowell 90) Not only is the tale of the Tortoise and the Birds narratively associated with the women of Okonkwo's household, but the role specifically gendered in the story as feminine is that of the wife who literally employs all the "glints of steel" hidden in her house and who is directly responsible for the destruction of Tortoise's shell. Okonkwo, not recognizing the rhetorical threat of Ekwefi's steel, dismisses the story as foolishness.

### "We can eat the chick": Textual Institutions of Colonialism in Nigeria

"The village was astir," observes the narrator, reporting on the communal effects of the imprisonment of Umuofia's leaders, insinuatively adding, "in a silent, suppressed way" (140). After Okonkwo and his family return to Umuofia from his motherland Mbanta, silence obtains greater import in the narrative description of life among Okonkwo's people. During Okonkwo's absence, not only had the missions established their presence, but the colonial administration had "built a court where the District Commissioner judged cases in ignorance" (123). *Things Fall Apart* represents the threat of both institutions in terms of generic inclusion and exclusion. That is, the intrusions of the church and the state radically transform the life of the natives not only by challenging the social, cultural, and political institutions of Umuofia but also by restructuring the kinds of speech and language in which life is conducted. The threat represented by the "new religion," in the form of the stories and songs that seduced Okonkwo's son Nwoye to convert, has its parallels in the juridical/administrative genres of testimony and palaver. While the narrator increasingly stresses the imposition of silence in

Umuofia, the plot foregrounds the encounters between Igbo individuals and the colonial institutions. Silence, then, becomes the paradigmatic medium of negotiation, resistance, and resignation.

Before the silence imposed by colonial administration infects the relationships between the characters in the novel, Obierika, Okonkwo's level-headed neighbor, delivers the news of the destruction of Abame to Okonkwo's clan in his motherland. Robert M. Wren has examined the historical and documentary sources for Achebe's fictionalization of the British raid on the Aro Igbo in relation to *Things Fall Apart*. Rather than reiterate the historical evidence and precedents for the relation, I want to look at the illustrative story Okonkwo's uncle Uchendu tells the younger men from Umuofia. Uchendu inquires of Obierika the details of the encounter between the white man and his Igbo killers that precipitated the massacre of Abame: "What did the white man say before they killed him?"(98). "He said nothing" is the initial reply; "He said something, only they did not understand him" is the revised response (98). Uchendu continues to listen and then delivers his tale and judgment:

"Never kill a man who says nothing. Those men of Abame were fools. What did they know about the man?" He ground his teeth again and told a story to illustrate his point. "Mother Kite once sent her daughter to bring food. She went, and brought back a duckling." "You have done very well," said Mother Kite to her daughter, "but tell me, what did the mother of this duckling say when you swooped and carried its child away," "it said nothing," replied the young kite. "It just walked away." "You must return the duckling," said Mother Kite. "There is something ominous behind the silence." And so Daughter Kite returned the duckling and took a chick instead. "What did the mother of this chick do?" asked the old kite. "It cried and raved and cursed me," said the young kite. "Then we can eat the chick," said the mother. "There is nothing to fear from someone who shouts." "Those men of Abame were fools" (98–99).

Okonkwo, not understanding the allegorical nature of this story, preferring as he does metonymic narratives, concurs with Uchendu's assessment that the men of Abame were indeed fools. His concurrence, however, demonstrates his misapprehension of the story: "They had been warned that danger was ahead. They should have armed themselves with their guns and their matchets even when they went to market" (99). Uchendu's story establishes a contest of genres, a clash of speech functions. The fact that Achebe locates this all-female-cast story, told by a brother of Okonkwo's mother, in his motherland after he has committed a "female" crime of inadvertently killing a clansman, all but overstates Okonkwo's ignorance in not learning "feminine" rhetoric. After listening to Uchendu's explanation about the virtues of having both a fatherland and a motherland, Okonkwo names his first born Nneka ("Mother is Supreme"). Yet, as the narrator tells us, "two years later when a son was born he called him Nwofia—'Begotten in the Wilderness'" (115). Okonkwo's belief in the protective powers of Mother follows the rigid distinction he maintains between mother-tales and father-tales. "Mother is Supreme" is a suitable name only for a daughter; a son must learn to negotiate physical danger from the start. Biodun Jeyifo attributes the maintenance of this dichotomy to psychology: "Okonkwo both loathes the memory of his father and represses the lore of his mother; in the process he distorts both the 'masculine' and the 'feminine,' by keeping them rigidly apart and by the ferocity of his war on the 'feminine'" (851).

Beyond the gendering of story types, of speech functions, Uchendu's story turns the discourse of European colonialism on its head. The colonial infrastructure demands from its subject's language of self-contempt, self-incrimination, and/or self-abnegation that seems to insist upon the importance of the native speaking but instead perverts that speech to relegate the native to silence. Uchendu's story reinvests silence with a kinetic potential, hidden as a glint of static steel that can never be accounted for by the oppressors. Achebe's text investigates this rhetorical paradox in the meetings that most immediately lead to Okonkwo's suicide. The District Commissioner responds to the moment when Umuofia speaks with the force of a singular voice, in the form of the *egwugwu* Ajofia, by inviting the leaders of Umuofia to the table.

But the pretense of palaver is violently perverted when the District Commissioner actually enters the conversation. "Ogbuefi Ekwueme rose to his feet and began to tell the story," explains the narrator, describing the scene at the courthouse (137). The District Commissioner interrupts, saying that he would like others to hear the story; "They sat together with the men of Umuofia, and Ogbuefi Ekwueme began again to tell the story of how Enoch murdered an *egwugwu*" (137). The pretended dialogue ends with the abduction of the tribal leaders, ending days later only with the "judicial" ransom by the village. The narrator describes the experience as silencing; "Even when the men were left alone they found no words to speak to one another" (138). The silence, as described in the early part of this section, is, however, one with kinetic force and potential. And after the man's release, Okonkwo's sense of impotence overboils at the moment he produces his matchet, usurping the decision making powers from the rest of the village with his murder of a colonial messenger. Neither the silence nor the violence serves to repair wholly the social, cultural, and political wounds that colonialism has visited on Umuofia. But, Okonkwo's personal fate is exacerbated by colonialism and missionary adventurism. The text suggests that his inability to accommodate and adapt to the social and cultural structures of Umuofia made him not long for its world.

The colonial record was, of course, no better than commercial enterprises at depicting or admitting the existence of the peoples of Southeastern Nigeria. The categories of description changed, but the itemizing discourse remained. The "history of record," as distilled and refined in the British colonial account books, commonly known as the Blue Books, categorized and atomized the shape of the new nation in terms established by the colonizers. The article from the early constitutions that mandated the form and substance of the Blue Books provides the categories under which information about Nigeria was to be organized: "The Governor shall punctually forward to Us from year to year, through one of Our Principal Secretaries of State, the annual book of returns for the Colony, commonly called the Blue Book, relating to the Revenue and Expenditure, Defence, Public Works, Legislation, Civil Establishments, Pensions, Population, Schools, Course of Exchange, Imports and Exports, Agriculture, Produce, Manufactures, and other matters in the said Blue Book more particularly specified, with reference to the state and condition of the Colony" (Wight 184). These categories of knowledge, meant to describe the "state and condition" of the colony, circumscribe the bureaucratic language available to the colonial officer for representing the order of the nation.

These Blue Books were to be read in the Colonial office in England and presented to Parliament. They often did not see publication until a couple of years after the period over which they report. In their general shape, any single Blue Book is as revealing as any other. In the 1951 report, for instance, the book opens with a typical account of "important" events from the previous year: "In annual reports of this kind it is sometimes not easy to pick out this or that event or series of events as the most important of the year" (3). Before moving on to report on the mandated categories of Commerce, Production, Art, Literature and Sport, the book rehearses the history of Nigeria and its people as it has come to be indexed in the colonial accounts. "Nigeria has been described as 'an arbitrary block of Africa'. Its ancient history is largely lost in the mists of legend and little accurate data are now available," the history begins (92). The rehearsal of the history functions simultaneously to "educate" the metropolitan reader in England and, in Prosperonian fashion, to "remind" the native of, or the lack of, her own history. Speaking directly to the subject of the Igbo, the Blue Book reports that "The tribes of what is now southeastern Nigeria have little or no known early history prior to British occupation, with the exception of certain of the coastal peoples, who were long known as keen and enterprising traders" (94). Praising the natives' capacity for institutional service, the report explains that "Since the establishment of the Protectorate, however, the rapid spread of education has brought great changes and both the Ibos and the less numerous Ibibios now exercise a most important influence on the social, economic and political life of Nigeria" (94).

The distilling and reaffirmation of colonial history continues year after year in the Blue Books, reducing last year's events to the minor context in the larger history elaborated by the reports, a process of revision and excision that the District Commissioner undertakes mentally at the end of *Things Fall Apart*. This textual process parallels the physical imperial one and is itself characterized in the reports: "Neither the acquisition by the British crown of the colony of Lagos nor the establishment of a Protectorate over large areas of the interior was the result of deliberate long-range planning by the governments of the day" (94). The non-deliberative aspects of this process are retroactively described in terms of a courtship where "the events covering the whole period from the early discovery of Nigeria to the present day may roughly be set out under three heads, the period of exploration, that of penetration and finally that of consolidation of the ground won" (94). The consolidation of the colony, and thus of history itself, is textually represented by the marginalization of all resistance to the imperial process, locating the one defiant act about which the Blue Book reports after the official history: "In all this period there was only one major threat to law and order in the territory. This was the women's rising which occurred in the Owerri and Calabar Provinces in 1929 and largely resulted in the destruction of the local system of government which had been set up and in the establishment of Native Administrations based closely on the indigenous customs of the people" (100).

The Blue Book categories prescribe a certain kind of narrative description of individuals and events. That is, the colonial records do not merely provide a commercial/political accounting of Nigeria; they also establish the categories by which individual character and plot are to be constructed, measured, and evaluated. The employment of this atomizing discourse to describe the people of Nigeria is mostly clearly evident in P. Amaury Talbot's 1923 census, in which he undertook not only to count the colonial assets but to schematize the cultural, social, political, legal, and religious aspects of those "holdings." Talbot interprets his mandate in the Foreword to his four volume report: "The chief work has been an attempt to classify the tribes and sub-tribes and to define their boundaries" (vi). The use to which the work should be put is prescribed as "a brief description of the Southern Provinces with a few notes on their history—in the hope that they may be of interest to the people of this country and of some use to new administrators, who have had no opportunity of gaining knowledge on the subject" (vi). Talbot expresses regret about what he sees as a lack of scientific taxonomy in his work, placing the blame for that lack on the difficulties and delays presented by the very environment and people about which the study reports: "Unfortunately the provisional classification adopted has had to depend almost entirely on the basis of language, since ... the results of an anthropometrical survey of several thousand natives will arrive too late for use in the present volumes" (vi).

Despite his misgivings that the census is organized around linguistic, as opposed to corporeal affinities, Talbot provides an elaborate classification of the populations of Nigeria. For colonial administrative use, he supplies intricate tabular data that presume to arrange the collection of human details that describe a native's individual circumstance. One of his poster-sized renderings tabulates the cultural and judicial response of the native Nigerians to "manslaughter." I have excerpted below a number of his entries that demonstrate the range of possible reactions to the accidental killing of another human being that he identifies as Igbo justice.

TribeSub-TribeCases judged by Manslaughter Igbo Abam Chiefs, sub-chiefs, and elders Carries out burial and undergoes all expenses. Igbo (Onitsha) Chiefs, sub-chiefs, and elders Pay burial expenses or hand over daughter; in default, his family did so. Igbo Awtanzu (Awtanchara) Chiefs, sub-chiefs, and elders Runs away for three years. Igbo Awtanzu (Awtanzu) Chiefs, sub-chiefs, and elders Nothing done if escapes for three years; if caught substitution by daughter or son. Igbo Ezza "Titled man" and some sensible elders. Fined 2 cows, 1 goat and cloth given to parents, and fowl and goat sacrificed to Ala. Igbo Ngwa (Oloko) Chiefs, sub-chiefs and sensible old men. Hanged. Igbo Oru (Oru) Serious cases by Eze, sub-chiefs and Ndi-nze. Minor cases by "quarter" chiefs. If through negligence treated as murder. In other cases, has to pay funeral expenses. Igbo Ore (Olo) Chiefs, sub-chiefs, and elders has to run away for three years; on return, offers sacrifice. Compiled from P. Amaury Talbot's The Peoples of Southern Nigeria, 1923. Table 19. p. 677.

I have chosen the example of manslaughter because the crimes, procedures, and punishments Talbot describes would appear to apply to the plot of *Things Fall Apart*. Okonkwo's "female crime" of accidentally killing a fellow clansman would seem to fall under Talbot's British label of manslaughter, yet the resulting punishment described in Achebe's novel appears, as one might expect, nowhere in Talbot's schema. Talbot's 1923 census delimits, at least practically if not actually, the range of possible "cultural" practices that a young colonial officer might encounter in the "bush." Thus, from the perspective of a District Commissioner, Talbot's tables stultify the "full" range of plot, character, and setting over which he is to take control. I am not arguing about the obvious inaccuracies and incompleteness of Talbot's rubrics; rather, I want to be clear that the colonial administration must treat this tabulation as the complete representation of a finite number of responses to manslaughter. This tendency of the accountant's report to finitude stabilizes, stills, and makes manageable the story lines of the natives. Yet, it is from within the space of that "silence" that the stories of resistance and contest are created. From Uchendu's point of view, the relegation of the natives to silence superficially confirms the dismissiveness of British administrative discourse and the prejudicial rationalizations for the introduction of a culture of bureaucratic speech while it establishes a discursive negation from within which a culture can continue and threaten the very structure itself.

Although Talbot's census and the colonial Blue Books do not represent the full range of official accounting of the colonial/administrative experience, they do represent the general modes of ordering knowledge about the colony and its peoples. The narrative depiction of Umuofia in *Things Fall Apart* represents, in the context of the other writings on Igbo life, a re-inscription into the record of the complexities, contradictions, and range of the Igbo world. The novelized treatment of Okonkwo allegorizes, in some way, the competition over discursive representation. As narrative, it directly challenges the itemizing and atomizing tendencies of European scientific and colonial language that presumed to represent, at least for bureaucratic and imperial purposes, the data of empire. But while this colonial discourse presumes to speak about the "state and condition" of the colonies, it simultaneously monopolizes the generic conventions for representation, naturalizing itself as the only significant form of information necessary for ordering and knowing the colonial world. Achebe's novel debunks this naturalization by exploring the generic encounter not only between the European and the African but also by examining a similar contradiction internal to Umuofia society. Ultimately, Okonkwo's inability to negotiate the native genres of story telling—gendered as masculine and feminine—illustrates the larger failure of colonial discourse that silences him for his own silencing attempts.

Achebe's novel suggests that a complex reorganization of rhetoric and generic convention are necessary for the survival of Umuofia. Ultimately Okonkwo's suicide attests to his own inability to negotiate the new exigencies of narration that the colonial administration presents but also to his intransigence in the face of domestic cultural pressures that pre-exist the coming of the white man to Umuofia. That is, Okonkwo's own overvaluation of, and dependence on stories that itemize—stories of the land and of his first human head—exemplifies the inadequacy and misrepresentational aspects of a tabular, metonymic, mode of narration. A "masculine" order of things is thus revealed to be structured around as much a principle of secrecy and exclusion as the contractual orders that Lugard so readily agreed to observe. Okonkwo's own predilections for the tabular forms of story telling, and ordering things, place him in opposition to the more dynamically speech-oriented forms of knowing promoted within the Igbo society of the novel.

### "Africans come out": Challenges to Silence, Violence, and Speech
In 1967, Sir Rex Niven, ex-Administrator for the Northern provinces, writes of southern Nigeria that "Historically the area is disappointing" (54).

"No one," he says "has left us any reliable account of the coastal peoples; to them the local population were mere 'natives' who could be amusing, irritating or exasperating, according to their moods; the idea that they, their customs and their beliefs could be interesting would have been laughable" (54). Notwithstanding the terribly ambiguous relationships between Niven's pronouns and his antecedents, his comments accurately describe a general lack of written records about the Igbo and other southern peoples. Niven's remedy for that lack, however, is questionable: "There are some personal narratives, but the Africans come out of them as comic, ridiculous or brutal; there was no serious attempt to describe their way of life or their religions or even their superstitions, still less to trace their origins" (54). On whose part, the question might be asked, and Niven responds: "It was not—perhaps surprisingly—until the administration got into its stride that a real attempt was made to enquire into these important matters" (54–55). Niven's deprecatory remarks about personal narratives and his laudatory evaluation of colonial scholarship quite succinctly describe an administrative attitude towards language. Since Niven never names the "personal narratives" to which he refers, we are left to judge his apparent disdain for them based on the words he uses to characterize the narrative construction, and his warnings about the narratives are clear enough; "Africans come out of them." Whether as comic and ridiculous, in Niven's estimation, or as dignified, social, and complex in Equiano's or Horton's writing, the threat to a colonialist discourse of consumption and atomization on the Niger is precisely the emergence of Africans.

Achebe remarked in a recent interview that his desire to write responded to the wisdom of a proverb he values: "Until the lions have their own historians, the history of the hunt will always glorify the hunter.... Once I realized that, I had to be a writer. I had to be that historian" *(Art of Fiction)*. The need for "that historian" is suggested by the discursive principles of secrecy and inventory in colonial writing that seem to naturalize the underlying evolutionary notions of development that locate Igbo society in a pre-European, read "primitive," stage. Thus, it is difficult to determine precisely whether the mode of ordering knowledge about colonial Nigeria is produced by a belief that the colonizers are confronting and encountering the "barbarous," that is without language, or whether the mode of ordering itself imposes silence and secrecy.

Colonialist discourse in southern Nigeria, both through its conformity to the representational exigencies of secrecy and in the mode of its ordering, configures the native as speechless, and, having justified that relegation of the people to a pre-linguistic existence with an organic model of civilization, it proceeds to malign their capacity for action. That is, as Mill argues, the nineteenth century British notion of liberty and society is predicated on the idea that action can only legitimately be taken when the individual is capable of freely discussing the motives, a capacity rhetorically, generically, and politically disallowed Africans. The yoking of silence to violence, and the liberating potential of speech has been patently enshrined as the justification for international law in general (a full investigation is needed into the role of speech and violence as justificatory terms for the humanist rhetoric of ending slavery that underpinned the Conference of Berlin) and international human rights law in particular in the *1948 Universal Declaration of Human Rights,* where the freedom of speech is posited as the antidote to violence (preamble of UDHR). Achebe argues that "Nobody is, of course, going to be so naive as to claim for language the power to dispose of all, or even most, violence" (*Hopes* 128). *Things Fall Apart,* by allegorizing many of the modes of colonial discourse that claimed to represent a Nigerian reality, suggests that some mediating principle between speech and violence, some principle outside of an organic mode of knowing and an itemizing form of collection, needs to exist if humans are to exist. For Achebe that mode is narrative, as he explains in his aptly titled essay "What has Literature Got to Do with It?"; "The universal creative rondo revolves on people and stories. *People create stories create people;* or rather, *stories create people create stories*" (*Hopes* 162).

Things Fall Apart is, in part, a corrective to discourses structured by secrets and silence. It is not that *Things Fall Apart* fills out that which cannot be told in the colonial discourses, but rather that it explodes the very category of not telling. It rejects the capitalist, imperialist imperative of corporate and narrative secrecy (a rejection that is, of course, as important for Nigeria in the time it was written as in the time it is set and in the present circumstance), threatening the idea of narrative as secrecy. In his *1959* (one year after Achebe published his novel) statement to the Second Congress of Black Artists and Writers in Rome, Frantz Fanon argued that "We must rid ourselves of the habit, now that we are in the thick of the fight, of minimizing the action of our fathers or of feigning incomprehension when considering their silence and passivity" (206–207). Fanon's comments are intended to enlist the African intellectuals in the popular struggles against colonialism and for independence, but his remarks also suggest that a normative notion of silence (and therefore violence and speech) will not accurately describe the resistant history of the colonial peoples and ancestral participation in that resistance. Achebe's novel thematizes the impositions of silence and the equally important representations of silence, suggesting that no easy equation between silence and passivity is possible.

## Works Cited

Achebe, Chinua. "The Art of Fiction: An Interview with Chinua Achebe." Online. 16 April 1995.

———. *Things Fall Apart*. (1958) London: Heinemann, 1986.

———. *Hopes and Impediments*. New York: Doubleday, 1989.

Cohen, Sir Andrew. *British Policy in Changing Africa*. Evanston: Northwestern University Press, 1959.

Conrad, Joseph. *Heart of Darkness*. (1902) New York: Penguin Books, 1989.

Fanon, Frantz. *The Wretched of the Earth*. Trans. Constance Farrington. New York: Grove Weidenfeld, 1963.

Flint, John E. *Sir George Goldie and the Making of Nigeria*. London: Oxford University Press, 1960.

Foucault, Michel. *The Order of Things: An Archeology of the Human Sciences*. (1966) New York: Vintage, 1994.

Harlow, Barbara. "'The Tortoise and the Birds': Strategies of Resistance in *Things Fall Apart*." *Approaches to Teaching Achebe's Things Fall Apart*. Ed. Bernth Lindfors. New York: Modern Language Association, 1991.

Horton, James Africanus. *West African Countries and Peoples*. (1868) Edinburgh: Edinburgh University Press, 1969.

Isichei, Elizabeth. *The Ibo People and the Europeans*. New York: St. Martin's Press, 1973.

Izevbaye, Dan. "The Igbo as Exceptional Colonial Subjects: Fictionalizing an Abnormal Historical Situation." *Approaches to Teaching Achebe's Things Fall Apart*. Ed. Bernth Lindfors. New York: Modern Language Association, 1991.

Jeyifo, Biodun. "Okonkwo and His Mother: *Things Fall Apart* and Issues of Gender in the Constitution of African Postcolonial Discourse." *Callaloo* 16.4: 847–858.

Kirk-Greene, A. H. M. (ed.). *Lugard and the Amalgamation of Nigeria: A Documentary Record*. London: Frank Cass and Co., 1968.

Lubiano, Wahneema. "Narrative, Metacommentary, and Politics in a 'Simple Story'." *Approaches to Teaching Achebe's Things Fall Apart*. Ed. Bernth Lindfors. New York: Modern Language Association, 1991.

Mill, John Stuart. *On Liberty*. Ed. David Spitz. New York: W.W. Norton, 1975.

Newbury, C. W. (ed.). *British Policy Towards West Africa*. Oxford: Clarendon Press, 1971.

Niven, Sir Rex. *Nigeria*. New York: Praeger, 1967.

Obiechina, Emmanuel. "Following the Author in *Things Fall Apart*." *Approaches to Teaching Achebe's Things Fall Apart*. Ed. Bernth Lindfors. New York: Modern Language Association, 1991.

Pakenham, Thomas. *The Scramble for Africa: White Man's Conquest of the Dark Continent from 1876 to 1912*. London: Weidenfeld & Nicolson, 1991.

Perham, Margery and Mary Bull (eds). *The Diaries of Lord Lugard*. Four Volumes. Evanston: Northwestern University Press, 1963.

Pratt, Mary Louise. "Scratches on the Face of the Country; or, What Mr. Barrow Saw in the Land of the Bushmen." in *"Race," Writing, and Difference*. Ed. Henry Louis Gates, Jr. Chicago: Chicago University Press, 1986.

Rousseau, Jean-Jacques. *Emile*. (1762) trans. Barbara Foxley. Rutland, Vermont: Everyman, 1997.

Rowell, Charles H. "An Interview with Chinua Achebe." *Callaloo* (Winter: 1990): 86–101.

Said, Edward W. *Orientalism*. New York: Vintage, 1979.

Schipper, Mineke. *Beyond the Boundaries: African Literature and Literary Theory*. London: W.H. Allen and Co., 1989.

Soyinka, Wole. *Myth, Literature, and the African World*. Cambridge: Cambridge University Press, 1978.

Spurr, David. *The Rhetoric of Empire: Colonial Discourse in Journalism, Travel Writing, and Imperial Administration*. Durham: Duke University Press, 1993.

Talbot, P. Amaury. *The Peoples of Southern Nigeria*. (1926). Four Volumes. London: Frank Cass and Co., 1969.

Todorov, Tzvetan. *The Conquest of America: The Question of the Other*. trans. Richard Howard. New York: Harper Colophon, 1985.

Wight, Martin. *British Colonial Constitutions*. Oxford: Clarendon, 1952.

Wren, Robert M. *Achebe's World: The Historical and Cultural Context of the Novel*. Washington D.C.: Three Continents Press, 1980.

MAC FENWICK

# Realising Irony's Post/Colonial Promise: Global Sense and Local Meaning in Things Fall Apart *and "Ruins of a Great House"*

Locusts . . . were very good to eat.
                    —Chinua Achebe, *Things Fall Apart*

Ancestral murderers and poets.
                    —Derek Walcott, 'Ruins of a Great House'

The only thing that can be said for certain about irony is that it is the trope *par excellence* of uncertainty. This is why I have chosen to begin this study not with a statement about irony, but with a couple of ironic moments. Still, the term is so protean that even to claim that the above examples are instances of irony will undoubtedly be contentious. The purpose of this study, then, is not to generate a new theory of irony (the world has no need of that) but to realise what I will be calling the 'promise' of irony within post/colonial texts.[1] I use the word 'promise' in both of its senses: to indicate the potential of irony (a potential that is best realised, perhaps, in never being fulfilled), and as an oath or compact made between irony's co-conspirators: the reader and the text.

There has been, for a very long time now, a vast and ever-growing list of journal articles and books on the form, nature and use of irony. Given the breadth and intelligence of the work already extant on the nature of irony, I

*Kunapipi: Journal of Postcolonial Writing*, Volume 28, Number 1 (2006): pp. 8–21. Copyright © 2006 Mac Fenwick.

99

shall forgo even the attempt to address those issues here in any but the most cursory manner. Most standard definitions of irony identify three different kinds, each one of them motivated by a different form of opposition between the literal meaning of the said, and the figural sense of the unsaid. Verbal irony is the result of a statement in which the meaning of the words used is the opposite of their sense. Irony of situation occurs when a character acts in opposition to expectation. Dramatic irony (the only form of irony that is exclusively literary) arises when the audience perceives something that a character in the literature does not know; dramatic irony is, then, the opposition of the limited meaning of the situation as it is understood by the character, and the full sense of that situation as it is apprehended by the audience. The extra-linguistic capacity upon which all three of these 'types' depend is apparent in even the simplest form of irony, the sarcastic remark. If I were to say 'that sounds like fun', in such a manner as to make it clear that it does not, the literal meaning of my sentence is replaced by its 'real', extra-linguistic sense. Furthermore, with my sarcasm I am not just indicating my reluctance to undertake the proposed adventure (hang gliding would be a good example), but I am also indicating a certain amount of disdain for the proposition, and perhaps even for the person making it. The promise of irony is, therefore, that it enacts a moment of extra-linguistic communication in which the limitations of the literal—and even the *aporia* occasioned by the opposition of sense and meaning—is (apparently) overcome.

Irony thus enacts a relation between truth and falsehood. While the literal meaning of my statement is false, I am excused from the accusation of lying insofar as the true sense of my utterance is understood. If it is not, the failure to communicate truth is not the result of my false utterance, but of the auditor's inability to understand what I am saying, or of my inability to mark the irony clearly enough. By saying one thing while meaning another, it would appear That irony is a form of the lie; but with the appeal that irony makes to a figural meaning that is in excess of its literal falsehood, it avoids (or even transcends) the accusation of lying. In a sense, irony—in its suspension of falsehood during a clearly untrue statement—suspends or resolves the ethical tensions of the moment. The true sense of my utterance not only transcends its false meaning, but adds to that meaning extra-linguistically. Irony, then, even in the everyday form of the sarcastic quip, appeals to a realm in which the true sense of the utterance transcends its false and limited meaning.

This aspect of irony gains special significance in post/colonial texts. For irony to 'work', that is, for the reader to apprehend its true sense, the reader must apprehend its false or limited meaning. I may say that I like hang-gliding, but if I do so in a context that makes it clear that I do not, the true sense of this statement is revealed: not by the utterance itself, which conveys a false or limited meaning, but by an act of reference to the local and particular circumstances that surround and inform the utterance in such a way as to mark its falsity and point the way toward its true sense. In this respect, then, irony enacts a relation not only between truth and falsehood but also between local and global, insofar as it brings into contact an extra-linguistic sense that surpasses or exceeds the utterance, and a meaning (or set of discontinuous meanings) that can be understood only within the particular context of the utterance. Above, I spoke of irony's promise as both potential and compact, and it is in this interdependent relation of local meaning and global sense that I think this promise is fulfilled. There is within every ironic utterance the potential for the successful communication of a true sense despite false or limited meaning. Irony is thus the composite of a moment of global representation, as the true sense is apprehended despite the falsity of the meaning, and local reference, insofar as that global representation depends upon reference to the local circumstances of the utterance. The contact enacted by irony between global sense and local meaning is what has made it such a rich, and problematic, form of address for post/colonial critics and theorists.[2]

William New's *Among Worlds* (1975) is among the first works to address the relation between irony and post/coloniality and it remains one of the most comprehensive. New approaches irony as symptomatic of 'the dualities that abound in Commonwealth literatures', and argues that irony is a dominant method whereby post/colonial authors are able to 'express concretely this sense of incomplete options', which he argues characterises the condition of post/coloniality (1–2). New maintains this stance throughout, consistently arguing that the ironies in the texts that he examines are the literary manifestations of a preexisting condition of 'duality' endemic to and characteristic of post/coloniality. He does not attempt to reduce the rich multiplicity of the texts to any single version or theory of irony; on the contrary, New explicitly states that 'thematic and technical likenesses must not be allowed to obscure each writer's private viewpoint. Though dualities abound in the ironist's world, the stances he may take range from parody and innuendo through sarcasm and self-disparagement to absurdity and nihilism' (3). Despite this important acknowledgement that there is no specific kind or manner of post/colonial irony, New does go on to explain that 'at its best the ironic stance provokes serious deliberation into the problems that led to the dualities in the first place' (3). For New, then, the many different uses and forms that irony takes on in post/colonial writing spring from the same source and lead to the same end. That is, ironies in post/colonial texts symptomatically reflect and provoke inquiry into the specific 'duality' of the 'split loyalties and unresolvable tensions' (2) of the post/colonial condition.

In "'Circling the Downspout of Empire'" (1989) Linda Hutcheon both echoes and refines New's argument when she argues that

as a double-talking, forked-tongued mode of address, irony
becomes a popular rhetorical strategy for working within existing
discourses and contesting them at the same time. Its inherent
semantic and structural doubleness also makes it a most convenient
trope for the paradoxical dualities of . . . post-colonial doubled
identity and history. And indeed irony . . . has become a powerful
subversive tool in the re-thinking and re-addressing of history by
. . . post-colonial artists. (171)

Despite this move toward irony as a strategic response by post/colonial
authors against the conditions within which they must write, Hutcheon
retains New's formulation of irony as symptomatic of the post/colonial condition: 'irony is a trope of doubleness. And doubleness is what characterises
. . . the twofold vision of the post-colonial. . . . Doubleness and difference
are established by colonialism by its paradoxical move to enforce cultural
sameness . . . while at the same time, producing differentiations and dis-
criminations' (176). Like New, Hutcheon characterises irony as the literary
manifestation of a literal state that has been imposed upon the writer by
imperial history.

For both New and Hutcheon, irony is an effective means through which
to express the conditions of post/coloniality insofar as it embodies the nature
of those conditions. Hutcheon is quick to acknowledge the limitations that
this view places on irony within post/colonial texts: 'Irony is . . . a way of re-
sisting old yet acknowledging the power of the dominant. It may not go the
next step—to suggest something new—but it certainly makes that step possible. Often combined with some sort of self-reflexivity, irony allows a text to
work within the constraints of the dominant while placing those constraints
as *constraints* in the foreground and thus undermining their power' (177).
The only effective means of contesting 'the dominant' that irony would seem
to lend the ironist is the ability to highlight the nature of that domination.
There is, according to Hutcheon, neither liberation from nor replacement of
that domination with 'something new' but merely a suggestion of how that
'something new' might be possible.

Hutcheon's stance echoes the argument of Homi Bhabha in 'Representation and the Colonial Text' (1984) insofar as he argues that irony is a mode
of the imperialising power, and thus insufficient to the task of countering the
oppressive and possessive gaze of the European critic. Stating that 'behind
the realist irony [stands] a European philosophical tradition of ethical realism' (115), Bhabha concludes that the irony of post/colonial texts exists only
within the eye of the imperial-beholder. In his analysis of V. S. Naipaul's *A
House for Mr. Biswas*, Bhabha claims that '[t]o demonstrate thematically how
*House* resists its appropriation into the Great Tradition of literary Realism

would not be difficult. It would be possible to see . . . its mode of address as the "uncanny" rather than irony' (115). According to Bhabha, irony is not a strategic tool of the post/colonial writer, but an alien form of mimesis that is imposed upon post/colonial texts by the imperial reader. This imposition, however, is neither stable nor lasting. Bhabha argues that the irony which the Western critic 'finds' in post/colonial texts is symptomatic of the central and indeed defining irony of the European critic's own critical practice:

> Writing as the filling of a gap . . . linear time consciousness as the effect of the sequential practice of writing; teleology and unity, progression and coherence as convention-bound, formal productions—all these notions give writing a materiality, a productive position. . . . There are intimations here of the construction of the unity of the sign (as opposed to its primordial 'givenness'), and the resulting stability of the signified which, paradoxically, suggests the possibility of its arbitrariness, that is, the irony of its repression of discontinuity and difference in the construction of 'sense', those modes of *meaning* that we call realism and historicism. (96–97; emphasis added)

In this view of the relation between irony and the post/colonial, the irony that the European reader/critic imposes upon post/colonial texts is symptomatic of the difference and discontinuity that always/already exists within the imperial culture. In effect, the attempt to ironise post/colonial texts rebounds upon the European critic. According to Bhabha, the attribution of irony to post/colonial texts reveals how the critic's own practice is irretrievably ironic insofar as it depends upon a false sense of unity that has been constructed to 'repress' the discontinuous and different meanings which undercut that practice.

Despite their differences, for New, Hutcheon and Bhabha the promise of irony for post/colonial texts is realised insofar as it 'disturbs'—or highlights the inherent disturbances between—different cultural meanings without offering any way past or beyond this moment of recognition. For each of them, irony is a cognitive dead end. It is my contention that the protean nature of the ironic utterance promises a mode of understanding for the post/colonial (con)text in which global sense and local meaning are related to one another within a provisional transcultural truth that exceeds the *aporia* or disruptive discontinuities of the post/colonial 'condition'. However, just as there is no monolithic or singular way of 'being' post/colonial, so too is there no monolithic post/colonial form of irony. In order to preserve this recognition of multiplicity I have chosen to examine here two moments of irony from markedly different (con)texts. Chinua Achebe's *Things Fall Apart* dramatises the conflict between Igbo and British as the clash of binary opposites. Derek Walcott's 'Ruins of a Great House' dramatises the speaker's difficult and dramatic confrontation with a history which he feels yokes together through violence and oppression these same two cultural 'sides'. More importantly, these two moments allow me to explore the promise of irony within the post/colonial (con)text from the perspective of each of irony's co-conspirators: the reader and the text. In *Things Fall Apart,* the extra-linguistic sense with which the different and oppositional meanings of the situation are overcome is the reader's own. In 'Ruins of a Great House', this extra-linguistic sense is expressed by the speaker. Despite their different perspectives, then, these moments fully realise the promise of irony within and for the post/colonial (con)text insofar as they realise a mode of transcultural understanding in which global sense and local meaning are brought into a productive and equivalent relation.

Achebe's *Things Fall Apart* concludes with a moment in which the colonial divide would appear to be unbridgeable, as the District Commissioner turns his back on the hanged form of Okonkwo's suicide and contemplates the title of the book that he will write: *'The Pacification of the Primitive Tribes of the Lower Niger'* (148). This moment marks the violent and brutal eradication of the hope expressed elsewhere in the novel that reciprocity between coloniser and colonised might indeed be possible.[3] Despite this lack of effective communication on the part of the characters, the novel does not lead only to *aporia* and the failure of understanding. While the narrative may very well end with a moment of painful stasis, its conclusion is, I would argue, quite different. The novel is itself poised upon a particularly painful irony as the meaning of its final moments is counterbalanced by the sense of the whole. In effect, the final stasis of the novel is overcome by the dramatic irony that allows the reader to resolve the conflict that entraps the characters,[4] and even the Igbo Storyteller.

Nowhere is this dramatic irony more apparent than during the locusts' descent upon Umuofia:

> And then quite suddenly a shadow fell on the world, and the sun seemed hidden behind a thick cloud. Okonkwo looked up from his work and wondered if it was going to rain at such an unlikely time of the year. But almost immediately a shout of joy broke out in all directions, and Umuofia, which had dozed in the noon-day haze, broke into life and activity.
>
> 'Locusts are descending,' was joyfully chanted everywhere, and men, women and children left their work or their play and ran into the open to see the unfamiliar sight. The locusts had not come for many, many years, and only the old people had seen them before.

> At first, a fairly small swarm came. They were the harbingers sent to survey the land. And then appeared on the horizon a slowly-moving mass like a boundless sheet of black cloud drifting towards Umuofia. Soon it covered half the sky, and the solid mass was now broken by tiny eyes of light like shining star-dust. It was a tremendous sight, full of power and beauty.
>
> Everyone was now about, talking excitedly and praying that the locusts should camp in Umuofia for the night. For although locusts had not visited Umuofia for many years, everybody knew by instinct that they were very good to eat. (39–40)

This passage disturbs the Westernised reader, as our expectations are at first supported by the prose, and then overturned by it. The foreboding and even apocalyptic language of the passage's beginning ('a shadow fell on the world, and the sun seemed hidden behind a thick cloud'), gives way within three paragraphs to a radically altered vision of the event ('it was a tremendous sight, full of power and beauty'). This passage is ironic in the most direct sense insofar as its conclusion is directly opposite to what the reader is led to expect by its beginning. Beyond this relatively simple instance of situational irony, however, the passage enables a moment of dramatic irony in which the reader is able to apprehend the relation of the two 'sides' of the conflict between Igbo and British in a manner that exceeds the literal expression given that conflict in the text—in particular, as that conflict is presented as an oppositional binary in the novel's final paragraph.

This dramatic irony is evident in the statement that 'everybody knew by instinct that [locusts] were very good to eat'. Throughout the novel there are moments in which the Igbo Storyteller's view of events is directly at odds with the Westernised reader's perceptions[5]—but nowhere is the division between narrator/text and reader made so palpably clear, or so (apparently) unbridgeable. For the Storyteller, human 'instinct' dictates that 'locusts are good to eat'; but the instincts of the (vast majority) of Westernised readers are entirely different, and not just because of the different cuisines. Western forms of mass agriculture are susceptible to locusts in a way that traditional Igbo cultivation is not; more significantly, there are also the Biblical associations of locusts with the wrath of God. The meaning of the passage, then, is to signal to the Westernised reader in as shocking a manner as possible that we do not fully understand the Igbo culture that we are encountering in the text. This act of recognition is a salutary and necessary component of the novel, for it removes those readers who have this apprehension from the perspective posited at the novel's conclusion by the District Commissioner, who is absolutely certain that he knows—and is authorised to write down—all that is necessary about the 'primitives' under his control.

There is, however, a sense in the passage that is at odds with this meaning; a sense that is apparent (ironically) only to someone encountering the text
from within that same Western perspective that the meaning of the passage
disturbs. The swarm of locusts foreshadows the destruction of the Igbo by the
British—a point that is later made quite clearly when the Oracle warns the
people of Abame that the Europeans 'were locusts . . . and that first man [on
the bicycle] was, their harbinger sent to explore the terrain. And so they killed
him' (98). In the wake of this murder, the entire village of Abame is wiped out
by British troops. When regarded in this manner, the passage reverses itself
once more and the locusts change back from being 'a tremendous sight, full
of power and beauty' and recover the far more foreboding implications of the
passage's beginning, 'a shadow fell on the world, and the sun seemed hidden behind a thick cloud'. This passage is ironic, then, insofar as its meaning
signals the insuperable divide between the narrator/text and the Westernised
reader ('locusts are good'), while its full sense is revealed only to that same
reader (locusts are not good). The result of this passage is a moment of ex-
cruciating dramatic irony as the Westernised reader is put into the position
of knowing or perceiving more than the characters, and even the storyteller.
The Westernised reader is thus immediately constituted as a part of the same
imperial 'us' that encompasses the District Commissioner (who 'knows better'
than the 'natives'), but whose (illiberal) cultural chauvinism the reader rejects.
I would like to suggest, however, that this moment need not be an uneasy *aporia* in which different cultural meanings are irreconcilably opposed ('locusts
are good' versus 'locusts are bad'). Rather, this moment holds the promise of a
global sense within which the different local meanings lead not to the steril-
ity of binary opposition but to a new understanding of the relation between
Igbo and British cultures. The reader's ironic apprehension of the claim that
'locusts are good to eat' resolves the apparently irresolvable *aporia* of the cognitive conflict between Okonkwo and the District Commissioner.

I said at the beginning that irony appeals to a realm in which the true
sense of the utterance transcends its false and limited meaning. I went on
to argue that irony is the composite of a moment of global representation,
as the true sense is apprehended despite the falsity of the meaning, and local reference, insofar as that global representation depends upon reference
to the local circumstances of the utterance. With this in mind, we can say
that the ironic promise of Achebe's novel is realised only in and through the
dramatic irony of the reader's recovery or (re)construction of a true sense of
the text (that European and Igbo are both necessary to understand the text)
that surpasses its false and limited meaning (that European and Igbo are
insuperably divided from one another). This true sense is not, however, to
be understood as truth-as-object—as a singular or totalising form of truth
that concludes or resolves the ambiguities of the text. The promise realised

within the ironic statement that 'locusts are good to eat' is a provisional form of truth, insofar as the reader's ironic apprehension of that moment does not resolve the conflict between different intercultural truths, but enacts a relation between those truths. The statement 'locusts are good to eat' is neither a falsehood to be overcome with truth (as the District Commissioner would claim of that 'primitive' belief), nor a truth that rebuts the falsity of its contrary (as Okonkwo would argue). It is a stage upon which these truths are brought into contact and relation with one another.

As Hutcheon argues in *Irony's Edge*, 'irony is, a relational strategy in the sense that it operates not only between meanings (said, unsaid) but between people (ironists, interpreters, targets). Ironic meaning comes into being as the consequence of a relationship, a dynamic, performative bringing together of different meaning-makers, but also of different meanings' (58). As we have seen with *Things Fall Apart*, the 'dynamic, performative bringing together' enacted by irony within post/colonial texts entails a relation not just between different individual 'meaning-makers' but between different cultural perspectives. I have argued that the promise of irony is that it enacts a moment of extra-linguistic communication in which the limitations of the literal—and even the *aporia* occasioned by the opposition of sense and meaning—is (apparently) overcome. If this is so, then the promise of irony in post/colonial texts would be that it enacts a moment of extra-linguistic communication in which the differences between cultures is (apparently) overcome. It is precisely at this point where my analysis is sundered (perhaps irretrievably) from those of New, Hutcheon and Bhabha, each of whom characterises irony as disruptive with little or no reference to its potential for creating something new. For it is precisely this that I believe is happening in *Things Fall Apart* insofar as the dramatic ironies of the narrative allow the reader to move past (or through) the disturbing and disruptive clash of Igbo and British to a transcultural truth within which the two sides of this bipolar historical conflict meet and interact. In Achebe's novel, the promise of irony is realised insofar as it allows for a sense of transcultural truth that exists in the relation irony enacts between or amongst the discontinuous meanings of different cultural truths. This transcultural truth is neither homogenous nor stable, for it exists upon the protean stage and word of the ironic utterance. The provisionality of this truth does not necessarily condemn it to directionless or relativistic play, nor to inconclusive *aporia*. In fact, the speaker in Derek Walcott's 'Ruins of a Great House' seizes upon this very provisionality as the basis of a new transcultural truth that surpasses or overcomes the discontinuities and *aporia* of cultural difference which threaten to overwhelm him.

In 'Ruins of a Great House', the speaker addresses the ironic nature of his own poetic voice and persona(e), as the poem dramatically represents the speaker's struggle to understand the complicated relation of master and slave.

As a West Indian, the speaker of this poem does not have the option to retreat into any illusory form of cultural singularity—as do the characters of Achebe's novel who can identify themselves as or with Igbo or England. As the descendant of both 'sides' of the historical conflict between Africa (slave) and Europe (master) he must instead confront the ironic nature of the relation that exists between these two cultures which have together created his identity. In this sense, the speaker of 'Ruins' must realise the same promise of irony as was achieved by the reader of *Things Fall Apart*. For the first part of the poem, the speaker attempts to work through the relation of master and slave on a consciously intellectual level, but eventually the ironies overcome him:

> A green lawn, broken by low walls of stone,
> Dipped to the rivulet, and pacing, I thought next
> Of men like Hawkins, Walter Raleigh, Drake,
> Ancestral murderers and poets, more perplexed
> In memory now by every ulcerous crime. (20)

The ironies of this moment produce a complicated series of relations and realisations that spread outward to the rest of the poem; energies that simultaneously disturb and reconfigure the speaker's understanding of himself in such a way that the intent to resolve the opposition of meaning and sense merges with an acceptance of this opposition. In this manner, the speaker realises the promise of his ironic identity.

The ironic opposition of meaning and sense that motivates this poem is most apparent—and is at its most disturbing—in the verbal irony enacted by the speaker's recognition of his 'ancestral murderers and poets'. As the speaker himself realises, this is a moment of profound 'perplexity' as the line's fluid, almost protean meaning simultaneously confronts and confounds the sense that the speaker finds in it. The Renaissance figures he imagines are 'ancestral murderers' in at least two senses: first, as part of the enslaving culture that brought Africans to the Caribbean, they are the murderers of the speaker's ancestors; second, they are murderers who are ancestral to the speaker, who in this poem is confronting the disturbing fact that he is as Walcott puts it in 'A Far Cry From Africa', 'poisoned with the blood of both, / . . . divided to the vein' (18). The line is rendered even more ironic by the fact that it is to these 'murderers' that the speaker owes his very voice, inasmuch as they were also the 'poets' whose lyrics have produced the poetic form that he depends upon now in his attempt to reject their legacy. They are thus, ironically, both his 'ancestral poets' and his 'ancestral murderers' at one and the same time. The ironies of this moment come to dominate the poem as the speaker is able to conclude (or terminate) the complexities of this line only by, ironically, silencing his own voice and giving the conclusion of his poem over to one of his 'ancestral murderers and poets', in the form of John Donne's 'Meditation XVII' from his *Devotions:*

> Ablaze with rage I thought,
> Some slave is rotting in this manorial lake,
> But still the coal passion fought
> That Albion too was once
> A colony like ours, 'part of the continent, piece of the main',
> Nook-shotten, rook o'erblown, deranged
> By foaming channels and the vain expense
> Of bitter faction.
>      All in compassion ends
> So differently from what the heart arranged:
> 'as well as if a manor of thy friend's . . .' (20–21)

It is thus by sublimating his own colonial voice to the oppressive European 'Master' culture that the speaker, ironically, learns the lesson of 'compassion' that resolves his poem. At the same time, his deferral to Donne is perhaps an allusion to another figure that ironises this deferral. The principal character of Wilson Harris's *Palace of the Peacock* (1960) is also named Donne, and his journey into the heartland of Guyana dramatises the brutality of European conquest of the Caribbean. The speaker's 'turn' to Donne is thus doubly ironic insofar as even as he seems to be sublimating his own voice to that of the master, he is doing so, perhaps, through an appeal to a figure who has himself been ironically rewritten already by the Caribbean's most prolific, imaginative and formidable novelist.[6]

This ironic conclusion is, apparently, the only way that the speaker can effectively lay to rest the difficult and divided imagery that marks this poem. On the one hand, he attempts to fan the 'blaze of rage' that he feels in response to the idea of a slave 'rotting in this manorial lake'. On the other, is the 'coal of compassion' that seems, ironically, to extinguish the fire of rage rather than fuel it. The 'blaze of rage' with which the speaker first attempts to conclude the poem is highly reminiscent of the conclusion to *Things Fall Apart* insofar as it leads toward a moment in which the reader is suspended within the same manner of static opposition between coloniser and colonised embodied by the District Commissioner's book. The 'blaze of rage' that the speaker wishes to feel is sustained only by the opposition of the brutalised 'slave' and the 'manorial lake' that seeks to hide him or her. As in *Things Fall Apart*, this opposition is overcome by the dramatic irony initiated by the idea of the slave as 'rotting'. To this point in the poem, what has been 'rotting' is not the slave, but the Manor ('the manorial lake'). In the first verse paragraph, we are presented with a number of images of rot and decay, all of them grouped around the manor:

> Stones only, the disjecta membra of this Great House,
> Whose moth-like girls are mixed with candledust,
> Remain to file the lizard's dragonish claws.
> The mouths of the gate cherubs shriek with stain;
> Axle and coach wheel silted under the muck
> Of cattle droppings. (19)

The irony of the speaker's 'blaze of rage' is that it is the opposite of how he began his poem. At the beginning, his 'compassion' seems almost wholly reserved for the manor and for those who dwelt within it. The 'girls', who are presented as having been 'moth-like', present to his imagination no threat or evil, and are the ones who—like the rotting slave at the end—are now 'mixed with candledust'. The ruins of the Great House are themselves under continual threat from the 'lizard's dragonish claws'. As with the locusts in *Things Fall Apart*, the Biblical allusions do not distance the speaker from the manor, but close the distance with a sympathetic response. The loss of the manor is, in some sense (and quite ironically), regarded as an Edenic fall, in which the forces of evil have taken over, 'staining' the angelic guardians of this realm (the 'gate cherubs'). By the end of this opening verse paragraph, the rot that has overtaken the Manor becomes, possibly, a source of hope and redemptive fertility as the landscape is buried beneath 'cattle droppings'. The meaning that the speaker strives to give his experience at the conclusion of the poem by firing within himself a 'blaze of rage' is at odds with the very sympathetic meaning of his opening stance.

The provisional sense of the relation between past and present that the speaker here achieves redresses what New thought was a gap within West Indian literature. In a discussion of George Lamming and V. S. Naipaul, New argues that

> order is . . . an irony in any community embarrassed by its past, for the people in it are constantly alienating themselves from the experiences they share. Their grasp on the present is preserved by the satiric displacement of the past, but their identity is subsequently diminished. A different kind of satire, attracted to the human beings whose foibles were being exposed, would embrace the past rather than distance it, but it would at the same time announce a different apprehension of the human predicament.
>
> (9)

In his apprehension of the complicated relation of past and present, master and slave, the speaker of this poem is able to construct just such an ironic vision in which the past is 'embraced' rather than distanced. In this manner, Walcott's poem establishes the same mode of understanding the relation between coloniser and colonised achieved by the reader of Achebe's novel, insofar as the speaker moves beyond the relatively simple binary opposition of master and slave that confounds the beginning of the poem. This new understanding is realised when at the poem's conclusion the speaker's 'blaze of rage' is confronted and quelled by 'the coal of his compassion'. The fuel with which he keeps alight this 'coal' is the idea that 'Albion too was once / A colony like ours'. The ironies of this stance are many and profound. First and foremost, is the ironic nature of the utterance. The speaker is here attempting to construct for himself a space of resolution and retreat in his own landscape while predicating that retreat upon a valuation of the imperial power that has scarred and wounded that landscape. What is more, this ironic stance is initiated by the affirmation that England was 'a colony like ours'. There are within this statement two closely allied ironies that the speaker seems to be accepting. The first irony is historical, insofar as the speaker's claim that England was 'a colony like ours' is patently untrue. The 'colonisation' of England by Rome was of an altogether different nature than was the colonisation of the West Indies by England.[7] The speaker himself seems to recognise this in his lament for the 'vain expense / Of bitter faction'. The scars and wounds that be perceives upon the history of England are, apparently, self-inflicted in civil war and the internally enacted violence of 'bitter faction' rather than the legacies of imperial control. The speaker also seems to accept and pass over without comment the irony of the fact that a nation that was itself a colony should become a brutalising coloniser. The final irony of the speaker's stance, then, is that he is able to find 'compassion' for the imperial brutalisers of his own history by transferring onto them the violence that they have enacted acted on others. The fact that he may see that violence as having been self-inflicted only adds irony to irony.[8] Thanks to this ironic understanding of his circumstance—and of himself—he is able to move past the ironic opposition of meaning ('England and the West Indies are the same') and sense ('no, they're not') to his final moment of compassion. Of course, as I have already argued above, this final stance is also ironic insofar as he depends upon the voice and words of his 'ancestral murderer and poet' to resolve his conflict for him. By this point, however, the irony of this reaction is overlooked—or transcended—by the speaker's ironic mode of understanding the relation between coloniser and colonised.

Irony, as the trope *par excellence* of misdirection, ambivalence and doubleness generates a fluid kind of truth that puts into motion opposing or contradictory terms or positions that cannot be reconciled, but which in their (ironic) mobility can be conjoined and mutually experienced. The reader of *Things Fall Apart* is able, through the apprehension of dramatic irony, to realise a truth of the imperial encounter that escapes or exceeds the actors caught up within it: that the situation it explores is not one that can be apprehended from within the static polarities of binary opposition. Just as locusts are neither 'good' nor 'bad' to eat, neither side of the cultural conflict is in the right, and both have something to offer to our understanding of their mutual clash. This global sense of the text, however, subsists only insofar as the reader is willing and able to perceive and understand the local and particular circumstances and point of view of the Igbo Storyteller. The transcultural truth achieved by the reader is therefore mobilised by and within the process that relates the reader's own perceptions and understanding to the text's differing and different truths. While it is the reader who must realise the promise of irony in *Things Fall Apart*, in 'Ruins' it is irony's other co-conspirator, the speaker, who realises this promise when he is able to conclude his poem in compassion by neither rejecting outright, nor accepting unquestioningly, his 'ancestral murderers and poets'. This conciliatory gesture is maintained by the ironic conclusion of the poem in which the speaker finds his own voice only in and through the voice of the tradition that his poem began in rebellion against. Both works bring to fruition the promise of irony for post/colonial texts by becoming the stage or ground upon which a global sense of the historical relation between coloniser and colonised ('As well as if a manor of thy friends . . .') is brought into a reciprocal and equivalent relation with the local meanings of that history ('some slave is rotting in this manorial lake').

These texts realise the promise of irony insofar as they each construct a sense of the relation between cultures that not only surpasses the discontinuity of different cultural meanings, but which actively adds to that meaning extra-linguistically. This sense is, however, always/already provisional, insofar as it is maintained by the extra-linguistic (inexpressible) sense that irony both aspires to and depends upon. It is this always/already provisional sense of truth that I have in mind when I speak of the promise of irony in and for post/colonial texts, for there is no uniquely post/colonial form of irony any more than there is an identifiable and singular 'condition' of post/coloniality. The ironic utterance holds within it the promise of a mode of truth in which global sense exists in an equal and reciprocal relationship with local meaning. At the same time, this relation is maintained upon the strength of the promise that binds the reader to the text, and the text to the reader; it is the promise made in and by every reading act—that this act is not meaningless.

## Notes

1. I use this form (post/colonial) of this most contentious term in order to sidestep the difficult (and never-ending) question of the hyphen. Whether the writers I will be examining are post-colonial or postcolonial is, for the purposes of this study at least, secondary to their status, as ironists.

2. Interestingly, there have been very few works of sustained criticism on irony and the post/colonial. In fact, the three works that I examine in this study are the most substantive yet produced. There are literally hundreds of papers and books in which the role of irony is considered in specific post/colonial texts, but by and large these works do not address the specific function or nature of irony as it is realised in a post/colonial text.

3. A few pages before this moment we hear of the conversations between Mr. Brown—the more 'moderate' missionary—and Akunna, in which each was able to learn of the others' beliefs, but significantly in which neither 'succeeded in converting the other' (126).

4. The novel's one and only legitimately 'in between' character, Okonkwo's son, Nwoye, is radically incapable of enacting any form of fruitful or lasting understanding between the cultural forces represented by the District Commissioner and Okonkwo. Nwoye's own rebellion against his father is neither articulate, nor productive of a new or comprehensive understanding:

> It was not the mad logic of the Trinity that captivated him. He did not understand it. It was the poetry of the new religion, something felt in the marrow. The hymn about brothers who sat in darkness and in fear seemed to answer a vague and persistent question that haunted his young soul. . . . He felt a relief within as the hymn poured into his parched soul. The words of the hymn were like the drops of frozen rain melting on the dry plate of the panting earth. Nwoye's callow mind was greatly puzzled. (104)

5. For example, when Okonkwo beats his second wife for not preparing his meal the Storyteller explains that Okonkwo 'was provoked to justifiable anger' and condemns him only for beating his wife during the Week of Peace (21); the Storyteller also does not condemn the murder of Ikemefuna, the practice of leaving twins to die in the Evil Forest or the brutally callous treatment of Okonkwo's dying father.

6. Donne is not the only 'ancestral poet' whose voice we hear in these concluding lines. The description of England as 'nook-shotten' is found in Shakespeare's *Henry V* as the French Constable openly wonders, at the valour of the English given that the climate of 'Albion' is 'foggy, raw, and dull' (3.5.14). The ironies of this potential echo are compelling when we consider that in Shakespeare's play the Constable utters these lines for ironic effect insofar as the English are destined to conquer France—as they did the Caribbean. The speaker of Walcott's poem, then, is able to adopt the voice of an outsider, of one who contests the conquest of the English, only through a reference to that most canonical of all English authors, and only through the mask of a character who mistakenly believes he can defeat the English.

7. This passage thus opens yet another ironic allusion insofar as the reference to England as Albion—the Roman name for their English province—hearkens back to the beginning of Conrad's *Heart of Darkness,* in which Marlow compares

the Roman conquest of England to British imperialism. The irony of this reference stems from the fact that Marlow condemns Roman imperialism as 'robbery with violence' (65) in order to celebrate British imperialism by comparison. The speaker's alluded sympathy with this point of view thus (ironically) aligns him with Marlow's pro-imperial sentiments even as the speaker is attempting to align his own experience with the coloniser's in terms of their mutual status as colonised victims of imperial aggression.

8. The very practice and purpose of empire is ironised in this poem, insofar as the plantation that it presents was used to grow limes, which were required by British sailors to avoid scurvy. The imperial plantation was thus dedicated to growing a crop that was required to fight a disease that was itself caused by imperialism.

## Works Cited

Achebe, Chinua 1996, *Things Fall Apart*, Heinemann, Oxford.

Ashcroft, Bill, Gareth Griffiths and Helen Tiffin 1989, *The Empire Writes Back*, Routledge, London.

Bhabha, Homi 1984, 'Representation and the Colonial Text: A Critical Exploration of some Forms of Mimeticism', *The Theory of Reading*, ed. Frank Gloversmith, Harvester, Sussex, pp. 93–123.

Conrad, Joseph 1899, *Heart of Darkness*, Broadview, Peterborough.

Hutcheon, Linda 1989, *Irony's Edge*, Routledge, London.

———. 1994, 'Circling the Downspout of Empire', *Past the Last Post: Theorizing Post-Colonialism and Post-Modernism*, ed. Ian Adam and Helen Tiffin, University of Calgary Press, Calgary, pp. 167–189.

New, William H. 1975, *Among World*, Press Porcepic, Erin.

Walcott, Derek 1986, 'A Far Cry from Africa', *Collected Poems 1948–1984*, Farrar, Straus & Giroux, New York, pp. 17–18.

———. 1986, 'Ruins of a Great House', *Collected Poems 1948–1984*, Farrar, Straus & Giroux, New York, pp. 19–21.

OLIVER LOVESEY

# Making Use of the Past in
# Things Fall Apart

*T*hings Fall Apart is an almost iconic text in the postcolonial counter-canon, and over ten million readers have taken Achebe's palm oil to swallow his words. This grand "little kola" of a novel, that eventually inaugurated—and its profits sustained—Heinemann's African Writers Series, has initiated generations of readers into the histories of resistance in Nigerian, African, and postcolonial literatures.[1] Written during the intense introspection of Nigeria's self-fashioning on the eve of independence, Achebe's novel reflects on the imprint of the past at a time when oppositional cultural and national identities were being constructed to oppose the legacy of imperialism's othering of Africa. While Achebe famously identified his novelistic purpose as educational ("The Novelist" 42–45), Things Fall Apart also re-creates an Ibo world that writes back intertextually to the legacy of Kurtz's desire to "Exterminate all the brutes!" (mimicked in the District Commissioner's projected "pacification" of oral history) (Conrad 84), perhaps Achebe's first use of the "trope of the interpreter" (Ashcroft et al 80). This interpreter, standing at the boundaries of Okonkwo's story, prepares to render it hypodiegetic, or to collapse it into an embedded tale within his own account of Africa. Achebe's own use of this past for his different communities of readers[2] tells of the ways in which the past has been invented, appropriated, interpreted, re-written, and erased. Written against the grain of colonial histories,

*Genre: Forms of Discourse and Culture*, Volume 39, Number 2 (Summer 2006): pp. 273–299.
Copyright © 2007 University of Oklahoma.

ethnographic accounts like G. T. Basden's, colonial novels like Joyce Cary's *Mister Johnson* (Walsh 107–119), and Conrad's self-conscious palimpsest of ethnographic misreading, Achebe's metahistorical past issues from an alienated historical consciousness suspicious of the fundamental instability of historical narratives. Achebe's story of Umuofia is a work of historical affirmation deeply marked by the uncertainty and historical disenfranchisement from which it sprang.[3]

*Things Fall Apart*'s reading of the past enacts historical instability and the provisional nature of all historical accounts, as well as the ways such accounts are changed and lost, rewritten and reinvented. At the end of *Things Fall Apart,* when the District Commissioner appropriates the authority to create and edit the historical narrative, he effects, as V. Y. Mudimbe writes in a different context, "the historical dislocation of the colonial subject" (*Idea* 192). The novel presents Umuofia's past through its misuse and appropriation that alienate the colonial subject. *Things Fall Apart* is thus less a representation of the past than a preparation for its writing. The novel's subtle treatment of the tragic disenfranchisement from history is performed through a critique of false, pseudo-traditional history and also a thematic misreading that is an incursion into the isolated villages, mimicking the imperial advance in the person of the patronizing, paternalistic District Commissioner—a more gentlemanly, bureaucratic monster than Conrad's Kurtz—who will translate Okonkwo's life and death into an anecdote for an instructional book for colonial officers, demonstrating the banality of imperial evil. In the context of a consideration of historical and ethnographic misreading, this essay examines *Things Fall Apart*'s critique of false traditionalism as well as its thematized misreading of the past.

### Contexts of Historical and Ethnographic Misreading

The "social practice of history" in much African art, writes Mudimbe, was performed by "specialists of memory" (*Idea* 70), but Achebe's metahistory in *Things Fall Apart* is alienated from tradition, as its author was, by education and also by religious and cultural orientation. While there is no unmediated access to the fiction of a pure, fixed, changeless tradition, Achebe's past in his first novel is a self-consciously hybridized artifact. His construction of the past and the motives behind it are partly explained by his personal circumstances and the paternalistic historical and anthropological climate in which he was writing. His own knowledge of Ibo oral tradition, for example, was gained at the crossroads of cultures partly by listening to sermons (Ezenwa-Ohaeto 66). Growing up in a mission homestead, Achebe experienced the alienation that Homi Bhabha describes as "the otherness of the Self inscribed in the perverse palimpsest of colonial identity" (44). *Things Fall Apart* for Achebe was "an act of atonement with my past, the ritual return and homage of a prodigal son" (Achebe, "Named" 70) .[4] As Francis Ngaboh-Smart suggests, "narrating the past in a postcolonial context implies a desire to have or talk about the past, the present, and the future at once" (21).[5] Achebe's attempt to reclaim this past and the authority to write history operated under the sign of loss, amnesia, and silence. Such silence before the outrages of history is, as Mudimbe writes in a different context, "the massive and shameful silence of men who discover themselves incapable of explaining to their children what happened"; "African ideologies of self-affirmation," growing out of the encounter with this silence, "are also haunted by the specter of *cultural* death" (*Idea* 183). *Things Fall Apart* thematizes this historical haunting, for as Achebe writes in "The Novelist as Teacher," "I would be quite satisfied if my novels (especially the ones I set in the past) did no more than teach my readers that their past—with all its imperfections—was not one long night of savagery from which the first Europeans acting on God's behalf delivered them" (45). Achebe's careful, studied reclamation of the authority to tell a historical narrative strives to unpack the hesitations, compromises, contradictions, and silences behind the rendering of a "usable" African past.[6] His discourse in *Things Fall Apart*, bearing the imprint of a Eurocentric genre, language, intertextuality and gaze, is a strategy of resistance to historical and ethnographic verities.

The notion of Africa as Europe's other, writes Mudimbe, in Foucauldian guise, "is a product of the West and was conceived and conveyed through conflicting systems of knowledge" (*Idea* xi), and one of the discourses of its articulation, cultural anthropology, originates in "the Western desire to discover its own past, and it constructed an imaginary [historical] trajectory that begins with the so-called primitive and culminates in the attainments of European civilization" (*Idea* 186–187). Ethnographic description frequently allegorizes an arrival in a prelapsarian paradise or a departure from a dystopian hell, but ethnography is a murderous discipline operating under the sign of cultural death (Clifford, *Writing* 112). It inadvertently eradicates cultures because of the destructiveness of contact with Western monoculture and the reification implicit in culture's translation into ethnographic discourse. For Mudimbe, the West represented itself against geographical others, who "were nevertheless imagined and rejected as the intimate and other side of the European-thinking subject, on the analogical model of the tension between the being In-Itself and the being For-Itself" (*Idea* xi). Achille Mbembe, in an attempt to invent a new discourse to address contemporary African realities and the imperial legacy, furthers Mudimbe's analysis. Set against an extended critique of George Wilhelm Friedrich Hegel's denial of African history, Mbembe figures the colonial encounter as rape and reification, a process in which the colonizer's very being is contingent on the annihilation of the colonized

(173–206). Epistemic colonial violence is reproduced in the legacy of abjection and horror in the postcolony (196–206, 236–241).

*Things Fall Apart* was written in the context of 1950s colonial African historiography. Achebe was writing against older notions of Africa as Europe's other, and the dismissal by Hegel and historians like Hugh Trevor-Roper of the very possibility of African history. In colonial ideology, as for Thomas Macaulay in his infamous "Minute on Indian Education," anything other than Eurocentric "true History" would merely promote local "lying legends" or the "flattering [of] national prejudices" (429–430). With insidious honesty, the Belgian missionary Placide Tempels in *Bantu Philosophy* recognized a distinct African metaphysical system based on vital force, to which Christianity and a colonial ethos would be a superficial imposition, leading the Westernized elite of "pseudo-Europeans" to godless materialism (120), unless Western values were manipulated to appear to belong to the very roots of African tradition. Tempels' examination of "Bantu philosophy" is based on intimate observations during an extended residence so that "In the end, without knowing how, one attains the ability to think like the Bantu and to look upon life as they do" (29). His proposal is an outgrowth of his despair at other schemes to advance African social evolution, and his account is punctuated by extracts from colleagues' encouraging letters. Tempels writes that a missionary or lay person may reject his notion of Christianity as the inevitable "consummation" of "Bantu philosophy" because of African's incapacity (121). Such an individual, Tempels concludes, however, would be forced to accept that "he should systematically liquidate the Bantu; or, more wisely, that he should pack his bags and return to Europe!" (119).

Achebe wrote against the horizon of such views of the colonized, in the historical climate of the 1950s when the dominant African historiography was a romanticized celebration of heroic African empires, such as Zimbabwe, on which was grafted contemporary national aspirations. Achebe in *Things Fall Apart* resists references to, for example, the glories of Nri, Nok, or Benin, and neither does he applaud the origins of republican governance in Ibo tradition; "Umuofia" after all means "children . . . of the forest" (Wren 171). Another preoccupation of African historiography when Achebe wrote *Things Fall Apart* was a reassessment, by African historians such as Christopher Wilson and Basil Davidson, as well as Hugh Trevor-Roper, of the reasons for what was perceived as "Africa's age-long stagnation" as William Ochieng points out (48). Achebe strongly implies the notion of Umuofia's "stagnation" and thus its very readability as a static object, an embedded mis-perception that is part of his text's performance of misreading as we shall see in the third section of this essay. In addition, *Things Fall Apart* does not romanticize the Umuofian past as a golden age, with national overtones. Umuofia is not a metonym for Nigeria or Africa, though it often has been read as such.[7]

Moreover, Achebe's portrayal anticipates more recent understanding of multiple and overlapping allegiances in many African societies to family, clan, cult, guild, ancestors, and village, as well as ethnic group and nation,[8] and it acknowledges the seductive role of trade, medicine, and education in colonization along with that of military violence.

African intellectuals, like Achebe, as well as European intellectuals participated in the invention of Africa and the definition of its cultural and national traditions, and this project is in large part Achebe's subject in *Things Fall Apart*. As Philip Zachernuk argues in an account of intellectual history in colonial southern Nigeria, this process of invention belongs to "a complex world of inventions—mutual, antithetical, and unconnected" (6)[9] As he reminds us, "the struggle to 'decolonize' African minds began long before the postcolonial era" (10). However, the colonial creation of profoundly static, reified African tradition was politically motivated in various parts of Africa to legitimize settlers' roles and to counter African demands for reform and later independence (Ranger, "The Invention" 211, 247, 261–262). Such colonial creations of tradition operated by "freezing the original indigenous culture by turning it into an object of academic analysis" (Young 174). Invented African traditions "distorted the past but became in themselves realities through which a good deal of colonial encounter was expressed" (Ranger, "The Invention" 212). In particular, the authority to assess the cultural capital of the past was translated by indigenous elites into new "traditions" of law and land rights (Ranger, "The Invention" 250–251), and most importantly into cultural/ ethnic and nationalist groupings. The complex relationship between culture, the nation-state, and colonialism—as well as modernization[10]—at the historical "moment" of colonization is a subject beyond the scope of the present paper, but it has great importance in describing the historical period in which Achebe was composing his novelistic analysis of historical representation. If the sovereign nation-state is itself a Eurocentric idea, internationalized in the late nineteenth century, then as Nicholas Dirks argues the notion of a nationalist culture may be contingent on the experience of colonialism:

> Even as much of what we now recognize as culture was produced by the colonial encounter, the concept itself was in part invented because of it. Culture was also produced out of the allied network of processes that spawned nations in the first place. Claims about nationality necessitated notions of culture that marked groups off from one another in essential ways, uniting language, race, geography, and history in a single concept. (3)

Dirks defines "culture" as "the congeries of belief, value, assumption, and habitus identified by anthropology" (22) as well as "a site of intervention,

dislocation, and struggle" (10–11); he explains in this passage, in the context of a study of colonial India, that "culture" was produced along with the
nation-state. Kwame Appiah argues, moreover, perhaps following Frantz
Fanon's direction in "On National Culture" (206–248), that this construct
of "culture" may have been a strategy of resistance to imperialism (53–54),
though as Dirks cautions, the nation-state paradoxically both resisted and
reproduced colonialism (15). Thus, considering the historical and theoretical
contexts of its creation, Achebe's project in *Things Fall Apart* was itself a form
of resistance to colonialism though it was based on a construct of "Umuofian"
culture that was in turn at least partly based on anthropologist's accounts.

Achebe's construct of cultural archaeology in *Things Fall Apart* involves
a dialogue with the missionary, ethnographer, and apologist of empire G. T.
Basden.[11] Achebe clearly has a relationship of great ambivalence with Basden, who married Achebe's parents and whose work he first encountered in
the early 1950s when he studied comparative religion at University College
Ibadan (Ezenwa-Ohaeto 5, 43). Often compared to the Rev. Brown in *Things
Fall Apart* (Wren, "Things" 42), Basden was afforded much respect in the Ibo
community. Basden attempted to record the Ibo past, but he did so to bury
that past so deeply and finally that it could not rise again, and his ethnographic motives are paternalistic and sanctimonious, as well as openly racist
and hegemonic. Achebe's famous, modest words about his novelistic aims
being satisfied by revealing African history as other than "one long night of
savagery" could be a direct reply to Basden who wrote of his own project:
"The records of the past need not reflect upon the future. As dawn succeeds
darkness, so may it be with the Ibo People" (xxii).

In the introduction to his 1938 study *Niger Ibos*, Basden laments that
the traditional culture, law, and customs he describes are lost. This autobio-
graphical introduction, an example of what Mary Louise Pratt defines as the
ethnographic subgenre of personal narrative (7), is a boastful apology for the
impossibility of his task and a backhanded assertion of the noble motive behind its inception and the authority of its pronouncements. It functions in
part to entice the non-African reader with the prospect of the exotic and
also to caution the African reader against nostalgia. Basden's introduction is
based on a notional observation of the heart of darkness, and reminds us that
anthropology and imperialism developed in the same soil, relying on ideas of
providential history and social Darwinism (Mudimbe, *Invention* 17). Basden's
self-appointed project is less a description, however, than a work of salvage
or a forensic autopsy: "To contemplate conserving native law and custom, is
to concern ourselves very largely with a corpse. It will not respond as anticipated, because life has ceased to animate it" (xv). The older generation that
recalls the past is quickly vanishing, he asserts, and given the poverty of documentary evidence, the memory of the past will be lost. The anthropologist's

record, henceforward, he implies, will be the established authority on the culture of the past. Moreover, Basden acknowledges the very impossibility of delimiting the object of his search because "pure unadulterated forms" of ancient culture are a myth (xix). He admits the enormous local variations in customs, as a result of constantly changing conditions, including the disruptions of slave raiding and colonialism, and the ongoing influence and superimposition of ideas from neighboring areas and from abroad. Such change is not merely imposed from outside: "What I would emphasise is, *that it is the African who is choosing,* and he will continue to do so, whatever the foreigner may say, whether he be trader, missionary, government official, educationist or anthropologist" (xiii).

However, despite his scholarly hand-wringing about the lost object of his search, Basden's stated aim is to address "the need for an authoritative and complete book" (xxi). His totalizing vision is consistent with his contradictory claims to total objectivity. He claims that "I have done no more than act as scribe after tracing the facts and placing them in order" (xxii), yet he admits that as an anthropologist he is assembling diverse fragments while "befogged with antecedent presumptions" (xvii). The authority of his work comes from its being information delivered firsthand to his unconscious pen by friendly native informants. He stamps this claim to authenticity by ending his introduction with a drawing of an elephant tusk presented to him in acknowledgment of his status. In this location, it is virtually an all-access pass to insider knowledge.

Despite this claim, however, the anthropologist's involvement in recording supersedes simply ordering facts and merely archiving the past. Basden's massive catalogue of customs has a definite political agenda, predicated on assumptions about the essential character of his ethnographic subjects. He emphasizes "the difficulties that beset the seeker after truth when delving into the depths of the primitive mind" (xviii). His subject is imprisoned by taboos, prohibitions, and superstitions, unfathomable by European rationality, a theoretical obstacle requiring novel methodological innovation:

> Hence, it is extremely difficult to draw up a rational account of native law and custom. It is to be *felt* rather than expressed. This is particularly the case about midnight when surrounded by a company of highly excited dancers, or taking note of blood-stained fetishes. There are moments when one positively *feels* a sinister influence, though this need not necessarily interfere with one's investigations, especially if he is present by invitation and, therefore, enjoying a fair measure of freedom. (xvii–xviii)

Basden's account thus reinforces a perception of the fundamental irrationality of his subjects. As a result, his text may be employed to resist any colonial attempt to adapt traditional laws and customs to present uses. Not only are such modernized traditions a "travesty" of their originals (xiii), but clearly the very attempt at creating them is ill-advised given the "sinister" nature of things past. Writing amid rumblings about colonialism and nationalism, Basden recommends the principle of British governance and Christian morality to restrain Ibo aspirations and also to prevent a descent into pure, godless materialism. He warns against a reversion to earlier forms, an historical atavism that resembles reverse evolution. His account of the dark past, he hopes, will serve to intensify the brightness of the future.

### False Traditionalism

Achebe deftly dispenses with the nagging desire for a myth of origin, such as that designated a fondness for nostalgia by Basden, at the beginning of *Things Fall Apart* with a concise rendition of Okonkwo's fame as a wrestler: his fight with Amalinze the Cat that "the old men agreed was one of the fiercest since the founder of their town engaged a spirit of the wild for seven days and seven nights" (3). Okonkwo wrestles not only with Amalinze but also with his ancestors, and by implication with his *chi* in his attempt to fashion a new tradition.[12] Okonkwo is ashamed of his gentle father's boastful improvidence and poverty, failing to appreciate his flexibility and dexterity, as well as his vigorous love for life. He can't understand the strength of his father's deceptive weakness. He also overlooks the oral history likely contained in his father's songs and the wisdom of his words. Okonkwo's life is put in danger by these words, spoken after his near calamity during the drought, that express a virtual prophecy he is doomed to fulfill: "Do not despair. I know you will not despair. You have a manly and a proud heart. A proud heart can survive a general failure because such a failure does not prick its pride. It is more difficult and more bitter when a man fails *alone*" (24–25). Attempting to purge Unoka from his memory, Okonkwo enacts an Oedipal compact that also entails the rejection of tradition, the very pillar on which he attempts to erect his own self-creation as a successful man of iron will who embodies the best of Umuofia's cultural heritage. As he acknowledges later, foreseeing "himself and his fathers crowding round their ancestral shrine waiting in vain for worship and sacrifice and finding nothing but ashes of bygone days," a son's rejection entails "the prospect of annihilation" (153), and he threatens his other sons with vengeance from beyond the grave if they follow Nwoye and join the missionaries (172). Okonkwo's symbolic annihilation of his father and of the living historical memory that he represents divorces Okonkwo from history. He wants to re-create his own past, beginning with the erasure of the memory of his father. He then attempts to remake history in his own image with the fame of his wrestling that becomes for him a new, reinvigorated myth of origin announced at the beginning of the novel. He promotes his veneration for tradition, but his inadvertent murder of Ezuedu's son and his own suicide are abominations that pollute the earth. He has embarked on what will become a prodigal, anti-bildungs narrative of the shame-faced son who re-creates himself as a murderous father. As an aspiring member of the egwugwu, Okonkwo should embody, behind his masquerader's mask, historic tradition, but instead he opposes his father, history, and tradition, attempting to create a pseudo-traditional history in its place.

Umuofia's communal ethos is grounded on three traditions, each of which Okonkwo violates: the land's sacredness, ancestors' right to respect, and the primacy of the clan's survival. Okonkwo in a series of petty and catastrophic violations of custom undermines each of these traditions. He initially disrupts the week of peace, endangering the yam harvest. His suicide, at the end of the novel, is an abomination defined by Achebe as a "*nso ani* (*nso*=taboo, *ani*=earth)—*that which the earth forbids*," an offence against the earth goddess Ani, who is also goddess of the arts and morality (Cott 82). However, most significantly his denial of his father and his attempt to orphan himself from the tradition his father represents render him a false father figure in the clan. While in this community the female spirit, represented by the earth, is a nearly divine force, Achebe's historical "Fathers and Sons" narrative progresses through a patriarchal line until Okonkwo is overtaken by historical forces he can't comprehend or control, and witnesses the supremacy of Umuofia's repressed and outcast.[13]

Okonkwo, who aspires to be leading patriarch of the clan, a champion of hegemonic masculinity, becomes his sons' enemy and even murderer. Okonkwo's violence as well as his eldest son Nyoye's dismay about the killing of twins drive Nwoye away from Okonkwo to the missionaries. Okonkwo wishes his daughter Ezinma and not Nwoye were his eldest son. Nwoye breaks his connection with his father as a direct result of Okonkwo's murder of Ikemefuna. Ikemefuna has become a kind of foster brother to Nwoye, and allows Nwoye to mimic the stereotypically male behaviors Okonkwo admires. Ikemefuna's attention allows Nwoye a place in the shadow of Okonkwo's self-fashioning as a great new patriarch who will be honored after his death. Ikemefuna, the child given in partial reparation for the murder of a woman of his village, combines the best of male and female tradition, in that he can appreciate "men's stories of conquest as well as women's stories of origins and ethics, and he manifests the essentialized male quality of courage along with female compassion. Ikemefuna is a peacemaker, prepared to shelter Nwoye's younger sister from Okonkwo's wrath, in addition to bridging the divide between father and son. He is an outsider in Okonkwo's village, who brings new aptitudes as well as new stories, and he would almost certainly have been a more skillful negotiator with the missionaries and the colonial forces.

While the representation of Ikemefuna's ritual death signals Achebe's unwillingness to sanitize the past, it also hints at his discomfort with pseudo-traditional limitations on cultural flexibility and adaptability of the sort advanced by Okonkwo.[14] In a rare passage of free indirect discourse in the novel, the childish innocence of the victim is naturalized. The account of Ikemefuna's murder shifts abruptly in the space of an ellipsis from reported narrative ("He had never been fond of his real father") to mediated interior monologue: ". . . of course she [his sister] would not be three now, but six. Would he recognize her now? She must have grown quite big. How his mother would weep for joy, and thank Okonkwo for having looked after him so well and for bringing him back. She would want to hear everything that had happened to him in all these years. Could he remember them all?" (59–60) Ikemefuna recalls his old method for resolving mysteries when he was a little boy. He remembers the words of the song from his favorite story about a land "where the ant holds his court in splendor and the sands dance forever" (35). We follow the child's return to an insect paradise and a yet more childish state that intensifies the horror of his murder. He wonders "Why had Okonkwo withdrawn to the rear?" (60–61). The blunt question and the stark description of action that follows recall, in reverse order, the staccato lines of Yeats's "Leda and the Swan"[15]: "Okonkwo looked away. He heard the blow. The pot fell and broke in the sand. He heard Ikemefuna cry" (61). Like Yeats's poem that inquires into the momentary violence of the encounter of human and divine, Okonkwo's involvement in violent ritual with the Oracle's sanction leads, because of his private trauma, to personal and collective catastrophe. In a child's version of the words from the cross in John's gospel, or Isaac's questioning of Abraham, Ikemefuna states with the stark matter-of-factness of those about to die: "My father, they have killed me!" His is not a tidy murder, however, and he runs in supplication to the one he claims with the name of father only to be struck down by his would-be savior. Driven by the intensity of his fear of resembling his own father, Okonkwo participates in the annihilation of Ikemefuna whose very name continues his plea for life: "let my strength not become lost" (Hoegberg 74). Okonkwo soon will cease even to refer to Ikemefuna by his proper name or by the more personal epithet "son." Instead, in a variation of metonymy, antonomasia, Okonkwo will replace his name with the indirect, impersonal epithet "boy" as he tries to make silence close over memory.

The horror of Okonkwo's murder of Ikemefuna and, to a lesser extent, Okonkwo's inarticulate response resonate throughout the rest of the novel, though clearly Okonkwo is a most flawed embodiment of Umuofian values and his personal Oedipal trauma does not allegorize the coming colonial encounter. Okonkwo's action, moreover, as Obierika says, is an abomination, an ethical violation "for which the goddess wipes out whole families" (67), even though it is consistent with the letter of the law. This action precipitates the novel's catastrophe, the hero's death. The more immediate consequence of Okonkwo's violation—seemingly part of the bizarre chain of cause and effect in the workings of the irony of fate in the narrative tragedy—however, is his inadvertent murder of the son of the oldest man in the village, a symbolic violation of ancestors and a strike against the clan's very survival. The warning about the potential violation has been brought to Okonkwo by Ogbuefi Ezeudu, the oldest man in Okonkwo's quarter of Umuofia. He repeats to Okonkwo that because Ikemefuna calls him father, Okonkwo should avoid the scene of his death. For Okonkwo, by this time, Ikemefuna has gone from being virtually an adopted son and Nwoye's elder brother to being merely "a boy" and "that boy" (65, 66). Okonkwo's murder of Ikemefuna, a product of his desire to conquer his own tenderness, displayed in his affection for Ezinma and Ikemefuna, indicates that Okonkwo opposes his chi and its promptings to gentleness and balance. While Okonkwo, resembles the proverbial man who challenges his chi to a wrestling match, he also wrestles with his culture that finally, as Achebe has commented, "betrays" him by being "devious and flexible, because if it wasn't, it wouldn't survive" (Jeyifo, "Literature" 118).[16] When Ezeudu dies, one of the ancestral spirits calls on him to haunt anyone who might have caused his death, and in the seven years after Okonkwo's flight into exile, events accelerate out of anyone's control and by the time of Okonkwo's return the community's memory of his past glory has faded, and he begins to fall out of collective history. During his exile, Okonkwo is suspended outside of Umuofian time and its colonial encounter in a limbo that, as Simon Gikandi writes, "compels the hero to confront his repressed feminine space" ("Poetics" 7). By Part Three of the novel, the reader, too, has a new perspective on events.

### Re-Reading the Past

One of the greatest achievements of *Things Fall Apart* is its construction of a seemingly objective, impartial narrator with a detached, self-effacing, implied author in the background.[17] The narrator appears to have an inexhaustible fund of cultural knowledge, as if combining Basden's ethnographic curiosity with the intuitive understanding of his native informants. The narrator appears to initiate readers into the practices of everyday life and the secrets of an isolated society. As in ethnographic discourse, the novel's first two parts present a fantasy of a traditional society going about its traditional ways unobserved. The novel's extended first part presents a methodical, multi-layered record, blending the community's seasonal folkways with the lives of a handful of individuals, merging private and public domains, the commonplace and the extraordinary. The novel has often been interpreted as anthropological.[18] The notion that *Things Fall Apart* presents "untrammeled cultural authenticity," however, is a fantasy belonging to the construction of "a European anthropological exotic" as Graham Huggan points out in a perceptive reading of the novel (43). After surveying the legacy of misguided anthropological "theories of Africans," including Tempels', Christopher Miller argues that despite its obvious pitfalls, anthropology is the necessary mediator between African literature and the non-African reader or African reader from a different cultural area (4). With its shifting focalization, the pacing of its seemingly opaque, transparent exposition, and the austere simplicity of its style, *Things Fall Apart* conveys the impression of being an ethnographic document, but it begins with a wrestling match and the reader is lulled early into a sense of complacency before being thrown at the end.

The reader begins to accumulate insider knowledge, and even the warnings implicit in the example of other outsiders fail to guard against complacency, because their ineptitude and arrogance elicit laughter or pity, binding the reader more closely within the periphery of the narrator's gaze. The growing assumption of insider knowledge leads the reader to a seemingly benign respect for Ibo culture, cultural difference, and even the unknowability of culture that initially disguise an awareness of misreading. As if able to distinguish different Ibo dialects, for example, the reader shares in the laughter at the missionary interpreter who calls himself "my buttocks" (144). The reader also shares in the outrage when Tortoise, who takes on the role of authoritative cultural mediator, betrays his compatriots. As Bruce Henricksen has argued, the novel's "familiarizing discourse . . . may have helped to plant the trap of universalizing interpretations" (300). The novel presents what Huggan describes as being "in part a deconstructive exercise in ethnographic parody, a series of pointedly exaggerated, at times caricatural, cultural (mis)readings aimed at a Western model reader confronted with the limits of his/her cultural knowledge and interpretive authority" (43). While *Things Fall Apart*'s fallible Western reader is less a "model" than merely being one of the novel's readers or implied readers, ethnographic parody is a frequently overlooked aspect of Achebe's complex aesthetic. However, while some of the parodic play is "pointedly exaggerated," much of it is not. *Things Fall Apart* is more subtle than Huggan allows in constructing the reader's gaze. This gaze is mediated through the seemingly detached, objective stance of the narrator, and it initially fosters a respect for the unknowableness of culture.

The novel carefully lays the groundwork for its embedded misreading not only in the introduction of false interpreters, but also in its careful construction of customs, language, and cultural change. When Chielo, for instance, leads the sickly Ezinma on an epic march through the nine villages, the reader is never allowed into the secrets of the priestess of Agbala's strength or the mysteries of the Oracle's cave or the reason for the walk, though we do learn that Chielo has a particular affection for the girl.[19] The focus in this scene is on the tenderness of a mother and even a violent, obtuse, awkward father for a beloved daughter. Whatever humor there is in the account heightens our sense of Okonkwo's inept concern. Moreover, like Okonkwo, we have no explanation of why things are happening. The would-be anthropological narrator does not intrude with an ethnographic quick fix, and we are not given material explanations such as that Ekwefi's immune response is triggered by excessive fatigue. There is no authoritative voice or center in the text to explain away cultural verities. Instead, we are presented bare facts, and left to ponder the mystery of cultural practices that most villagers would be unable to fathom. We are left to emulate the narrator's quiet respect for cultural artifacts.

The clearest instance of the cultivation of readerly respect and the sophisticated preparation for misreading lies in the justly famous ogbanje episode that anticipates Chielo's night walk. Okagbue, the medicine man who unearths the *iyi-uwa*, does not have a stone in his loin cloth; we aren't told there was an earlier shrine or village under this ground where such objects may have been littered; and we are not even told that such legends may have helped to explain high infant mortality rates. Rather, as with Chielo's night walk, the realism of presentation is psychological, and we appreciate the youthful Ezinma's humorous self-importance. The absence of explanation and the presentation of bare details convey a respect for cultural mysteries. The reader, constituted here as a comparative anthropologist, leaves such scenes a detached observer, allowed to witness the manifestation of mystery, but encouraged to respect its authenticity without an irritable rush to facile explanation. Moreover, the mode of presentation cultivates a sense of insider knowledge and insider respect for cultural taboos.

*Things Fall Apart* also seemingly facilitates the reader's introduction to an Ibo linguistic medium and to a resulting misreading. Like Basden, Achebe provides a glossary of Ibo words and phrases, italicized in the text, and he also provides simultaneous translation. In such instances, language functions as a metonym for an entire culture, as Ashcroft et al suggest (62), but it may also serve as a two-way gate allowing an outsider endowed with "global" English ready access to the essential cultural artifact. *Things Fall Apart* appeared in paperback on June 17, 1958 at a time when paperback publication, designed for the educational market, was somewhat unusual (Currey et al 149–159). The novel was published by the division of Heinemann responsible for the marketing and distribution of school textbooks in Africa. The novel's glossary, added to the 1967 edition, which has a problematic diegetic status in the postcolonial text (Ashcroft et al 61), would facilitate the novel's use as a school text, a function embraced by both Achebe and Heinemann. Typically, in the novel's use of Ibo, we are introduced to a word or concept in English and then provided with the English word connected to the Ibo word by a correlative conjunction, and then left with the Ibo word alone, with presumably the possibility of reference to the glossary again if necessary.[20] The first reference to a "hut," in English with no Ibo word attached, is on page five, and then on page 14 we progress to "hut, or *obi*," and by page 29 we have "*obi*" alone. Similarly, "personal god" is used on page 14, and then "*chi* or personal god" on pages 18 and 27; the next three references in the text are to *chi* alone. The reader is presented a kind of Berlitz Guide to Ibo, "Ibo Made Simple," but also and more importantly a kind of shorthand authority over certain metonymic elements of a presumably static, unchanging linguistic medium standing for what the reader is lulled into misreading as a static, unchanging, exotic culture, complete and frozen in time. The reader thus is led into misreading by being encouraged in a species of seemingly benign cultural appropriation. The very linguistic medium of the text thus embeds a misreading that is based on an implied sense of cultural stasis. We have a carefully manufactured "Ibo Survival Guide" to facilitate life in a carefully controlled fictional model village; it allows ready access to representative concepts and linguistic markers, useful for time travel back to the "past."

Similarly, Ibo proverbs offer mediated access to cultural heritage, presented through careful explanation, repetition, and directed interpretation. The novel carefully but subtly explains proverbs, sometimes providing first the general principle the proverb illustrates, then the proverb itself, followed by its specific application. For example, when Okonkwo moves from success to success as wrestler and farmer, we learn in a condensed model of how this pattern will subsequently operate: "Age was respected among his people, but achievement was revered. As the elders said, if a child washed his hands he could eat with kings. Okonkwo had clearly washed his hands and so he ate with kings and elders" (8). The proverb is groomed and dressed for general consumption. Elsewhere, repetition fosters the perception of understanding as with the proverb "A toad does not run in the daytime for nothing" that is first introduced after the explanatory paraphrase "There must be a reason for it" (20). A variation of this proverb repeated later in the novel is followed by the speaker's contextualized explanation: "My father used to say to me: 'Whenever you see a toad jumping in broad daylight, then know that something is after its life.' When I saw you all pouring into this meeting from all the quarters of our clan so early in the morning, I knew that something was after our life" (203). A partial familiarity with the proverb is flattered, as if the reader now belongs to the discursive milieu.

A similar gradual immersion in cultural lore and a preparation for misreading occur in the telling of folktales. Nwoye loves his mother's stories of origins, conflict resolution, and morality. Just before he hears the tale of

Vulture's embassy to Sky to acquire rain for parched Earth, there is a reference to a category of "stories of the tortoise and his wily ways" (53), preparing us for the more extended narration of the tale of tortoise and the birds. However, before this narrative, Okonkwo, waking from his first sleep after murdering Ikemefuna, recalls his mother's story of Ear's dismissal of seemingly feeble Mosquito's marriage proposal. Humiliated Mosquito reminds Ear of his continuing vitality each time he passes. In context, we clearly see the allegorical importance of the tale and of Okonkwo's rejection of such women's stories as "silly" (75). He fails to appreciate the endurance of the weak and the triumph of memory. The reader is gradually led to perceive the extension of allegorical significance in such tales, so that when we hear Ekwefi's story of cunning Tortoise going to a feast in the sky and stealing all of the food, and his betrayed compatriots allowing him to shatter on the ground, we know the story's significance supersedes explaining the origin of the tortoise's patterned shell. We are led to perceive the consequences of selfish behavior and perhaps to interpret the account as a colonial allegory of the cultural mediator (Tortoise) who abuses his role. Thus, the careful presentation of essential cultural lore fosters the reader's self-confidence in feeling like an insider and even in opposing alien incursion.

Part One of *Things Fall Apart* presents a cultural mosaic that is clearly fluid and pluralistic, but the novel thematizes a misreading whereby the accumulation of insider knowledge, including a grasp of the metonymic function of language, strongly implies that there is a knowable cultural object that remains static. There are numerous signs that there has been change within Umuofian society, but the process of change remains mysterious, and this complicates the dilemma of men like Nwoye, Obierika, and Uchendu facing the seeming inevitability of the murder of twins. It also constructs a solid if fragile cultural identity whose encounter with colonialism it may not withstand without breaking to pieces and being massively restructured. Early in the novel and long before the Rev. Brown and Akunna's discussion of comparative religion, Achebe's subject of study when he first encountered Basden's *Niger Ibos,* there is a discussion of the merits of changing customs regulating the Week of Peace. Punishment for violating the Week of Peace has cooled in a number of generations from execution to a fine, because the older sanctions "spoiled the peace which it was meant to preserve" (31). In a different clan, those dying during that week are cast into the Evil Forest, resulting, says Ogbuefi Ezeudu, in the clan's being haunted by "the evil spirits of these unburied dead" (32). Okonkwo and Obierika later ruminate on the restrictions placed on titled men tapping palms, and the absence of such restrictions in other clans. Obierika complains, "I don't know how we got that law" (69), but he proceeds to find its justification in upholding the status of titled men. While there is often little indication of exactly how customs change, they obviously do change and there is an open discussion among senior clan members of the relative merits of maintenance and innovation. This is apparent when Obierika recalls the discussion of titled men and tapping, and reflects that other clans bargain a bride price rather than using sticks. This discussion in turn leads to the question of maternal or paternal child ownership, and, after Okonkwo's comment on the variety of customs in the world, to a reference to rumors of the toeless white men. Despite the evident fluidity and plurality existing in Umuofian culture, the process for changing customs and laws is not explained, and because of the prominence given the predicaments of Nyoye, Obierika, and Okonkwo, the reader may well misperceive that the clan's inflexibility contributed to or even caused its decline. Nwoye breaks with his father and appears to oppose tradition when he joins the missionaries. He is motivated by Okonkwo's violence, and by his revulsion at the murder of Ikemefuna and the slaughter of twins. Similarly, Obierika is puzzled by the necessity of driving Okonkwo into exile after his accidental shooting of Ogbuefi Ezeudu:

> But although he thought for a long time he found no answer. He was merely led into greater complexities. He remembered his wife's twin children, whom he had thrown away. What crime had they committed? The Earth had decreed that they were an offense on the land and must be destroyed. And if the clan did not exact punishment for an offense against the great goddess, her wrath was loosed on all the land and not just on the offender. As the elders said, if one finger brought oil it soiled the others. (125)

Finally, too, Okonkwo murders the District Commissioner's messenger to trigger a war against the colonial forces or to signify his last act of violation against community norms and collective decision making in favor of his own version of tradition. His act is a gesture of individual will, though based on the traditional heroic warrior values that he embodies. It acknowledges his grief at the community's weakness and his acceptance that for him "there is no future" (Moses 131). He dies, however, and Nwoye and Obierika survive, and the catharsis within the text and within Umuofia will soon begin with the cleansing of the earth.

Okonkwo's own inflexible devotion to initiative, violence, and power, and his disregard for pluralistic cultural traditions and ancestral history, result from his traumatic upbringing and do not represent the totality of the cultural norms of the clan. The very different responses to changing circumstances shown by Nwoye and Obierika, men of different generations, display the clan's flexibility: "The clan was like a lizard; if it lost its tail it soon grew another" (171). They will remember Okonkwo in ways that he refused to honor the memory of his father, whose unburied spirit roams the earth from the Evil Forest, a site that enabled the missionaries' survival. Okonkwo is the son of an outsider, but Okonkwo became an insider by creating his own tradition of exclusion. Okonkwo's rise is enabled by cultural flexibility, but so too is his fall. Nwoye and Obierika, unlike Okonkwo, have adapted according to the flexibility and plurality of the old ways. Okonkwo severs Nwoye from his family after. Okonkwo beats his silent son. For the wise Uchendu silence may be ominous. The near silence of the white man who cycles into Abame, for example, is unsettling he says. Uchendu, Okonkwo, and Obierika agree on Abame's foolishness, but disagree on its cause. Uchendu says Abame erred by killing an ominously silent man and failing to conceive of the possibility of unknown abominations; Okonkwo and Obierika criticize Abame's failure to anticipate a massive armed assault. Uchendu gestures to a living tradition of tolerance when he refers to the presence of albinos in the clan who must have a nation elsewhere: "'There is no story that is not true,' said Uchendu. 'The world has no end, and what is good among one people is an abomination with others'" (141). Okonkwo, however, refuses alternate interpretations, and is impatient with fine words whatever their truth. Okonkwo should have come to see the wisdom of his father's words about the bitterness of personal failure; instead, he disdains his advice: "Unoka was like that in his last days. His love of talk had grown with age and sickness. It tried Okonkwo's patience beyond words" (25). Okonkwo's contempt for those with a "love of talk" will finally position him with another who is prepared to close off Umuofia's pluralistic history and who is infuriated by the clan's "love of superfluous words" (206), the amateur anthropologist and future Africanist, the District Commissioner.

Until the sudden appearance of the District Commissioner in Okonkwo's village, the reader's sympathetic identification with Umuofia and the reader's assumption of a stance of cultural relativism like the Rev. Brown's are fostered by the text. The reader attains a carefully nurtured confidence in the possession of insider knowledge and a paternalistic if not mildly patronizing attitude, bordering on that of the sanctimonious and condescending Basden's. The text appears to initiate the reader in the secrets of an isolated society, but this constructed pretense of understanding positions the reader not with Obierika or even Brown, but with the District Commissioner. In Yeats's "The Second Coming," from which Achebe takes his novel's title, the poem's speaker, standing on the verge of a cataclysmic historical paradigm shift, is able to gaze into the past and future. For Yeats, the configuration of the gyres at this instant enables a type of lucid dreaming that permits the telescoping of history and prophecy. Standing at the diagetic border of Achebe's text of Umuofia and at one crossroads of a continent's history, the reading District Commissioner gazes at the projected annihilation of Umuofia and of stories like Okonkwo's. There is a radical constriction of time and space, as in Yeats's poem, and the periphery of Umuofia has been breached. The District Commissioner fails to recognize that just as the West can rise and fall in apocalyptic time, so too can Umuofia (Ten Kortenaar 34). Operating under the sign of an apocalyptic vision of the dissolution of civilizations, Achebe in Part Three of *Things Fall Apart* reduces the historic cataclysm of imperialism to the banality of a bureaucrat's colonial history.

Hearing of Okonkwo's suicide and of Umuofia's methods for dealing with the abomination, the District Commissioner enacts catachresis. He anticipates writing an account that will falsify and shrink Okonkwo's narrative, the rich diversity of Umuofia, and in fact the entire novel to a paragraph. He will thus reduce and distort Okonkwo's story, and erase history. Moreover, he will superimpose his own project, "The Pacification of the Primitive Tribes of the Lower Niger," that will reinterpret and rewrite Okonkwo's history. He projects a discursive shift from an indigenous oral history to a history and anthropology of the conquered. His title and the annihilation it entails refer to *Heart of Darkness* and the paternalistic Kurtz's projected genocide. As James Clifford has argued, *Heart of Darkness* self-consciously draws attention to its own ethnographic self-fashioning (*Predicament* 110). Conrad has "built into his work a vision of the constructed nature of culture and language" (95). Like Conrad's narrator, in Clifford's reading, Achebe's District Commissioner self-consciously anticipates the selecting, deleting, and editing that will focus and polish his ethnographic study. Drawing on Clifford's insight, Huggan notes that *Things Fall Apart* is also an "ethnographic parody" (40), its intertextual dialogue with *Heart of Darkness* a "postcolonial parody-reversal" (42).

Achebe's District Commissioner is a reading character who considers himself to be both a participant in the unfolding events and a self-conscious interpreter of his own performance in these events, as if he were standing akimbo on the diagetic border of the textual thoughtworld of Umuofia. The last part of *Things Fall Apart* shows that there is no such thing as a benign imperial reading. Like the District Commissioner who assumes insider knowledge, the reader has acquired a carefully packaged pretense of grasping Umuofian culture in Part One. In what appears to be a novelistic *deus ex machina,* the omnipotent District Commissioner descends to adjudicate Umuofian affairs, but he is judge and destroyer, whose patronizing dismissal of "superfluous words" performs a narrative and historical erasure. He is a participant in "the glamour of empire building" that conferred instant gentility (Ranger, "The Invention" 215), a man readying himself for a career after his tour of duty, when his imperial memories will be domesticated into colonial theory. He will write an ethnographic account in the service of the globalizing ideology of empire that will classify, reduce, distort and destroy the society it describes. Achebe's narration ends with the commencement of the narrative of ethnographic representation, that annihilates the social forms it describes.

The third part of the novel projects into the future uses made of an African past and onto the construction of ethnographic, colonial, and post-colonial discourses of history. The novel is a tragedy, but one that is multi-dimensional.[21] The tragedy operates because of the reader's identification with, not Okonkwo, but Umuofia, but the catastrophe is the recognition that the reader is an outsider who has believed him/herself to be a sympathetic insider and is now positioned with the arrogant, myopic, annihilating District Commissioner. The novel thematizes this misreading whereby the reader performs the appropriation of culture, and then experiences historical alienation. Like Marlow in *Heart of Darkness* who is compelled to repeat his story because of his complicity in lying to the Intended, a lie of the kind that perpetuated the fiction of King Leopold's saving mission in the Congo, *Things Fall Apart*'s reader is at least notionally complicit with the District Commissioner in perpetuating the appropriation of cultural memory. This aesthetic dislocation reflects the historical alienation of a subject from history.

*Things Fall Apart* thus anticipates the uses that will be made of the past. It thematizes interpretation and misinterpretation. Achebe ironically reduces the District Commissioner's momentous plan for Africa to five paragraphs, and at least gestures forward to the uses that will be made of Africa's past in postcolonial theory, an area in which Achebe's own vital contribution is often ignored (Moore-Gilbert 4).[22] Achebe reminds us, more than four decades after his novel first appeared in a modest print run of 2000, of the uses made of Africa's past. Written under the sign of the loss of the past, his novel addresses the fundamental instability of historical accounts of fluid, pluralistic, and flexible cultures, that have been fought over with such violence by competing powers. Like the tradition of Mbari, about which Achebe has written so eloquently ("African" 1–3), his achievement in *Things Fall Apart* is one with its destruction and dissolution. *Things Fall Apart* foregrounds the provisional nature of all narratives of the past, the ways they are lost, changed, re-written, and reinvented.

## Notes

1. Bernth Lindfors concludes a 1998 survey of the novel's impact: "*Things Fall Apart*, both in Africa and elsewhere, remains the most widely read and durable of African literary masterworks and a truly international classic" ("Achebe" 16).

2. The question of *Things Fall Apart*'s readership has been controversial. The novel has a wide variety of readers, real, intended and implied, and Achebe has said the novel is intended for all readers though he clearly assumed a certain familiarity with Western languages and genres and a lack of familiarity with Ibo folkways, though he also wrote for a broadly-defined African audience, divorced from its

history, and also for the audience of Conrad and Cary, to serve as an antidote. Bruce Henricksen offers a valuable discussion of universalizing, exoticizing, ethical, and political readings of the novel, though he assumes that "the Western reader is Achebe's intended audience" (302).

In a binary study of *Things Fall Apart* and Ben Okri's *The Famished Road*, in light of Mudimbe's notion of African gnosis, and using an approach, that while theoretically sophisticated, inadvertently recalls one member of the Troika's match-up of Achebe and Soyinka, and their evaluative and legislative approach to African discourse, Ato Quayson argues that *Things Fall Apart*'s realist mode is designed to package African traditions for a Western audience in order to justify independence. Achebe's realist mode, for Quayson, does not attempt to conjure a "pristine past"; instead, this mode is formulated for a future when indigenous oral genres would be engulfed by ethnographic and realist discourses (146). However, Quayson seems to overlook the fact that Achebe's is clearly a constructed, mediated past, and that the fragmentation of traditional history and its discursive appropriation began well before he began writing in the 1950s. Quayson claims, moreover, that *Things Fall Apart* fails to represent supernatural actions or motivation, or to allow the supernatural to overwhelm linear narration, as in Okri's mythopoetic manner, and that "[e]ven when the narrator seems to be leaving a margin for the supernatural, everything is explained to the reader in order to locate it within the pattern of real-world causality" (144). Achebe's novel, on the contrary, avoids such explanation of supernatural events, characteristic of ethnography, and the aesthetic distancing produced, as Quayson allows, by Okri's omnipresent supernaturalism. Quayson's discussion of indigenous oral genres, furthermore, draws on the practice of writers within a western Nigerian tradition (Tutuola, Soyinka, and Okri), with the exception of Onitsha Market literature, and the discussion tends to overlook the fact that when Achebe wrote his first novel there was not a single national literature, though perhaps Achebe was attempting to produce one in anticipation of independence. Moreover, Okri's novel is not divorced from its ideological context, and the shape-shifting abiku partly allegorizes the changing nation to which he tentatively belongs, and Azaro also figures the artist, and the inspiration provided by one with the ability to live amidst the beauty and terror of creation.

3. Achebe has spoken of the sense of personal and collective betrayal he experienced in reading European fictions of Africa, like Conrad's, and being led to identify with White invaders. In a 1984 interview, Achebe made a similar point about reading Joyce Cary's *Mister Johnson:* "We should have immediately identified with the Africans but this was impossible because the dice was loaded against them, the way the story was told, the way the author took sides" (qtd in Ezenwa-Ohaeto 44). In fact, Achebe said in an interview in 1983 that "anger" with *Mister Johnson* "inspired" him to write (Nkosi 13). In an 1983 interview he said: "the moment I became conscious of the possibilities of representing somebody from a certain standpoint, from that moment I realised that there must be misrepresentation, there must be misjudgment, there must be even straightforward discrimination and distortion" (Jeyifo, "Literature" 112). In 1995, he said that he encountered "colonial ideology, for the first time in fiction, as something sinister" (Rowell 183). Recognizing this narrative double-cross awakened him to the ideological embedding of all stories, and inspired his own writing.

4. A similar awareness of generational responsibility informs the purpose of other African cultural historians. Mudimbe, for example, refers to his work in

*The Idea of Africa* as "stories to my children" (209), and Kwame Anthony Appiah dedicates *In My Father's House* to his family's children (viii).

5. Ngaboh-Smart's essay argues that Achebe's novel calls for a nationalist response to the colonial imposition of silence (17), a subject Joseph R. Slaughter explores farther in his account of colonial silence and narrative voice (140–143), concluding "Achebe's novel thematizes the impositions of silence and the equally important representations of silence, suggesting that no easy equation between silence and passivity is possible" (147). These two essays begin and end the first part (focused on *Things Fall Apart*) of volume one of *Emerging Perspectives on Chinua Achebe*, edited by Ernest N. Emenyonu. A number of essays in this first part argue that Achebe's novel presents a complex account of a coherent if multifaceted past and of integrated integrity in national (Ngaboh-Smart 3–23), individual (Onyemelukwe 35–47), and gendered (Azodo 49–65) terms. "Things Do Not Fall Apart" is the provocative title of Joseph Obi's essay (77–83).

6. I am employing an expanded sense of the evocative phrase employed in Terence Ranger's survey of African historiography (Ranger, "Towards" 17) Referring to the crisis in African historiography in the 1970s, following the dominance of heroic history in a period when "there was a demand for some—almost any—past" (19–20), Ranger advocates approaches to social history that are relevant to problems of poverty and underdevelopment (17–30). Appiah refers to *Things Fall Apart*'s "usable past" (150), but he does not cite Ranger, instead reading the novel as an instance of what Frederic Jameson generalized as a "national allegory." Appiah writes that novels like *Things Fall Apart* "seem to belong to the world of eighteenth- and nineteenth-century literary nationalism; they are theorized as the imaginative recreation of a common cultural past that is crafted into a shared tradition by the writer; they are in the tradition of Scott . . . The novels of this first stage are thus realist legitimations of nationalism: they authorize a 'return to traditions' while at the same time recognizing the demands of a Weberian rationalized modernity. From the later sixties on, these celebratory novels of the first stage become rarer: Achebe, for example, moves from the creation of a usable past in *Things Fall Apart* to a cynical indictment of politics in the modern sphere in *A Man of the People*" (149–150).

7. See the discussion of Umuofia and Africa in Kalu Ogbaa's *Understanding Things Fall Apart* (1–2), and Chidi Amuta's interpretation of Okonkwo as an "embodiment of the spirit of his age" and his class (134).

8. See, for example, Terence Ranger's "The Invention" (248).

9. Zachenuk doesn't discuss Achebe and avoids literary endeavors in his account of intellectual history, but his definition of his focus "medial community," involving a colonial-educated elite trained for colonial service, would include figures like Achebe (13, 14).

10. See Michael Valdez Moses's Hegelian analysis of the role of modernization in what he reads as Achebe's progressive view of history is *Things Fall Apart*, a novel prophetic of postcolonial crises (107–109).

11. Robert Wren documents Basden's influence on Achebe in *Achebe's World*, but he sets out to critique Basden and then cites him as an authority.

12. Wresting also signifies society's ordering of chaos, as Chidi Okonkwo indicates (84–86), though Okonkwo both subdues and perpetuates chaos.

13. Zohreh T. Sullivan argues that in the novel "the presence of the slippery and unstable female code disturbs the unstable rigidity of masculine codes in all three sections of the novel" (106). Jeyifo notes that "the fragmentary stories and

motifs of the *agbala* and the *efulefu* move this social category to restitution at the end of the novel" ("For Chinua" 64).

14. David Hoegberg shows how Ikemefuna's ritual murder violates Umuofian sanctions against killing outsiders and judging sons according to their fathers' value: "[b]y the time he killed, Ikemefuna has become a symbol of blurred boundaries between self and other" (73).

15.
A sudden blow: the great wings beating still
Above the staggering girl, her thighs caressed
By the dark webs, her nape caught in his bill,
He holds her helpless breast upon his breast.

How can those terrified vague fingers push
The feathered glory from her loosening thighs?
And how can body, laid in that white rush,
But feel the strange heart beating where it lies?
. . .

16. Achebe tells of the proud wrestler who goes to the spirit world and defeats everyone but is defeated by his chi, an "unimpressive" figure "very weak and hungry-looking, thin as a rope" who "with one finger picks him up and smashes him on the ground" (Cott 84).

17. Simon Gikandi notes that in *Things Fall Apart* "the narrator's position, identity, and perspective change often" (30).

18. Ato Quayson, for example, surveys unproblematized approaches to the novel's "cultural authenticity" and "Africanness" ("Realism" 119, 121), paradigmatic of much early African literary criticism.

19. Neil Ten Kortenaar reads this scene as an example of the novel's use of "double-consciousness," the bifurgated vision of a holistic world of absolute integrity and the abstracted stance of rational observation" (36–37). For Ten Kortenaar, the novel employs double-consciousness to present "the history of a society that did not conceive of itself historically" for a "modern audience" (38) that cannot conceive of anything else. Achebe historicizes the Ibos, Ten Kortenaar argues, by making Okonkwo a self-conscious agent who narrates his life thus allowing, through his confrontation with the Whites, "the Igbos' entry into history" (45). Ten Kortenaar's argument is based on a dichotomous view of Western and African conceptions of the novel's modern, universal audience, composed of both African and Western readers. His argument is underwritten with a suspicion of the viability of oral history.

20. This does not apply to single uses of individual words, like *inyanga* (43), explained in the glossary, or single uses of words followed by extended definitions, such as *osu* (155, 156).

21. Richard Begam's study of the novel's three endings in three historical modes classifies four types of tragedy designated in the critical literature: classical, modern, Igbo, and historical (399).

22. Bart Moore-Gilbert implies that the District Commissioner's projected title anticipates the wars of postcolonial theory and his own dilemma of choosing between adjudication or synthesis in treating the subject (202).

# WORKS CITED

Achebe, Chinua. "African Literature as Restoration of Celebration." *Chinua Achebe: A Celebration.* Eds. Kirsten Holst Petersen and Anna Rutherford. Oxford: Heinemann, 1990. 1–10.

——— . "Named for Victoria, Queen of England." *Morning Yet on Creation Day: Essays.* London: Heinemann, 1975. 65–70.

——— . "The Novelist as Teacher." *Morning Yet on Creation Day: Essays.* 42–45.

——— . *Things Fall Apart.* New York: Anchor, 1959.

Amuta, Chidi. *The Theory of African Literature: Implications for Practical Criticism.* London: Zed Books, 1989.

Ashcroft, Bill, and Gareth Griffiths and Helen Tiffin. *The Empire Writes Back: Theory and Practice in Post-Colonial Literatures.* London: Routledge, 1989.

Appiah, Kwame Anthony. *In My Father's House: Africa in the Philosophy of Culture.* New York: Oxford University Press, 1992.

Azodo, Ada Uzoamaka. "Masculinity, Power and Language in Chinua Achebe's *Things Fall Apart.*" *Emerging Perspectives on Chinua Achebe.* Ed. Ernest N. Emenyonu. 49–65.

Basden, G. T. *Niger Ibos.* London: Frank Cass, 1966.

Begam, Richard. "Achebe's Sense of an Ending: History and Tragedy in *Things Fall Apart.*" *Studies in the Novel* 29.3 (Fall 1997): 396–411.

Bell, Richard H. "African Philosophy from a Non-African Point of View: An Exercise in Cross Cultural Philosophy." *Postcolonial African Philosophy: A Critical Reader.* Ed. Emmanuel Chukwudi Eze. Cambridge, Massachusetts: Blackwell, 1997. 197–220.

Bhabha, Homi K. *The Location of Culture.* London: Routledge, 1994.

Chinweizu, Onwuchekwa Jemie and Ihechukwu Madubuike. *Toward the Decolonization of African Literature.* Washington, D. C.: Howard University Press, 1983.

Clifford, James. *The Predicament of Culture: Twentieth-Century Ethnography, Literature, and Art.* Cambridge: Harvard University Press, 1988.

Clifford, James and George E. Marcus, eds. *Writing Culture: The Poetics and Politics of Ethnography.* Berkeley: University of California Press, 1986.

Conrad, Joseph. *Heart of Darkness.* Ed. Robert Hampson. London: Penguin, 1995.

Cott, Jonathan. "Chinua Achebe: At the Crossroads." *Conversations with Chinua Achebe.* Ed. Bernth Lindfors. Jackson: University of Mississippi Press, 1997. 76–87.

Currey, James et al. "Working with Chinua Achebe: The African Writers Series. James Currey, Alan Hill and Keith Sambrook in Conversation with Kirsten Holst Petersen." *Chinua Achebe, A Celebration.* Eds. Kirsten Holst Petersen and Anna Rutherford. Oxford: Heinemann, 1991. 149–159.

Dirks, Nicholas B. "Introduction: Colonialism and Culture." Colonialism and Culture. Ed. Nicholas Dirks. Ann Arbor. University of Michigan Press, 1992. 1-25.

Emenyonu, Ernest N., ed. *Emerging Perspectives on Chinua Achebe. Vol. 1. Omenka: The Master Artist.* Trenton, New Jersey: Africa World Press, 2004.

Ezenwa-Ohaeto. *Chinua Achebe: A Biography.* Oxford: James Currey, 1997.

Fanon, Frantz. "On National Culture." *The Wretched of the Earth.* Trans. Constance Farrington. New York: Grove, 1963. 206–248.

Gikandi, Simon. "Chinua Achebe and the Poetics of Location: The Uses of Space in *Things Fall Apart* and *No Longer at Ease.*" *Essays on African Writing, A Re-Evaluation.* Ed. Abdulrazak Gurnah. Oxford: Heinemann, 1993. 1–12.

————. "Chinua Achebe and the Signs of the Times." *Approaches to Teaching Achebe's* Things Fall Apart. Ed. Bernth Lindfors. New York: The Modern Language Association of America, 1991. 25–30.

Hegel, George Wilhelm Friedrich. *The Philosophy of History.* Trans. J. Sibree. New York: Dover, 1956.

Henricksen, Bruce. "Chinua Achebe: The Bicultural Novel and the Ethics of Reading." *Global Perspectives on Teaching Literature: Shared Visions and Distinctive Visions.* Eds. Sandra Ward Lott, Maureen S. G. Hawkins, and Norman McMillan. Urbana, Illinois: National Council of Teachers of English, 1993. 295–310.

Hoegberg, David. "Principle and Practice: The Logic of Cultural Violence in Achebe's *Things Fall Apart.*" *College Literature* 26.1 (Winter 1999): 69–79.

Huggan, Graham. *The Post-Colonial Exotic: Marketing the Margins.* London: Routledge, 2001.

Jaggi, Maya. "Storyteller of the Savannah." *Guardian Weekly.* Dec. 28, 2000–Jan. 3, 2001. 10–11.

Jeyifo, Biodun. "For Chinua Achebe: The Resilience and the Predicament of Obierika." *Chinua Achebe, A Celebration.* Eds. Kirsten Holst Petersen and Anna Rutherford. Oxford: Heinemann, 1990. 51–70.

————. "Literature and Conscientization: Interview with Chinua Achebe." *Conversations with Chinua Achebe.* 110–123.

Lindfors, Bernth, ed. *Conversations with China Achebe.* Jackson: University Press of Mississippi, 1997.

Lindfors, Bernth. "Achebe at Home and Abroad: Situating *Things Fall Apart.*" *The Literary Griot* 10.2 (Fall 1998): 10–16.

Macaulay, Thomas. "Minute on Indian Education." *The Post-Colonial Studies Reader.* Eds. Bill Ashcroft, Gareth Griffiths, and Helen Tiffin. London: Routledge, 1995. 428–430.

Mbembe, Achille. *On the Postcolony.* Berkeley: University of California Press, 2001.

Miller, Christopher L. *Theories of Africans: Francophone Literature and Anthropology in Africa.* Chicago: University of Chicago Press, 1990.

Moore-Gilbert, Bart. *Postcolonial Theory: Contexts, Practices, Politics.* London: Verso, 1997.

Moses, Michael Valdez. *The Novel and the Globalization of Culture.* New York: Oxford University Press, 1995.

Mudimbe, V. Y. *The Idea of Africa.* Bloomington: Indiana University Press, 1994.

————. *The Invention of Africa: Ghosts, Philosophy, and the Order of Knowledge.* Bloomington: Indiana University Press, 1988.

Ngaboh-Smart, Francis. "Worldliness, Territoriality, and Narrative: *Things Fall Apart* and the Rhetoric of Nationalism." *Emerging Perspectives on Chinua Achebe.* Ed. Ernest N. Emenyonu. 3–23.

Nkosi, Lewis and Wole Soyinka. "Conversation with Chinua Achebe." *Conversations with Chinua Achebe.* Ed. Bernth Lindfors. 111–117.

Obi, Joseph. "Things Do Not Fall Apart." *Emerging Perspectives on Chinua Achebe.* Ed. Ernest N. Emenyonu. 77–83.

Ochieng, William R. "Undercivilization in Black Africa." *Kenya Historical Review* 2.1 (1974): 45–57.

Ogbaa, Kalu. *Understanding* Things Fall Apart: *A Student Casebook to Issues, Sources, and Historical Documents.* Westport, Connecticut: Greenwood, 1999.

Okonkwo, Chidi. "Chinua Achebe: the Wrestler and the Challenge of Chaos." *Postcolonial Literatures: Achebe, Ngugi, Desai, Walcott.* Eds. Michael Parker and Roger Starkey. Houndmills, Basingstoke: Macmillan, 1995. 83–100.

Onyemelukwe, Ifeoma. "Search for Lost Identity in Achebe's *Things Fall Apart.*" *Emerging Perspectives on Chinua Achebe.* Ed. Ernest N. Emenyonu. 35–47.

Quayson, Ato. "Protocols of Representation and the Problems of Constituting an African 'Gnosis': Achebe and Okri." *The Yearbook of English Studies* 27 (1997): 137–149.

———. "Realism, Criticism, and the Disguises of Both: A Reading of Chinua Achebe's *Things Fall Apart* with an Evaluation of the Criticism Relating to It." *Research in African Literatures* 25.4 (Winter 1994): 117–136.

Pratt, Mary Louise. *Imperial Eyes: Travel Writing and Transculturation.* London: Routledge, 1992.

Ranger, Terence O. "Towards a Usable African Past" *African Studies Since 1945.* Ed. Christopher Fyfe. London: Longman, 1976. 17–30.

———. "The Invention of Tradition in Colonial Africa." *The Invention of Tradition.* Eds. Eric Hobsbawm and Terence Ranger. Cambridge: Cambridge University Press, 1983. 211–262.

Rowell, Charles H. "An Interview with Chinua Achebe." *Conversations with Chinua Achebe.* 165–184.

Slaughter, Joseph R. "'A Mouth with Which to Tell the Story': Silence, Violence, and Speech in Chinua Achebe's *Things Fall Apart.*" *Emerging Perspectives on Chinua Achebe.* Ed. Ernest N. Emenyonu. 121–149.

Sullivan, Zohreh T. "The Postcolonial African Novel and the Dialogic Imagination." *Approaches to Teaching Achebe's* Things Fall Apart. Ed. Bernth Lindfors. New York: The Modern Language Association of America, 1991. 101–106.

Tempels, Placide. *Bantu Philosophy.* Trans. Margaret Read. [Paris]: Collection Presence Africaine, 1953.

Ten Kortenaar, Neil. "How the Centre is Made to Hold in *Things Fall Apart.*" *Postcolonial Literatures: Achebe, Ngugi, Desai, Walcott.* Eds. Michael Parker and Roger Starkey. Houndmills, Basingstoke: Macmillan, 1995. 31–52.

Walsh, Chris. "A Balance of Stories or Pay-back: Chinua Achebe, Joyce Cary, and the Literature of Africa." *Emerging Perspectives on Chinua Achebe.* Ed. Ernest N. Emenyonu. 107–119.

Wren, Robert M. *Achebe's World: The Historical and Cultural Context of the Novels of Chinua Achebe.* Washington, D. C.: Three Continents, 1980.

———. "*Things Fall Apart* in Its Time and Place." *Approaches to Teaching* Things Fall Apart. Ed. Bernth Lindfors. New York: The Modern Language Association of America, 1991. 38–44.

Yeats, W. B. "Leda and the Swan." *The Poems Revised.* Ed. Richard J. Finneran. New York: Macmillan, 1989. 214–215.

Young, Robert J. C. *Colonial Desire: Hybridity in Theory, Culture and Race.* London: Routledge, 1995.

Zachernuk, Philip S. *Colonial Subjects: An African Intelligentsia and Atlantic Ideas.* Charlottesville: University Press of Virginia, 2000.

FRANK SALAMONE

# The Depiction of Masculinity in
# Classic Nigerian Literature

Turning and turning in the widening gyre
The falcon cannot hear the falconer;
Things fall apart; the centre cannot hold;
Mere anarchy is loosed upon the world,
The blood-dimmed tide is loosed, and everywhere
The ceremony of innocence is drowned;
The best lack all conviction, while the worst
Are full of passionate intensity.
                    —"The Second Coming" (1921) William Butler Yeats

The writings of Chinua Achebe, Wole Soyinka, and Amos Tutuola rank among the world's great literature. They share with that literature the establishment of icons and the creation of classic types against which all subsequent writings are judged. These authors have set the terms for future discussion. Interestingly, they have focused on the meaning of masculinity in Nigeria and given it a central position in the cultural web of meaning within and between interacting groups.

In *Things Fall Apart*, for example, Chinua Achebe uses the opposition of masculinity and femininity to encapsulate the conflict between the British and Igbo, between the mission and traditional religion. Wole Soyinka in *Aké* and other writings addresses the issue of the confusion of gender roles under

*JALA: Journal of the African Literature Association*, Volume 1, Number 1 (Winter–Spring 2007): pp. 202–213. Copyright © 2007 Frank Salamone.

colonial rule and in the postcolonial era and the problems that such confusion raises. While Tutuola's *Palm Wine Drinkard* may appear to be a good-natured romp derived from various Yoruba folk tales, it has important things to say about the Yoruba concept of masculinity. In his later works, such as *The Brave African Huntress,* Tutuola examines the significance of women and gender roles in the Nigerian scene.

Each of these authors, thus, approaches major issues of identity amid change through the lens of gender. Gender, moreover, is wrapped up in all aspects of life, including religion, education, hunting, and drinking. The details each author painstakingly presents allow their worlds to emerge whole and complete and paradoxically entice from readers the creation of parallels from their own worlds and lessons applicable to their lives.

Moreover, masculinity may appear to exist in certain works as somehow independent of femininity or in absolute opposition to it. However, even in Achebe's fictional world which sometimes appears to be dominated only by males, there is clear evidence that definitions of masculinity are strongly dependent on cultural constructions including the feminine. That is as true of *Things Fall Apart* as *Anthills of the Savannah.* Soyinka focuses on gender confusion resulting from colonialism and all that is encompassed and contingent on it while much of Tutuola's humor results from explicit or implicit gender conflict.

These major authors, then, address cataclysmic defining issues in Nigerian history from the perspective of gender relations. The overall disruption, an integral part of the colonial heritage, struck at the core of indigenous values. Concepts of religion, politics, and family came under attack. Masculinity became a metaphor for resistance to these assaults since both colonial culture and society and the indigenous cultures and societies it sought to transform in theory were male-dominated ones. Sexuality, additionally, and eroticism were integral discourses in the colonial dialogue, symbolizing power and control.

Nevertheless, the reality was far more complex than its abstractions. Women played a more significant role than either side often acknowledged in the power struggles that rocked the Nigerian cosmos. Soyinka clearly recognizes the role women played in anti-colonial movements and Achebe was influenced by the Onitsha Market Women's rebellion. Tutuola's drinkard is certainly asserting his masculinity through his drinking. He does so as one knowing that such behavior offends women and symbolizes his masculinity.

### Colonialism and Masculinity in the Literature

In *Things Fall Apart,* Achebe sets the Igbo, a farming people, in opposition to the effete British colonial establishment. Rather than cloaking this conflict in vague or didactic generalities, though, he personifies Igbo ethos through the protagonist Okinawa. Okinawa champions the old masculine virtues in which weakness threatens the individual's as well as group's survival.

Achebe elaborates through Okinawa the Igbo belief in an essential link between a human and God, called "chi". Chi is a person's destiny, part of a person from conception. Chi is an integral part of a person's personality. Chi is not God but God chooses a person's chi. However, chi is not a passive thing. It actively chooses from among the packages God places before it. Each package contains an individual's destiny.

The package contains all of a person's luck and misfortunes which a person will encounter in life. Chi, thus, can mean either this package of destined good and evil and the guardian spirit who guides a person in life. There is no escaping chi. A good Igbo, therefore, sets as a goal the achievement of his or her chi, which can be read on an individual's palms.

The quest to achieve one's chi guides a person's behavior throughout life. Chi is an expression and reinforcement of the individualistic nature of Igbo social organization. It is also an essential part of Igbo religion and daily values. However, chi is not absolute. Reflecting another Igbo value, Igbo hold that an individual who is wise enough can manipulate his chi just as his chi seeks to manipulate an individual. Struggle and ambition are prized Igbo values. Overcoming obstacles is a way of life and highly honored among the Igbo, and Achebe makes this struggle part of his plot, adding to the tension and interest of his tragic tale.

Igbos believe that predestination is not an irrevocable determination of a person's life. People may change their destiny. Destiny, as so much of Igbo life, is a transaction in which the partners negotiate. In this case it is the individual and Destiny that negotiate. In this negotiation between destiny and Chi lies the root of the conflict between British colonialism and the Igbo. Thus, the strong masculinity of Okinawa's Chi leads him into a tragic conflict with British imperialists. Their Chi is greater than his. It is a hopeless conflict but Okonkwo yields to his Chi, helping to bring himself and his people down.

Achebe, moreover, depicts the Church as diluting the masculinity of the Igbo through their imposing English on them, thus easing them into a loss of their own language on proverbs. Everywhere the Igbo turned there was a force at work undermining traditional laws and religion. Ethnocentrism, on both sides, hindered any real hope of mutual understanding between the two cultures.

On an individual level, Okonkwo wishes to distinguish himself from what he perceives as his father's weaknesses. Okonkwo, consequently, wishes to be a warrior, a strong man in the traditional Igbo value system. For Okonkwo Christianity is the antithesis of the masculine values of the Igbo. He believes that these masculine values have preserved the Igbo throughout their history. The feminine values introduced by colonial rule, then, appear, then, to threaten the very existence of the Igbo people.

Okonkwo believed that masculinity was the glue that held the Igbo together. This belief was reinforced in him because he had no inheritance. Therefore, the Igbo belief in the value of hard work as a means for advancement was reinforced. He had to advance on his own or not at all. First, he excelled at wrestling and then became a sharecropper. Moreover, Okonkwo blames his father for wasting his time by spending it making music on his flute, socializing and communing with nature instead of amassing wealth and prestige for his family. Instead of making money he borrows it and accumulates debt.

In reaction, Okonkwo work endlessly, sowing his fields. He embraces traditional Igbo values, appreciating the value of the yam, accepting the significance of wrestling and hard work. Moreover, he pays his debts and keeps his wife and children in line with a strange hand.

## A Yoruba View of Masculinity

There are similarities between Soyinka's *Aké* and Achebe's *Things Fall Apart*. However, there are significant differences. Soyinka is relating a memoir, albeit a kind of nostalgic and somewhat idealized one. Moreover, while not having fallen apart the world of the village of Ake is a mixture of traditional, modern, and changing. The young Soyinka is growing up in the period just before and during World War II, to about the age of ten. It was a period at the height of British Colonialism in Nigeria, when it seemed as if the British rule would last forever.

Soyinka grew up in a privileged position firmly in the middle of British ideological sway. His mother was a Christian market woman and his father was a schoolmaster. There were, to be sure, strong remnants of Yoruba culture and tradition in the overall mix of life. Moreover, Soyinka notes the transactions that occurred between the two cultures.

Thus, Soyinka relates the understanding of Yoruba masculinity to the complexities of the Yoruba place within Nigerian colonial reality. These complexities include strong market women who revolt against taxation, led by his own mother; buffoons in British uniforms; traditional Yoruba rites; and his own Christian indoctrination. Christian missionaries by naming his play areas in English change their realities for him, impressing on him the power of language.

Soyinka's themes are powerful ones. They deal with the clash of cultures, the power of language to define and create reality, and the social construction of gender roles. These views have led to actions which have caused his imprisonment on a number of occasions. His criticism of fraud in the Western Nigerian elections led to his first imprisonment.

Shortly after these elections triggered off events that led to the Nigerian Civil War, Yakubu Gowon's government arrested him for seeking to aid the breakaway region of Biafra in its resistance to Nigeria. Soyinka was in prison from 1966–1969, eighteen months of it in solitary confinement. In part pressure from Lillian Hellman and Robert Lowell among other prominent writers effected his release.

During this period Soyinka managed to write poetry and his prison notes. The book *The Man Died* resulted from these efforts. 'Live Burial' appeared in *The New Statesmen* on the 23rd of May, 1969 before Soyinka's release from prison. Its lines, "Sixteen paces / By twenty-three. They hold / Siege against humanity / And Truth / Employing time to drill through to his sanity" captured the literary imagination of the time and directed more anger against the Federal Government of Nigeria. Indeed, the Nigerian government banned *The Man Died* (1972) on its publication.

However, Soyinka has practiced in his life the words he used in his acceptance speech for the Nobel Prize, words which reflect his nuanced understanding of masculinity.

> There is a deep lesson for the world in the black races' capacity to forgive, one which, I often think, has much to do with ethical precepts which spring from their world view and authentic religions, none of which is ever totally eradicated by the accretions of foreign faiths and their implicit ethnocentrism. (Nobel Lecture, 1986)

## Amos Tutuola and the Comedy of Masculinity

Comedy is the other side of tragedy. It can only exist, in fact, in the presence of tragedy. Through its mocking of the serious side of life, it brings it into deeper perspective, focusing light on the shadow of tragedy. Tutuola chose to master the field of comedy, inheriting in the process the role of the clown, the truth sayer, whose jokes and jibes hide and reveal nuggets of deep truth.

It is altogether appropriate that the rhythms of his prose reflect the riffs of Yoruba music. Like Yoruba music, and much of the African-American music derived from it, there is rhythmic and structural repetition, insinuating the message deep into the unconscious of the listener, touching on archetypal themes. These themes, moreover, are overlapping ones, supporting a lead voice that soars over the top. This style, common to Yoruba storytelling, involves the listener into the creation of the story, riffing and improvising on common themes.

He begins his most famous work with these sentences, "I was a palm-wine drinkard since I was a boy of ten years of age. I had no other work more than to drink palm-wine in my life." Although many of his fellow Yoruba objected to the novel because of the language and accused Tutuola of falsification, the book reflects Yoruba life accurately in the later period of British colonialism. It is also a morality tale, depicting what happens to a man who gives himself up to the pursuit of pleasure instead of living a morally responsible life as delineated in Yoruba culture.

The magical elements of the story in which the hero follows his palm wine tapper down a hole to Dead's town evoke the magic of the folk tale, where anything can and usually does happen. There are ghosts, wondrous deeds and events. Along the way many lessons are transmitted and the narrator, in turn, puts these into perspective.

### Views of Women in Yoruba and Igbo Colonial Culture

Soyinka has a felicity of touch which enables him to present women in an equable light with men. He appreciates the importance of women and their contribution to both traditional and colonial culture. He relates the role strong women played in his life from his older sister whom he accompanied to school before he was officially old enough to attend through his mother who led a market revolt and the influence of his aunt, Funmilayo Ransome-Kuti, mother of the famous musician Fela and a leader of the Nigerian feminist movement. She organized and led the women's revolt in Abeokuta against British tax policy. Soyinke served as a messenger between members of that revolt.

On the other hand, there are those who argue that male dominance did not arrive with European colonialism but was merely strengthened by it.

> Women, therefore, were socialized to fill specific roles in their society. However, it is important to note that these women, while assigned to different social strata, did not necessarily view themselves as victimized or downtrodden (Ufomata). Women's roles in pre-colonial Nigerian society were often complementary to those of men, rather than divergent. (Rojas). Women had household and farming duties, but the burdened was eased and their lives became easier as time went on and they bore children, proving their value to the society as a whole (Rojas). There was no concept of a full-time housewife, however. Each woman had responsibilities ranging from caring for children and the aged to farming and other agricultural activities (Ufomata). As Okonkwo noted, His mother and sisters worked hard enough, but they grew women's crops, like coco-yams, beans and cassava. Yam, the king of crops, was a man's crop. (Achebe, 22–23). So although their contribution was less significant overall to the status of the group,

women had an important job in growing the food with which to supplement the family's income and diet. They also had the chance to acquire political influence through marriage, but it remains clear that differences also exist[ed] in the power relations between the sexes men typically being expected to be dominant over their wives and to have greater control over economic resources (Spence, 4).

This male dominance was increased with British colonial rule. The Igbo, too, experienced a female headed riot against British colonial practices.

The Aba Women's Revolt was one of the most significant events that occurred in Nigerian history during colonialism. It was for example, the first major revolt of its type that was organized and led by rural women of Owerri and Calabar Provinces which contained a population of two million people, located in a total land mass of about 6,000 square miles (Van Allen 1981, 60). Like other major events of its magnitude, the revolt has continued to attract much scholarly inquiry and discourse, unparalleled in Igbo history until the Nigeria-Biafra war (Oriji http://www.icaap.org/iuicode?101.2.1.14).

The revolt took place as a protest against colonial interference in the acknowledged privileges of women not to pay taxes in Igbo society. Thus, the interpretation of traditional women as being totally oppressed needs refinement since the Abba revolt of 1929 demonstrated that women were fully capable of taking powerful and unprecedented action against colonial men and wanted to protect privileges they deemed essential to their status as Igbo women. The Abba revolt, moreover, led to the emergence of numerous female heroes, further demonstrating the need for care in arriving at facile generalities regarding gender relations in African societies.

These subtleties and ambiguities in gender relationships help explain the writings of Soyinka, Tutuola, and Achebe in their overt and covert delineation of masculinity. After all we define ourselves against the other and in interaction with the other. It is clear that Achebe, for example, depicts Okonkwo's struggle for Igbo masculinity as a result of his belief in his father's failure to achieve it. It is also clear that Okonkwo does not fully appreciate the boundaries of the real as opposed to the ideal Igbo perception of masculinity.

His socialization into that masculine ideal was patently flawed. To slip into jargon we can say that his role model was sadly lacking. His father was unable to pay his own way, a true Igbo ideal, and support his family. It is clear that Okonkwo is struggling to right his father's wrongs, to make up to his family for those weaknesses and become a model of true male Igbo righteousness. Overcompensation is a common behavior among those seeking to restore family honor and Okonkwo was no exception.

On the other hand Amos Tutuola decided to examine the world of women and shows great skill in so doing. In *Simbi and the Satyr of the Dark Jungle* (1955) and *The Brave African Huntress* (1958), he makes women heroines who drive the plot. Adebisi is a formidable woman. She is a huntress, following in her father's profession. Adebisi is a charming as well as brave person, who endeavors to rescue her four elder brothers. These brothers, who appear less brave and charming than she, went off on an expedition to the Jungle of the Pygmies and were never heard from after that.

Adebisi went after them and survived numerous perils. As expected, she emerges from her ordeal unscathed. She also has her four brothers, many other captives of the people in the Jungle of the Pygmies, and a good deal of precious coin. Needless to say, she becomes a rich and honored woman.

Earlier Tutuola approached the topic of lesbianism in a more understanding manner than most European writers, male or female, of his day. In 1954 he returned to his magical "Bush of Ghosts". His hero winds up magically in The Nameless Town off the "Queer Way Homeward". His words tell it best.

> There I noticed that all the inhabitants are ladies and women, no single man is living there or coming there at all and to my surprise all these ladies and women have long brown moustaches under their lower jaws, so every woman married a lady, because there are no men to marry them. But when I asked the "Super-Lady" or my wife—"Why all the ladies and women have moustaches in this town like he-goats?" she replied—"those women with moustaches had been betrayed by their husbands after their marriage, but now none of them could marry any male again except to marry ladies as husbands". After we took a stroll round the village and saw many terrible and wonderful things for some hours, then we came back home (*My Life in the Bush of Ghosts* 123).

Without delving deeply into the patent symbolism of the passage, it is clear that Tutuola is aware of the deep ambiguity of Yoruba gender relationships and the blending of Western concepts of male and female. Interestingly, like Soyinka, he is apparently not troubled by this fact. His own "Super-Lady" in the novel has a moustache that makes her, as well as others, look like a goat.

Unlike the Igbo Achebe, then, the Yoruba Tutuola and Soyinka appear to have no need to prove their masculinity or, to be more accurate, to have their male characters establish their masculinity. There is the Yoruba tolerance for "this" and "that, too" in their artistic and religious imagination. Perhaps, this Creole characteristic of syncretism has allowed a more nuanced view of gender among their writings.

## Conclusion

It is always useful to go back to essentials, especially when dealing with power relations and the ability to impose definitions on social constructions of reality. While sex is biological, gender is cultural. Each society determines what it means to be "male" or "female;" that is; each society imposed its own construction of gender on its people. However, colonial and African definitions of gender were at odds with one another.

Therefore, a significant part of being a man for the generation of Achebe, Soyinka, and Tutuola was resistance to colonial authority and the construction of a new order to replace it. A significant part of the construction of that new order had to do with the construction of gender and the definition of appropriate gender relationships. Each author agreed that the colonial order was indeed fragile. However, each approached the depiction of that fragility in a different way just as each had a different vision of what should replace the colonial state.

Soyinka envisions the New Africa as a synthesis of feeling and reason. Thus, he rejects the concept of Negritude because in Leopold Senghor's vision it is a static embodiment of non-rational feeling. It is a stereotype under another guise. Soyinka is too much of a rational humanist to embrace the vision of the instinctive noble savage, who sings and dances without any conscious thought or effort.

His rejection of absolutes, moreover, mirrors Yoruba tolerance and even embrace of ambiguity and the Creole world of syncretism. This embrace of contradiction and rejection of absolutism is completely in keeping with Soyinka's rebuff of colonialism. For Soyinka and his fellow Yoruba Tutuola the totalitarianism of colonialism cannot be replaced with any other absolutism. The world must be embraced as it is, with all its blurred genres and even genders.

## WORKS CITED

Chowdhury, Kanishka. "Afrocentric Voices: Constructing Identities, [dis]placing Difference." *College Literature* 24.2 (1997): 35–56.

Coyle, Martin, et al., eds. *Encyclopedia of Literature and Criticism*. London: Routledge, 1990.

Gandhi, Leela. *Postcolonial Theory: A Critical Introduction*. St. Leonards, N.S.W.: Allen & Unwin, 1998.

Gardiner, Judith Kegan, ed. *Masculinity Studies & Feminist Theory: New Directions*. New York: Columbia University Press, 2002.

Griswold, Wendy. "Recent Moves in the Sociology of Literature." *Annual Review of Sociology* (1993): 455–467. Questia. 25 Apr. 2005 <http://www.questia.com/>.

Hawley, John C., and Emmanuel S. Nelson, eds. *Encyclopedia of Postcolonial Studies*. Westport, CT: Greenwood Press, 2001.

Irele, F. Abiola. *The African Imagination: Literature in Africa & the Black Diaspora*. New York: Oxford University Press, 2001.

Iyasere, Solomon O., ed. *Understanding* Things Fall Apart: *Selected Essays and Criticism*. Troy, NY: Whitston Publishing, 1998.

Janmohamed, Abdul R. *The Politics of Literature in Colonial Africa*. Amherst: University of Massachusetts Press, 1983.

Moore, Gerald. *Seven African Writers*. London: Oxford University Press, 1966.

Moore-Gilbert, Bart. *Postcolonial Theory: Contexts, Practices, Politics*. London: Verso, 1997.

Njoku, Benedict Chiaka. *The Four Novels of Chinua Achebe: A Critical Study*. New York: Peter Lang, 1984.

Chinweizu, Onwuchekwa Jemie, and Ihechukwu Madubuike. *Toward the Decolonization of African Literature*. Washington, DC: Howard University, 1983.

Osei-Nyame, Kwadwo. "Chinua Achebe Writing Culture: Representations of Gender and Tradition in *Things Fall Apart*." *Research in African Literatures* a.2 (1999): 148–164.

Podis, Leonard A., and Yakubu Saaka, eds. *Challenging Hierarchies: Issues and Themes in Colonial and Postcolonial African Literature*. New York: Peter Lang, 1998.

Thomas, Valorie D. "'1 + 1 = 3' and Other Dilemmas: Reading Vertigo in *Invisible Man, My Life in the Bush of Ghosts,* and *Song of Solomon*." *African American Review* 37.1 (2003): 81–94. Questia. 25 Apr. 2005 <http://www.questia.com/>.

Tobias, Steven M. "Amos Tutuola and the Colonial Carnival." *Research in African Literatures* a.2 (1999): 66–74.

Tutuola, Amos. *The Columbia Encyclopedia*. 6th ed. 2004.

Tutuola, Amos. *The Palm-Wine Drinkard and His Dead Palm-Wine Tapster in the Dead's Town*. New York: Grove Press, 1962.

———. *Women in Literature: Reading Through the Lens of Gender*. Eds. Jerilyn Fisher and Ellen S. Silber. Westport, CT: Greenwood Press, 2003.

## References

Achebe, Chinua. *Hopes and Impediments: Selected Essays*. 1988. New York: Anchor-Doubleday, 1990. [COCC Library: PR9387.9.A3 H6 1990]

———. *Morning Yet on Creation Day: Essays*. London: Heinemann, 1975.

———. *Things Fall Apart*. [First published 1958.] Expanded edition with notes. 1996. London: Heinemann, 2000.

Bakhtin, Mikhail. *The Dialogic Imagination*. Eds. Michael Holquist and Caryl Emerson. Austin, TX: University of Texas Press, 1981.

Begam, Richard. "Achebe's Sense of an Ending: History and Tragedy in *Things Fall Apart*." *Studies in the Novel* 29.3 (Fall 1997): 396–411.

Gallagher, Susan VanZanten. "Linguistic Power: Encounter with Chinua Achebe." *The Christian Century* (12 March 1997): 260–262.

Nnolim, Charles E. "Achebe's *Things Fall Apart*: An Igbo National Epic." *Modern Black Literature*. ed. Okechukwu Mezu. New York: Black Academy Press, 1971. 55–60.

Obiechina, Emmanuel. "Narrative Proverbs in the African Novel." *Research in African Literatures,* 24, 4 (1993): 123–140.

Okafor, Chinyere Grace. "From the Heart of Masculinity: Ogbodo-Uke Women's Masking." *Research in African Literatures,* 25.3 (1994): 7–17.

Oriji, John N. (2000). IGBO WOMEN FROM 1929–1960. *West Africa Review,* 2.1. [iuicode: http://www.icaap.org/iuicode?101.2.1.14]

Traore, Ousseynou. "Matrical Approach to *Things Fall Apart:* A Poetics of Epic and Mythic Paradigms." *Approaches to Teaching Achebe's* Things Fall Apart. ed.

Gregory Gipson. *Mutable Semantics: Three Texts and the Term Postcolonial.* Gregory Gipson, *English* 27 (Autumn 1997).

Ashcroft, Bill, Gareth Griffiths, and Helen Tiffin, eds. *The Post-colonial Studies Reader.* Routledge, New York, NY, 1995.

Emecheta, Buchi. *The Slave Girl.* George Braziller, Inc., New York, NY, 1977.

Soyinka, Wole. *Aké: The Years of Childhood.* Vintage International, New York, NY, 1989.

ANDREA POWELL WOLFE

# Problematizing Polygyny[1] in the Historical Novels of Chinua Achebe: The Role of the Western Feminist Scholar

*I believe that in our situation the greater danger lies not in remembering but in forgetting, in pretending that slogans are the same as truth; and I believe that Nigeria, always prone to self-deception, stands in great needs of reminders.*

—Chinua Achebe, *Morning Yet on Creation Day* XII

In "Chinua Achebe and the Invention of African Culture," an article in the special issue "Chinua Achebe at Seventy," published in *Research in African Literatures* in 2001, Simon Gikandi lauds Achebe's novels as the "Ur-texts of our [African] literary tradition" (6). He goes on to extol the "tremendous influence [Achebe's] works have had on the institutions of pedagogy and interpretation and the role his fictions have come to play in the making and unmaking of African worlds" (6). Certainly, with the publication of his first novel, *Things Fall Apart* (1959), Achebe was almost immediately taken up in literary circles as the father of African literature and has since remained at the center of African literary studies. Furthermore, and perhaps more significantly, Achebe occupies a position of great importance for his African readers. In general, his writing is regarded as having restored a sense of pride to Africa (see Moore; Omoyele; Williams). Early in his career, Achebe seemed to recognize and, most honorably, to take on the

*Research in African Literatures*, Volume 39, Number 1 (Spring 2008): pp. 166–185. Copyright 2008 The Indiana University Press.

difficult responsibilities that came with his privileged position. In his essay "Novelist as Teacher" (1965), Achebe describes his own perception of his role as a prominent African writer: "I would be quite satisfied if my novels (especially the ones I set in the past) did no more than teach my readers that their past—with all its imperfections—was not one long night of savagery from which the first Europeans acting on God's behalf delivered them" (72). In many regards, Achebe has achieved his goal. In his historical novels, *Things Fall Apart* and *Arrow of God* (1964), Achebe depicts precolonial Igbo life with great complexity. Although his characters are not without flaws, Achebe portrays their lifestyles and belief systems as worthy of respect. Achebe recalls his African heritage with pride and "teaches" others to do the same. If only for this reason, Gikandi and others are certainly justified in considering Achebe's novels foundational for teachers and scholars of African literature.

As feminist critics have long noted, though, Achebe's novels, especially his early novels, reveal real blind spots when it comes to important gender issues that continue to plague many postcolonial African countries.[2] In his two historical novels, in fact, Achebe consistently side-lines the place of the postcolonial woman in order to focus on postcolonial manhood. Women's lives often serve as little more than fodder for the exploration of masculinity. And because Achebe does hold such a high-profile position in African studies, his gender-determined blind spots demand careful scrutiny. The apparent dismissal of women's issues in Achebe's early novels suggests a "first things first" approach to nationalism, an approach which dictates that Africans deal with national problems before they move on to "less important issues," such as gender politics on local levels. We know, however, despite the immediate attractions of the "first things first" movement, that gender issues are indeed integral to nationalist causes. Certainly, in order for African nationalism to serve all Africans, women's issues must make their way into public discourse and, ultimately, women must take part in the actual formation of African nations. Polygyny, or the marriage of one man to more than one woman at the same time, is one system, still prominent in many African communities, that keeps women from taking part in this important business of nation-building. Ironically, in his historical novels, Achebe seems to dismiss the issue of African polygyny, which I consider an important gender concern for feminists the world over, as a nonissue.[3]

In this essay, I analyze Achebe's portrayal of polygyny in *Things Fall Apart* and *Arrow of God* and then illuminate some of the social realities and lasting legacies of this system of marriage. Perhaps more important, I consider the place of the Western feminist critic in relation to the matter of polygyny. How can we discuss African polygyny without discounting its very real benefits for women? Furthermore, how can we talk about polygyny in a productive way, in a way that advances the agenda of African feminism, without projecting a "West is best" ideology onto our discourse and without further silencing the women who are actually involved in polygynous relationships? I propose that the framework of feminist postcolonial theory, specifically bell hooks's conception of "solidarity," can provide us with a useful way of approaching this complex issue and, ultimately, lend us the authority that we need in order to create contexts in which women can envision and pursue alternatives to oppressive polygyny. Moreover, I assert that we can teach Achebe's historical novels in ways that provide our students with meaningful opportunities to think through the implications of Achebe's centrality to the canon and the consequences of his lack of attention to gender concerns in general and to the issue of polygyny in particular.

Polygyny is certainly the preferred type of marriage for the men of the precolonial Igbo villages in both *Things Fall Apart* and *Arrow of God,* but it is in the latter novel that we gain the most insight into the negative effects of this marriage custom for Achebe's female characters. Polygyny, in *Arrow of God* at least, seems to cause perpetual tension between women of the community. In fact, for the female characters in the polygynous households of Achebe's *Arrow of God,* set in late nineteenth- or early twentieth-century Africa, bickering seems a way of life. Ezeulu, the Chief Priest of his village and the protagonist of Achebe's text, has two wives, Matefi and Ugoye, who squabble incessantly throughout the story. Even in the novel's opening scene, in which Ezeulu and his wives and children observe the new moon, Matefi and Ugoye quarrel over whether the moon appears to have an evil "posture" (2). Their rivalry becomes more and more apparent as the novel progresses. Matefi resents Ugoye because the latter wife is beautiful and young enough to bear children and is thus still attractive to their husband. Her jealousy surfaces mostly in the form of malicious gossip. When Nwafo, Ugoye's son, shows interest in Matefi's cooking, she insinuates that Ugoye starves her children in order to accumulate personal funds for jewelry. She asks her own daughter, "What do you expect a boy to do when his mother cooks soup with locust beans for fish? She saves her money to buy ivory bracelets" (9). In this way, the bitterness between the two women infects every interaction that occurs within Ezeulu's compound.

The competition between the two wives reaches a peak after a physical battle between Oduche, another of Ugoye's sons, and Ojiugo, Matefi's daughter. Matefi sees that Oduche has caused a welt to surface on her daughter's face and takes advantage of the opportunity to publicly humiliate Ugoye. She wails loudly that her daughter has been wounded by the son of her husband's other wife. Ugoye reacts to Matefi's accusations by running into the senior wife's hut and shouting, "Let nobody call my name there [ ... ]. I say let nobody mention my name at all" (129). Ezeulu, who has by this time dismissed the battle between his two children as a normal instance of sibling rivalry and of minimal consequence to him, promptly advises both of his wives to shut up. When Ugoye protests again that Matefi has criticized her unfairly, Ezeulu retorts, "And if she did? . . . Go and jump on her back if you can" (129). With this response, Ezeulu demonstrates that not only is he accustomed to the bickering between his wives, but that, at least on some level, he takes pleasure in their rivalry. Most of all, though, Ezeulu makes it clear that the relationship between his wives is of little significance to him.

In this way, we begin to see that competition among women is expected, acceptable, and, ultimately, inconsequential in Achebe's polygynous society. Even outside of Ezeulu's immediate family, women of the community pit themselves against each other in a number of scenes. When Oduche and Ojiugo fight, for instance, the crowd of women surrounding them are "immediately divided" (128). Two of the women, long-time rivals, become verbally and physically aggressive toward each other. They "[measure] themselves against each other," and one of them recommends that the other "go and eat shit" before the crowd finally disperses (128). Furthermore, during a spiritual reenactment ceremony at the feast of Pumpkin Leaves, the women "all [struggle] to secure positions in the front" (71). Jealousy between women is apparently even legendary in Achebe's Igbo community, for the one story that Ugoye relates to her children throughout the novel depicts the troubled relationship of competing wives. The story begins: "Once upon a time there was a man who had two wives. The senior wife had many children but the younger one had only one son. But the senior wife was wicked and envious" (190). Certainly, we can understand Ugoye's storytelling as a way of her coping with the circumstances of her own life, but the fact that she shares a tale of such bitterness and jealousy with her young children implies that although rivalry between wives is a common occurrence in her culture, it is not considered a serious issue. Ugoye's willingness to relate this story to her children paradoxically indicates her sense of anxiety regarding her quarrelsome relationship with Matefi, her awareness that her situation is normal, and, finally, her denial that the rivalry causes her serious emotional distress even when it clearly does. Perhaps we can interpret the contention evident between these female characters as a consequence of their community's perception of them, and their perceptions of themselves, as no more than "wives." As the adjective "jealous" is attached to the noun "wives" in numerous passages throughout *Arrow of God*, we learn, as the women in Achebe's precolonial village have learned, that women (or wives) are expected to bicker and fight.

Reading the competition between women in Achebe's *Arrow of God* through a feminist lens is tricky, though, to say the least. First of all, we must understand the rivalries that develop between women in this novel within the broader context of rising tensions between men. Ezeulu's importance as Chief

Priest is seriously threatened, for instance, by the arrival of the Christian missionaries near his village; the new Christian deity, and the missionaries who
attempt to win over Ezeulu's neighbors, and, indeed, his own son, Oduche,
to a new type of religion, become his direct rivals throughout the course of
the novel. Furthermore, Ezeulu engages in several struggles with another local Chief Priest, Ezidemili, in attempts to prove the supremacy of his god
over that of the other's god and, thus, his position of supreme power over the
community. In fact, Ezeulu's refusal to declare the harvest, a decision that ultimately causes his people to turn to faith in the Christian god, is one way in
which Ezeulu tries to position himself as more important than Ezidemili. Indeed, in some ways, *Arrow of God* is about rivalry; tensions between colonizer
and colonized and between individual male characters drive the novel's plot.
The tensions between female characters can be read, then, much as Ezeulu's
hunger for power can be read, as mere symptoms of the impending sickness
of colonization. In this way, though, the women's rivalries are perhaps all the
more disturbing. Clearly, women such as Ugoye and Matefi are victims of
that which many postcolonial scholars have described as double colonization.
These women are subordinated, not only to the colonizing powers, but also to
their own men. Even if the colonial forces at work in the novel intensify the
conflicts between these two women, and other women in the text, polygyny
remains at the core of their rivalries.

Certainly, polygyny, as portrayed in the novel, seems to breed a "male supremacist ideology," which, according to feminist scholar bell hooks, teaches
us "that women are 'natural' enemies, that solidarity will never exist between
us because we cannot, should not, and do not bond with one another" (396).
Due to the particular realities of polygynous living, then, the women of Ezeulu's village do not demonstrate that which hooks calls "solidarity" (396). They
do not support one another despite their differences or stand united against
their oppressors, as hooks suggests that women can and should do. The difficulty with assessing this aspect of Achebe's female characterization, though,
lies in determining if his depiction of women simply represents the social reality of his setting or if Achebe himself actually endorses the sexist treatment
of women in the novel.[4] Rose Ure Mezu, who discusses Achebe's treatment
of gender, explains that "in creating a masculine-based society, Achebe was
merely putting literature to mimetic use, reflecting existing traditional mores"
(n.p.). Mezu goes on, however, to fault Achebe, not for depicting women as
subordinate to men, but for rendering his women "inconsequential" and thus
keeping them "on the fringe of their universe—neglected, exploited, degen-
erated, and indeed made to feel like outsiders." For Mezu, then, "Achebe's
sexist attitude is unabashed and without apology." Thus, although Achebe's
portrayal of women may be historically accurate, his disregard for the

negative circumstances of his female characters' lives is apparent throughout *Arrow of God*.

Let us also recall, as we consider the parallels between Achebe's portrayal of polygyny in *Arrow of God* and his personal attitude toward this system of marriage, Achebe's own words in his important essay "An Image of Africa: Racism in Conrad's *Heart of Darkness*" (1975), now anthologized as a seminal text of postcolonial theory. Besides using examples from Joseph Conrad's personal writings to prove this canonical author "a bloody racist" (215), Achebe points to specific passages within *Heart of Darkness* that demonstrate Conrad's own perceptions of Africans. Achebe does consider the possibility "that the attitude to the African in *Heart of Darkness* is not Conrad's but that of his fictional narrator, Marlow, and that far from endorsing it Conrad might indeed be holding it up to irony and criticism" (214). Ultimately, though, Achebe rejects this interpretation: "But if Conrad's intention is to draw a *cordon sanitaire* between himself and the moral and psychological malaise of his narrator, his care seems to me totally wasted because he neglects to hint however subtly or tentatively at an alternative frame of reference by which we may judge the actions and opinions of his characters" (214). Much as Achebe finds nothing in *Heart of Darkness* to suggest an ironic depiction of racism, I find nothing in *Arrow of God* to suggest an ironic depiction of sexism. In fact, I propose that Achebe reveals his own attitude toward polygyny, an intrinsically sexist institution, at several points during the novel.

Achebe reveals his dismissive attitude toward polygyny partially with his use of numerous perspectives in *Arrow of God*. Throughout the novel, Achebe provides us with not only insights into Ezeulu's own attitude toward his wives, but also glimpses of the attitude of the voice that narrates the text and, perhaps most disturbingly, indications of the attitudes of the women toward each other. All of these perspectives point to Achebe's own lack of interest in the real, material concerns of his female characters. We know, for instance, that Ezeulu regards rivalry between wives as common and inconsequential. Besides ignoring the very real concerns of his warring wives, he squelches an argument between his eldest two sons by calling them "'jealous wives,'" implying that jealousy is antithetical to masculinity and a sentiment that belongs in the feminine sphere (13). The narrative voice affirms Ezeulu's assessment of rivalry as unimportant. When Ezeulu returns to his home after imprisonment, the narrator informs us, essentially, that things return to normal: "Even in Ezeulu's compound the daily rounds established themselves again. Obika's new wife had become pregnant; Ugoye and Matefi carried on like any two jealous wives [ . . . ]" (193). The most disturbing perspective on the bickering between women is that stated by Adeze, Ezeulu's eldest daughter, born of Ezeulu's deceased first wife. Adeze is already married and resides in her husband's village when she visits with her sister Akueke at the feast of Pumpkin Leaves. Like Ugoye, Akeuke has also experienced numerous conflicts with Matefi. When she notices Akueke's negative reaction to Matefi's presence at the feast, Adeze teases Akueke, "Are you two quarrelling again? I thought I saw it on her face. What have you done to her this time?" (74). Achebe uses this exchange between Adeze and Akueke to demonstrate to his readers, in case we have remaining doubts at this point in the text, that the negative interactions that occur between the Igbo women in his novel are just a part of traditional African life. Because these words of dismissal are spoken by a woman, they serve to prove Achebe's assumption that rivalry between women is normal and not to be taken too seriously. Adeze, as a woman herself, powerfully validates the gender norms of precolonial Africa that stimulate competition among women.

Although it is not such a central issue as in *Arrow of God,* polygyny is also the common model of marriage in *Things Fall Apart,* Achebe's first novel and the only other of his major works set in precolonial Africa. *Things Fall Apart* takes place a generation or so before *Arrow of God,* and, like the latter novel, is set in an Igbo village. Having multiple wives is clearly a marker of masculinity and prestige in the precolonial African society of the text. Okonkwo, the central character, resents his father, Unoka, who only had one wife and was not successful according to his sons' standards, but he honors the memory of his father's friend, Okoye, who "had a barn full of yams and [ ... ] three wives" (6). In this way, wives are equated with property in Igbo culture and, especially, in Okonkwo's mind. Okonkwo takes great pride in holding dominion over his wives. He beats them regularly and quite brutally. Although we have no reason to suppose that his community members condone his treatment of his wives, it is certainly accepted as nobody's business but Okonkwo's. Additionally, Okonkwo believes that "[n]o matter how prosperous a man [is], if he [is] unable to rule his women and his children (and especially his women) he [is] not really a man" (53). Tellingly, Okonkwo's desire for women is the same desire that he experiences as he prepares for battle; it is "the desire to conquer and subdue" (42). Okonkwo's three wives "[live] in perpetual fear of his fiery temper" (13). Scholars have paid ample attention to Achebe's portrayal of gender in *Things Fall Apart,* though not specifically to the institution of polygyny as it is presented in the novel (see notes 2, 3, and 8). Although rivalry among women is not an issue brought to the forefront in *Things Fall Apart* as it is in *Arrow of God,* I assert that the custom of polygyny influences women's lives greatly, and negatively, in both novels. The institution of polygyny itself promotes the male perception of women as mere acquisitions and necessarily subordinates them to men and the maintenance of patrilinear culture.

After conducting studies into the realities of polygyny in contemporary African communities, feminist scholar Anne Nasimiyu-Wasike asserts that polygyny creates "a world of uncertainties, jealousies, and rivalries" (113). We find that Nasimiyu-Wasike's conclusion rings true as we consider the tensions that exist between Achebe's female characters, especially in *Arrow of God*. Perhaps more important, though, polygyny, as a cultural system, simply dehumanizes women. Intrinsic to the institution of polygyny is the privileging of male status and the denial of female subjectivity. In general, polygyny assumes that women exist solely for the benefit of the men in their families and as trading collateral for their larger communities. As teenagers, young women are commonly given in marriage to much older men from neighboring communities, and, in these exchanges, they create bonds between their home communities and their new husbands' communities. Anthropologist Eugene Hillman states that "polygamy is a function of social solidarity on the level of the extended family, the clan, and the tribal or ethnic community" (118). He goes on to explain: "Each new marriage sets up new relationships of affinity between two different kin groups" (118). In this way, the more wives (and later, daughters) a man has, the more patronage ties he has to other communities. In *Arrow of God*, for instance, messengers from Umuaro feel safe visiting Okperi because several wives and mothers of the first village were born and raised in the second village (20). The two communities are thus linked by the transfer of women from one to the other.[5] This type of patronage system is not exclusive to polygynous African communities, of course, or even to African communities in general, as it has operated in many Western cultures throughout the ages in similar ways; however, polygyny certainly multiplies the effects and injuries of this patriarchal system.

Frequently in polygynous cultures, once women are married, they become the property of their husbands' communities. We see this shift of property in *Arrow of God* when Obika marries Okuata, a young woman from a neighboring Igbo community. Okuata's parents and several friends from her community deliver her to Obika, and when they leave her, to live out the rest of her life among the people of her new husband (who, we must remember, is himself a stranger to her), "Okuata felt like an orphan child and tears came down her face" (117). The next day, "[e]very child in Ezeulu's compound wanted to go to the stream and draw water [ . . . ] because *their* new wife was going" (123; emphasis added). Okuata is now claimed, not only by her husband, but also by her husband's family and by the community at large. After marriage, women are often valued most highly for the children that they produce for their husbands' communities. In general, men prefer for their wives to bear male children to secure the patrilinear continuance of their families, but they value female children for the patronage ties that they will bring to their communities when they eventually marry. Children also become property of their fathers' communities, and mothers have virtually no voice in the raising of their own children. When Ugoye protests Ezeulu's order that their son, Oduche, participate in a Christian missionary church, for instance, Ezeulu's responds, "How does it concern you what I do with *my sons?*" (46; emphasis added). With this comment, Ezeulu reminds Ugoye that, as only a mother, she does not have the authority to question his decisions regarding her children.

Besides bearing children, women in polygynous societies are often expected to do most of the planting and harvesting and to cook and clean for their husbands and children.[6] A man who has multiple wives multiplies his family's labor force and also his chance at having many healthy children. In *Arrow of God,* Ezeulu's brother, Okeke speaks on the issue of marriage: "Different people have different reasons for marrying. Apart from children which we all want, some men want a woman to cook their meals, some want a woman to help them on the farm, others want someone they can beat" (64). Okeke's point is certainly not that beating women is acceptable; on the contrary, this is the only reason of those that he states that is not acceptable to him and to most of the men in his community. It is interesting, though, that Okeke begins his speech by asserting that "people" have various reasons for wanting to marry but immediately slips into a description of what "men" want and need from the bond of marriage. A woman's needs are not only not valued here, they are not even acknowledged. In a system so centered on male wants and needs, then, it is no wonder that Achebe's female characters bicker and demonstrate discontent in various ways throughout *Arrow of God.*

Yet, in his BBC documentary series *The Africans: A Triple Heritage,* Ali A. Mazrui assures those of us who might find plural marriage based on male supremacist ideology disturbing that "polygamy is one of Africa's most misunderstood institutions." Mazrui assumes that polygyny works for those who practice it and that Westerners simply do not understand this form of marriage. Certainly, polygyny in practice is a complicated custom and, although I have described it in general terms and with specific attention to its negative aspects, resists reduction to a simple definition. Though polygyny is an institution undeniably constructed on principles of male superiority and dominion, it serves women's interests in several important ways. In theory, at least, polygynous unions provide women with built-in support systems. Hillman says that in polygynous households, "the joys and sorrows of family life are shared" (119). Furthermore, if one wife cannot bear children, another wife might give one of her own children to the childless wife for upbringing (Hillman 119). Wives share work responsibilities as well, and in areas where "subsistence food production depends on the labor force that each family provides for itself," a polygynous household is more efficient in providing for its family members (Hillman 114). In his documentary, Mazrui claims that in his experience, polygynous families function well. He speaks about his own "two mothers" sharing responsibilities for his dying father and comments that, in general, "if there is jealousy between two wives, it does not interfere with daily work."[7] Another positive aspect of polygyny is that it provides social stability for all women within a community. It is almost unheard of for a woman of marriageable age to be unmarried in a polygynous community. Also, widows are quickly remarried, usually by relatives of their deceased husbands (Hillman 121). In a material sense, then, polygyny provides comfort and financial security for women. A proverb mentioned in *Arrow of God* affirms the sense of stability, even amid general unhappiness, that polygyny provides for some women: *"Let my husband hate me as long as he provides yams for me every afternoon"* (176; emphasis in original). In fact, Carole Boyce Davies claims that although polygyny as a system functions for an African woman's "repression and submission," it is also a feature of her culture "which make[s] for her independence and control" ("Motherhood" 242). Besides, polygyny is an institution that, although sexist in nature, is perpetuated by women as much as it is perpetuated by men, as Hillman explains:

> Where it is believed and seen and felt that polygamous, much more than monogamous, families produce for their members greater security, prosperity, and prestige, the women themselves will be seen to favor the custom of plural marriage. Since the wives, together with their children, share in all the benefits of belonging to the polygamous family, they themselves will sometimes pressure their husbands into seeking additional wives. Some women regard it as a disgrace to be the only wife of a man. (120)

Clearly, the custom of polygyny is deeply ingrained in many African cultures, and, thus, even though it is so "oppressive to women," polygyny is one of "the most difficult of traditions to eliminate" (Boyce Davies, Introduction 8).

Indeed, despite the European influence of colonialism, polygyny has not ceased to exist in Africa. In fact, although it may look slightly different among the many diverse cultures on the continent, it continues as a widespread custom. In a 1998 study, sociologist Paul Spencer estimates that three out of four African societies practice polygyny (51). Some scholars have argued that polygyny will become less common as Africa becomes more and more industrialized, but Samuel Waje Kunhiyop, who claims that the Christian Church should accept African polygyny as a legitimate form of marriage, challenges this assumption, stating, "It is evident that polygamy is not dying out as argued but rather is still present and needs serious attention" (14). Polygynous marriage is especially common in rural areas, having "remained an ideal in those areas where it is still an economic asset rather than a liability" (Spencer 53). The Igbo of Nigeria, whose history and heritage Achebe portrays in his novels, are exceptional among cultural groups in Africa in that the custom of polygyny *has* become almost obsolete.

In fact, the majority of Igbo today consider themselves to be Christians and have abandoned the custom of polygyny in accordance with Christian teachings.[8] According to Daniel Jordan Smith, an anthropologist who has published widely on various aspects of Igbo culture, "Polygamy, once fairly common, is exceedingly rare among the younger generation" (139). He goes on to explain, however, that many Igbo men have lovers:

> That Igbo men can and will have extramarital affairs is widely accepted. A man who cheats on his wife risks little social condemnation, assuming he continues to provide for his wife and children [ . . . ]. In fact, among Igbo men there is a certain pride in taking lovers. Being able to have lovers is sign [sic] of continuing masculine prowess and of economic success, because, increasingly, women expect their lovers to perform economically as well as sexually. (141)

In this way, then, polygyny has left behind a powerful legacy even in cultures that have, in theory at least, abandoned the practice. In fact, the system that Smith describes is, in some ways, much worse for women than polygynous marriage. The women who engage in extramarital affairs with Igbo men are not in stable social positions; their male partners do not have financial obligations to these women as they do to their wives. Moreover, the custom of married men taking lovers involves other risks, such as unwanted pregnancy and the spreading of AIDS and other sexually transmitted diseases. Many Igbo men continue to engage in extramarital affairs despite the risks and problems associated with this custom, however; some even regard it as their cultural right to do so: "To hear Igbo men tell it, access to multiple women is part of their African heritage. 'It is our culture,' many men said, 'and it cannot be changed.' Implicit in men's version of traditional culture is the belief that women do not and have never had the same rights of extramarital sexual access" (Smith 146). Clearly, gender politics in Igbo communities, which have ostensibly abandoned the practice of polygyny, continue to validate its powerful legacy.

Interestingly, in Western academic research, scholars have largely ignored polygyny throughout the past several decades. Certainly, very few critics of Achebe's two novels, *Arrow of God* and *Things Fall Apart*, have focused on the polygynous lifestyles that he presents in the texts. In early reviews of both novels, critics either ignored the issue of polygyny, or they presented it as a quaint aspect of Achebe's rendering of local color. Phoebe Adams, in her 1959 review of *Things Fall Apart*, which is representative in content and tone of many of the other initial reviews of the novel, was quite entranced by Achebe's portrayal of precolonial Africa, but she failed to understand that

Achebe's characters represent real people and real customs and especially that the customs presented in the texts were at the time (and remain today) prevalent in many African cultural groups: "Here are all the primitive rites, the witchcraft, and superstitious savagery as well as the more acceptable facets of heathen existence depicted with a historical insight available to few white men" (101). When *Arrow of God* was published in the United States in 1967, most reviewers treated its portrayal of Africa in much the same way as Adams regarded Achebe's Africa in *Things Fall Apart*. The review in *Booklist*, for instance, labeled the novel "a slow-moving but evocative novel of African village life in the 1920's" (824). Clearly, critics were attracted to these early Achebe novels for the charming pictures they conjured of natives in a place far away and were much less interested in the gender politics presented in the books or the legacies of these politics for actual African people. In dangerous ways, I think, Westerners read their own colonialist stereotypes into these early postcolonial texts.

Especially as we endeavor to unpack the political import of Achebe's portrayal of polygyny, we must consider the ways Westerners have tended to ignore the issue of polygyny. Our reluctance to address Achebe's depiction of this system of marriage is perhaps indicative of our reluctance to address polygyny at all and, let alone, to declare a strong stance on the issue. Although some critics of Achebe have considered issues of gender in his fictional works, virtually none have addressed polygyny.[9] In fact, very few feminists have written about polygyny at all, as it exists in literature or in the real world, at least in formal scholarship. The topic of polygyny did come up recently, however, on WMST-L, an international email forum for the discussion of Women's Studies issues. This list-serv conversation, which occurred between March 26 and March 30, 2006, began with a discussion of the HBO series *Big Love* and ways to use this program to talk about polygyny in the classroom. Because *Big Love* portrays the trials of polygyny in an American Mormon family, the discussion necessarily focused on polygyny in the United States. As the discussion broadened to a more general debate on polygyny, though, attitudes toward polygyny itself surfaced. An immense division emerged between those who argued that polygyny is oppressive to women and, thus, a system that must be demolished and those who believed that polygyny is simply an alternative type of marriage and, though admittedly sexist in nature, a bond ultimately agreed upon among consenting adults. In the end, no conclusions were reached in the list-serv discussion except that we need to talk about polygyny in nuanced terms, that polygyny is experienced differently by different individuals, and that this system of marriage exists for multiple purposes, not all of which disservice women. It is interesting that the topic of African polygyny only entered into the discussion one time and then merely as an example of how drastically opinions on polygyny can differ; even in Africa, one contributor stated, women disagree about whether or not the practice should be continued.

Besides recognizing that polygyny is a multidimensional custom with deep roots in many African communities, feminist scholars have avoided discussing this topic for various other reasons. We must examine our rationale for evading the topic of polygyny in the past in order to begin to consider appropriate ways to deal with it in the present. For instance, one motive for avoiding polygyny is that feminists do not want to associate themselves with the Christian missionaries who, beginning in precolonial times and continuing up until the present day, have gone to extremes to eradicate polygynous customs among their African converts. Polygyny has frequently been considered by Christians "a state of adultery" (Kunhiyop 43). In many cases, in fact, when a polygynous man has converted to Christianity, he has been required to choose just one of his wives and to divorce the others. The results of polygynous divorces have been severe; some abandoned wives, unable to marry again due to cultural beliefs, have turned to prostitution, and abandoned children have struggled with poverty and the stigma associated with illegitimacy (Kunhiyop 44). As Christianity has become one of most dominant, and domineering, religions in Africa, many African countries have criminalized polygyny and, in some cases, pronounced it punishable by imprisonment (Mazrui). Because organized Christianity has taken a stance of rigid condemnation against it, then, polygyny has clearly come to represent a disjuncture between the understanding of Western peoples and the cultures of indigenous Africa. Feminist scholars may be hesitant to align themselves with the Church and the often merciless ways in which Christians have handled the custom of polygyny.[10]

Another deterrent to Westerners speaking out against polygyny is that it is an ancient custom, one that existed well before the age of European colonialism. Since Westerners had no hand in creating this marriage system, oppressive to women though it may be, many believe that it is not within our rights as outsiders to question it. While it is true that Westerners did not create the institution of polygyny, the colonial system certainly contributed significantly to the plight of African women. As many historians have pointed out, though, the colonial structure powerfully reinforced the patriarchal systems that already existed in precolonial Africa. For one thing, the introduction of capitalism often subordinated women, who had previously held important roles as laborers for their families, to their wage-earning husbands. Mineke Schipper claims that under capitalism, "the value of traditional women's labor was reduced considerably because the home and the work-place were separated [and] the state and industrial concerns reserved most urban wage labor for men" (157). The capitalist system made women even more dependent on men, of course, for providing for their material needs. Colonial laws also devalued women by determining that "they had no rights to ownership of land or control over the produce they cultivated" (157). In addition, colonialism narrowed the possibilities for women within their communities and the world at large: "Their traditional powers of healing and other functions (spirit mediums, midwives, brewers of ritual beer) were undermined by Church and State. Women received little or no education because neither African nor colonial patriarchs regarded it as important" (158). Furthermore, in some cases, colonial forces *did* directly influence the increase of polygyny. In his study of the history of the Yoruba, another cultural group from Nigeria, Andrew Apter claims that the cocoa trade, which increased dramatically in Nigeria from 1900 through 1960, caused "an increase in polygynous households among farmers who traded in cocoa, with their wives as managers" (120). In these cases, men needed multiple wives to manage large cocoa businesses. Without a doubt, European imperialism has done its part in keeping African women on the lower rungs of the traditionally patriarchal hierarchy that still exists in many African cultures, preventing them from achieving independence and suitable quality of living.

Indeed, then, Western feminists and African feminists alike must question the polygynous customs of Africa, as they are represented in literature such as Achebe's and as they exist in actuality, and, in doing so, make strides toward empowering the women of polygynous societies. As Boyce Davies asserts, "[F]orms of oppression intrinsic to various societies which still plague African women's lives [ . . . ] must inevitably be at the crux of African feminist theory" (Introduction 7). Nasimiyu-Wasike takes Boyce Davies's assessment a step further and states specifically, "It is only by uniting and focusing on the common enemy that women will be able to expose the evils of polygamy" (113). Our goal is not necessarily to eradicate the practice of polygyny, though, and certainly not to punish or ridicule members of polygynous families, as missionaries have done in the past. Instead, we must work toward the creation of safe contexts from which women can talk openly about the gender politics that influence and control their lives and, ultimately, make their own decisions about marriage without risking condemnation from their communities. Certainly, though, we must resist envisioning and treating women involved in polygynous relationships as agentless and endeavor to listen to their own expressions of subjectivity, in whatever forms these may take. Also, as Chandra Talpade Mohanty reminds us, feminists must refuse to give in to the temptation of homogenization, which she regards as "discursively coloniz[ing] the material and historical heterogeneities of the lives of women in the third world, thereby producing/re-presenting a composite, singular 'Third World Woman'—an image that appears arbitrarily constructed, but nevertheless carries with it the authorizing signature of Western humanist discourse" (260). Theorist Anne McLeer presents an alternative to reproducing the Third

World Woman as Other. She says that we must "embrace notions of sister-hood and a global condition of women without erasing difference or negating other aspects of women's identity, such as culture, ethnicity, nationalism, and so forth" (46). As feminists of the WMST-L list-serv have mentioned, we cannot assume that all women in polygynous marriages have lived similar experiences or even that they are oppressed in the same way. Perhaps most importantly, we cannot ignore the very real benefits of polygyny or fail to rec-ognize the material reasons why women choose to perpetuate this institution. Ultimately, as Benita Parry points out, "discourses of representation should not be confused with material reality" (37). Feminists must respect women's decisions regarding how they will live their lives, because, of course, no system should override a woman's right to choose.

As outsiders, though, we in the West face definite challenges as we venture to create change even in the discourses surrounding polygyny and certainly in the social practice of African marriage customs. First of all, be-cause imperial nations have frequently used women's rights issues as justifi-cations, or excuses, for colonization, we must fight to differentiate ourselves from the protofeminists of the imperialist age. We must avoid transposing a "West is best" ideology onto the issue of African polygyny. I believe that we can best work against polygyny by forming alliances with African women themselves. However, even the women among us cannot base our alliance with African women simply on gender. As Mohanty suggests, "Sisterhood cannot be assumed on the basis of gender; it must be formed in concrete, historical and political practice and analysis" (262). Even the term "sister-hood" is problematic in that it signifies gender as the defining factor of re-lationships between women. hooks takes Mohanty's suggestion further and proposes that the consolidation of diverse forms of feminism not necessarily take the shape of sisterhood but of "solidarity," which, as mentioned earlier, accommodates difference:

> Women do not need to eradicate difference to feel solidarity. We do not need to share common oppression to fight equally to end oppression. We do not need antimale sentiments to bond us together, so great is the wealth of experience, culture, and ideas we have to share with one another. We can be sisters united by shared interests and beliefs, united in our appreciation for diversity, united in our struggle to end sexist oppression, united in political solidarity. (411)

The most pressing question, then, seems to ask the following: How can we be united in solidarity with those who do not speak about their oppression?

Studies have shown that many African women are dissatisfied with their roles in polygynous families but that they are reluctant to speak out about their struggles. Summarizing the results of an anonymous 1992 survey of female Nigerians' attitudes toward gender and gender roles, Nasimiyu-Wasike says: "This shows that many women are not happy with their lot, despite their seeming acceptance [ . . . ]. They quietly reject and resent what society and men have imposed on them" (112). Gayatri Chakravorty Spivak affirms Nasimiyu-Wasike's findings. In the 1988 version of her groundbreaking essay "Can the Subaltern Speak?" Spivak asserts that women in postcolonial nations, especially underprivileged women, are generally unable to voice their experiences:

> Within the effaced itinerary of the subaltern subject, the track of sexual difference is doubly effected [ . . . ] both as object of colonialist historiography and as subject of insurgency, the ideological construction of gender keeps the male dominant. If, in the context of colonial production, the subaltern has no history and cannot speak, the subaltern as female is even more deeply in shadow. (28)

Here Spivak suggests that women in postcolonial countries are silenced both by the traditional patriarchy under which many Africans construct their lives and by the legacy of colonialism. Thus, I claim that a part of solidarity, as defined by hooks, is directing our attention to the silent suffering of women.

I do not claim that we can speak for African women in polygynous relationships; instead, I insist that we must speak about the circumstances of these women's lives and work toward incorporating their voices into our discourse. As Western feminists, we can envision and begin to create cultural change by speaking out against polygyny. Because feminists live diverse lives and work in diverse fields, we can speak out against polygyny in diverse ways. As teachers, we can teach Achebe's historical novels with attention to the voices that Achebe excludes. We can ask our students to consider the portrayal of polygyny in *Things Fall Apart* and *Arrow of God*. These texts, and the depictions of polygyny within them, can provide our students with opportunities to discuss the place of the Western feminist in these matters. As literary scholars, we can begin to change the oppressive marriage customs in Africa by discussing polygyny in general, much as the contributors to the WMST-L list-serv did earlier this year. Participants in discussions such as this one, however, would do well to remember hooks's idea of solidarity. The primary disagreement that occurred during this discussion was over whether or not Western feminists have the authority to take a stand on the issue of polygyny. On this issue, list-serv comments, unfortunately, turned personal and took on highly aggressive tones. Instead of squabbling with one another, as if playing the parts of "jealous wives" in an Achebe novel, over our authority, or lack of authority, to judge polygyny, let us recall that neither differences of opinion among those who speak about polygyny nor differences in experiences between Western women and African women need prevent us from working toward the empowerment of all women. We need not fear telling the truth, which is, of course, that polygyny, as a system that so clearly subjugates women to the needs and desires of men, is intrinsically oppressive. Thus, as feminists, we must stand united against the marriage custom of polygyny.

I begin this process by bringing to light, for the purposes of discussion, Chinua Achebe's portrayal of polygyny in *Things Fall Apart* and *Arrow of God*. As stated previously, Achebe essentially writes polygyny off as a non-issue—it is not something that he is particularly interested in or considers to be much of a problem. In order to understand the significance of Achebe's attitude toward polygyny, however, we must return to his reputation within and outside of the academy. Mezu describes Achebe's success in terms of "the eagle on the iroko":

> In this metaphor the iroko [the tallest tree in African landscape] represents the field of African literature; the eagle [the king of birds], Chinua Achebe. Achebe has, of course, literarily climbed and soared above the iroko several times. More than those of any other African writer, his writings have helped to develop what is known as African literature today [ . . . ]. Having been the first, so to speak, to scale the top of the iroko, this eagle Achebe, and other male eaglets after him, arguably have appropriated all that they have found there. (n.p.)

Mezu first reports on the undeniably prominent position that Achebe has secured for himself in the field of African literature. She goes on to reveal his sexist portrayal of African culture and insinuate that this particular aspect of Achebe's work has resulted in negative consequences for the real African women whom his female characters represent. Especially because Achebe regards himself as something of a "teacher" to his African readers, his dismissal of women's issues, such as polygyny, is problematic.[11] Of course, Achebe may simply regard his stance toward polygyny as only a necessary postponement of a more in-depth analysis of women's issues in Africa. He may assume that attention to women's issues should follow a securing of national identity in postcolonial nations. Postcolonial feminist scholar Kristen Holst Petersen explains how women's issues have been swept aside in African literature for the purposes of nationalist causes:

An important impetus behind the wave of African writing which started in the '60s was the desire to show both the outside world and African youth that the African past was orderly, dignified and complex and altogether a worthy heritage. This was obviously opting for fighting cultural imperialism, and in the course of that the women's issue was not only ignored—a fate which would have allowed it to surface when the time was ripe—it was conscripted in the service of dignifying the past and restoring African self-confidence. (253)

In his early novels, Achebe does exactly what Petersen describes; he assumes both that women's issues are not integral to the nationalist cause and that they can wait. Achebe is certainly not the only African or postcolonial writer to make these dangerous assumptions regarding the place of women's issues within the larger nationalist movements, but he is perhaps the most significant figure to do so in the field of African literary studies.

In his critique of Conrad's *Heart of Darkness,* Achebe condemns the tendency of Western writers to depict Africa as the antithesis of Europe. He describes this much-employed literary trope as evidence of "the desire—one might indeed say the need—in Western psychology to set Africa up as a foil for Europe, a place of negations at once remote and vaguely familiar in comparison with which Europe's own state of spiritual grace will be manifest" ("Image" 210). In his historical novels, however, Achebe uses women in much the same way as Conrad uses Africans. Certainly, Achebe does not systematically dehumanize his women as he claims Conrad does to his Africans, but Achebe consistently uses female characters to throw male characters in relief. The bickering between Matifi and Ugoye, for instance, is presented as insignificant when measured against Ezeulu's rivalry with Ezidemili and downright trivial when compared to the threat that the Christian missionaries pose to Ezeulu's spiritual leadership. Achebe's depiction of polygyny in *Things Fall Apart* and *Arrow of God* situates his female characters firmly in a masculine tradition that prevents them from moving into the positions of power, positions that women in Africa must occupy in order for their nations to serve their needs. More significantly, Achebe provides us with no alternative way of reading his portrayal of polygyny. So if "Heart of Darkness" reveals Conrad's deliberate racism, Achebe's historical novels reveal his, probably subconscious, sexism. Furthermore, if Conrad's depiction of Africa points to his darkest fear that, in an uncivilized land, a European might mentally and morally deteriorate to the level of an African, then Achebe's representation of polygyny points to his fear that under the colonialism of the early twentieth century or the neocolonialism of today, a man might decline to the state of a "jealous wife." Postcolonialism has often involved reclamation of native male power and, as a result, has sometimes encouraged the romanticizing of precolonial forms of masculinity. Certainly, polygyny has traditionally served as a system through which African men could demonstrate power and stature within their communities. In this way, Achebe's portrayal of polygyny suggests his anxiety, influential to his work at least during the period of time in which these texts were written and published, over dispensing with this particular avenue of "proving" African manhood.

Achebe proposes that the reason that Western readers have so long accepted Conrad's representation of Africa as factual is because this representation is consistent with a typical Westerner's system of thought: "That this simple truth [Conrad is a racist] is glossed over in criticism of his work is due to the fact that white racism against Africa is such a normal way of thinking its manifestations go completely undetected" (215). Likewise, perhaps we have not attended to Achebe's dismissal of polygyny because, as primarily an African women's issue, this matter has somehow fallen off our radars. It is a seemingly forgotten issue—an issue not usually considered with the respect that it is due. Certainly, Chinua Achebe's two historical novels fail to represent the full significance of this issue for African women. Thus, Achebe is perhaps guilty of that which he warns against in his introduction to a collection of his essays, *Morning Yet on Creation Day* (1975) (a title that in itself alludes to the optimism of the nationalist movement). As Achebe points out in the epigraph that I use to open this essay, there is a real danger in forgetting the truth about the state of one's nation, especially as that nation is forming, and in imagining "slogans," such "first things first," more real than reality itself. And yet, in his quest to dignify African tradition and customs, Achebe has forgotten the true state of affairs in polygynous homes all across Africa. Like others in positions of power, Achebe has ignored that polygyny still exists and forgotten that this institution deserves and demands careful scrutiny. He has used polygyny as a way to talk about masculinity while ignoring the problems, for women like Matefi and Ugoye in *Arrow of God*, of this system of marriage. He has forgotten that polygyny is intrinsically destructive to women's autonomy, that it purposefully silences them. Perhaps most of all, at least in his early novels, Achebe forgets that in order for African nationalism to serve all Africans, women *must* take part in the formation of African nations, that women's voices *must* be heard.

As Gikandi suggests, Achebe has changed the face of African literature, revised the perception of Africa in the Western world, and done more than his fair share to instill a sense of cultural pride in his African readers. I do not argue that we should, or even that we could, remove Achebe from his position as such a prominent figure in African literary studies. Rather, I propose that we complicate some of the issues that Achebe has so successfully brought to international attention. Polygyny is one such issue that we must address more fully in scholarly studies and discourse. As Western feminist teachers and scholars, we can practice "solidarity," even with those who do not speak about their struggles, by taking a stand on this admittedly complicated issue. Certainly, we do not want to further appropriate women's lives, but we must remind Achebe, and others, that systems of marriage have to change in order for African women to be able to speak out and join the nationalist cause.

## NOTES

1. I use the term "polygyny," which refers specifically to the practice of a man having more than one wife at the same time, rather than "polygamy," which is a universal term that denotes plural marriage. I prefer "polygyny" because it is this type of plural marriage that is most common in African communities. Polyandry, the practice of a woman having more than one husband at the same time, is extremely rare among communities in Africa. In order to remain true to the words of other scholars and theoreticians that I use in this essay, I retain their use of the term "polygamy" even when "polygyny" would more accurately describe the systems of marriage that they discuss.

2. Merun Nasser and Mabel Segun explicitly argue that Achebe has disserviced his female readers.

3. Although I argue that his first two novels, *Things Fall Apart* and *Arrow of God*, dismiss important women's issues, I agree with critics such as Idowu Omoyele, Rose Ure Mezu, Kwadwo Osei-Nyame, Jr., and Sophia O. Ogwude, who have noted that Achebe does attend more fully to the positions of African women in his later novels. As Mezu asserts, "Achebe's newly envisioned female roles are to be expounded, articulated, and secured by woman herself" (n.p.). According to Mezu, Achebe even goes so far as to "[acknowledge] that the malaise the African party is experiencing results from excluding women from the scheme of things." I recognize, however, that the historical novels, especially *Things Fall Apart,* are the ones most often taught; thus, Achebe's treatment of women's issues in these novels seems especially important to the ways in which these issues are viewed in and outside of the academy.

4. Critics debate this issue hotly. In opposition to Mezu, Prafulla C. Kar reads Achebe's characterization as an attempt to render a realistic version of precolonial Africa and the people who lived within that world, asserting that Achebe "examines the nature of the traditional African without trying to idealise it" (152). See also Ogwude.

5. Mineke Schipper, in a 1996 issue of *Research in African Literatures,* says that in traditional African cultures, if a man wants a wife, she will have to be relinquished by another man [ . . . ]. In this exchange, the woman is not a subject but an object. Men [treat] women as living commodities, to be bartered in the interest of enhancing the greater glory of male status [ . . . ]. In a number of cultures, a woman is only known as some man's daughter or mother. Her identity is dependent on her father, husband, or son. (162)

6. As Juliet I. Okonkwo asserts, "The wife is to all intents and purposes servant" (148).

7. Interestingly, although he seeks to present polygyny in a positive light, Mazrui's comment demonstrates his assumption that jealousy is indeed inherent in the system of polygyny.

8. As literary scholar D. Ibe Nwoga points out, the Igbos are well known for their "receptivity to change" (36). This cultural group accepted Christianity quickly when missionaries introduced it in the early part of the twentieth century.

9. In opposition to Nasser and Segun, some scholars have positioned Achebe as sensitive to the interests of African women. See the articles of Nwando Achebe, Biodun Jeyifo, and Kwadwo Osei-Nyame.

10. Even though Achebe deals directly with the consequences of Christian missionary work for his characters in both *Arrow of God* and *Things Fall Apart,* he avoids any interrogation of polygyny even in this context.

11. Achebe demonstrates his perception of himself as a teacher in several passages of "Novelist as Teacher." In one such passage, he cites an example of a schoolboy who feels ashamed to write about the harmattan, the windy season in Africa, and he responds, "I think it is part of my business as a writer to teach that boy that there is nothing disgraceful about the African weather, that the palm tree is a fit subject for poetry" ("Novelist" 71).

## Works Cited

Achebe, Chinua. *Arrow of God*. New York: Anchor, 1984.

———. "An Image of Africa: Racism in Conrad's Heart of Darkness." *Postcolonial Discourses: An Anthology*. Ed. Gregory Castle. Oxford: Blackwell, 2001. 209–220.

———. Introduction. *Morning Yet on Creation Day*. Garden City, NY: Anchor/Doubleday, 1975. xi–xiii.

———. "The Novelist as Teacher." *Morning Yet on Creation Day*. Garden City, NY: Anchor/Doubleday, 1975. 67–74.

———. *Things Fall Apart*. New York: Anchor, 1994.

Achebe, Nwando. "Balancing Male and Female Principles: Teaching about Gender in Chinua Achebe's *Things Fall Apart*." *Ufahamu* 29.1 (2001–2002): 121–143.

Adams, Phoebe. Rev. of *Things Fall Apart*, by Chinua Achebe. *Atlantic* Feb. 1959: 101.

Anon. Rev. of *Arrow of God*, by Chinua Achebe. *Booklist*. 15 Mar. 1968: 824.

Apter, Andrew. "Atinga Revisited: Yoruba Witchcraft and the Cocoa Economy, 1950–1951." *Modernity and Its Malcontents: Ritual and Power in Postcolonial Africa*. Ed. Jean Comaroff and John Comaroff. Chicago: University of Chicago Press, 1993. 111–128.

Ashcroft, Bill, Gareth Griffiths, and Helen Tiffin, eds. *The Post-Colonial Studies Reader*. London: Routledge, 1995.

Boyce Davies, Carole. Introduction. Boyce Davies and Graves 3–26.

———. "Motherhood in the Works of Male and Female Igbo Writers: Achebe, Emecheta, Nwapa and Nzekwu." Boyce Davies and Graves 241–256.

Boyce Davies, Carole, and Anne Adams Graves, eds. *Ngambika: Studies of Women in African Literature*. Trenton, NJ: Africa World, 1986.

Gikandi, Simon. "Chinua Achebe and the Invention of African Culture." *Research in African Literatures* 32.3 (2001): 3–8.

Hillman, Eugene. *Polygamy Reconsidered: African Plural Marriage and the Christian Churches*. Maryknoll, NY: Orbis, 1975.

hooks, bell. "Sisterhood: Political Solidarity between Women." *Dangerous Liaisons: Gender, Nation, and Postcolonial Perspectives*. Ed. Anne McClintock, Aamir Mufti, and Ella Shohat. Minneapolis: University of Minnesota Press, 1997. 396–411.

Jefiyo, Biodun. "Okonkwo and His Mother: *Things Fall Apart* and Issues of Gender in the Constitution of African Postcolonial Discourse." *Callaloo* 16.4 (1993): 847–858.

Kar, Prafulla C. "The Image of the Vanishing African in Chinua Achebe's Novels." *The Colonial and the Neo-Colonial Encounters in Commonwealth Literature*. Ed. H. Gwoda and H. Anniah. Mysore: Prasaranga University, 1983. 149–159.

Kunhiyop, Samuel Waje. *Contemporary Issues Facing Christians in Africa*. Nigeria: Baraka Press, 2003.

Mazrui, Ali A., dir. *The Africans: A Triple Heritage*. Perf. Mazrui. Prod. WETA TV and BBC TV. Videorecording. Intellimation, 1986.

McLeer, Anne. "Saving the Victim: Recuperating the Language of the Victim and Reassessing Global Feminism." *Hypatia: A Journal of Feminist Philosophy* 13.1 (1998): 41–55.

Mezu, Rose Ure. "Women in Achebe's World." *Womanist Theory and Research* 1.2 (1995): n. p. Online. 30 Nov. 2005. <http://www.uga.edu/~womanist/1995/mezu.html>.

Mohanty, Chandra Talpade. "Under Western Eyes: Feminist Scholarship and Colonial Discourse." Ashcroft 259–263.

Moore, Gerald. "Chinua Achebe: A Retrospective." *Research in African Literatures* 32.3 (2001): 29–32.

Nasimiyu-Wasike, Anne. "Polygamy: A Feminist Critique." *The Will to Arise: Women, Tradition, and the Church in Africa*. Ed. Mercy Amba Oduyoye and Musimbi R. A. Kanyoro. Maryknoll, NY: Orbis, 1992. 101–118.

Nasser, Merun. "Achebe and His Women: A Social Science Perspective." *Africa Today* 27.3 (1980): 21–28.

Nwoga, D. Ibe. "The Igbo World of Achebe's *Arrow of God*." *The Literary Half-Yearly* 27.1 (1986): 11–42.

Ogwude, Sophia O. "Achebe on the Woman Question." *Literary Griot* 13.1–2 (2001): 62–69.

Okonkwo, Juliet I. "Adam and Eve: Igbo Marriage in the Nigerian Novel." *Conch: A Sociological Journal of African Cultures and Literatures* 3.2 (1971): 137–151.

Omoyele, Idowu. "Forty Years Since *Things Fall Apart*." *West Africa* 16–29 (1998): 349–350.

———. "The Legacy of Chinua Achebe." *West Africa* 16–29 (1998): 346–348.

Osei-Nyame, Kwadwo, Jr. "Chinua Achebe Writing Culture: Representations of Gender and Tradition in *Things Fall Apart*." *Research in African Literatures* 30.2 (1999): 148–164.

———. "Gender and the Narrative of Identity in Chinua Achebe's *Arrow of God*." *Commonwealth Essays and Studies* 22.2 (2000): 25–34.

Parry, Benita. "Problems in Current Theories of Colonial Discourse." Ashcroft 36–44.

Petersen, Kirsten Holst. "First Things First: Problems of a Feminist Approach to African Literature." Ashcroft 251–254.

Segun, Mabel. "Challenges of Being a Female Writer in a Male-Dominated Developing Society." *Matatu* 23–24 (2001): 295–302.

Spencer, Paul. *The Pastoral Continuum: The Marginalization of Tradition in East Africa*. Oxford: Clarendon, 1998.

Spivak, Gayatri Chakravorty. "Can the Subaltern Speak?" Ashcroft 24–28.

Schipper, Mineke. "Emerging from the Shadows: Changing Patterns in Gender Matters." *Research in African Literatures* 27.1 (1996): 155–171.

Smith, Daniel Jordan. "Romance, Parenthood, and Gender in a Modern African Society." *Ethnology* 40.2 (2001): 129–151.

Williams, Adebayo. "The Autumn of the Literary Patriarch: Chinua Achebe and the Politics of Remembering." *Research in African Literatures* 32.3 (2001): 8–21.

## ACKNOWLEDGMENT

I would like to thank Dr. Deborah M. Mix and Dr. Lauren Onkey for reading and commenting on drafts of this article.

CAREY SNYDER

# The Possibilities and Pitfalls of Ethnographic Readings: Narrative Complexity in Things Fall Apart

> The District Commissioner changed instantaneously. The resolute administrator in him gave way to the student of primitive customs. . . . As he walked back to the court he thought about [the book he planned to write]. Every day brought him some new material. The story of this man who had killed a messenger and hanged himself would make interesting reading. One could write almost a whole chapter on him. Perhaps not a whole chapter but a reasonable paragraph, at any rate. There was so much else to include, and one must be firm in cutting out details. He had already chosen the title of the book, after much thought: *The Pacification of the Primitive Tribes of the Lower Niger.*

These famous closing lines of Chinua Achebe's *Things Fall Apart* (1958, hereafter *TFA*) represent a dramatic shift of perspective, whereby the protagonist's life story, which has been the subject of the previous twenty four chapters, is unceremoniously condensed into a brief anecdote in a foreign text: we are thrust from what is figured as an intimate, insider's view of Igbo life to a jarringly alien one. The outsider's proposed ethnography of the region's purportedly primitive tribes exemplifies a tradition of colonial discourse that Achebe powerfully counters in *TFA*.[1] Okonkwo's tragic death—prefiguring for the reader the demise of the clan's traditional ways—

*College Literature*, Volume 35, Number 2 (Spring 2008): pp. 154–174. Copyright © 2008 West Chester University.

serves the government anthropologist merely as raw material to appropriate and possibly turn to a profit.[2] Not only is the prominent Okonkwo stripped of his individual identity as he is transformed into a nameless African in a Western text, but the particularities of the sophisticated Igbo culture, which the novel has taken pains to elaborate, are also erased as they are lumped together in the essentialist category of *primitive tribes*. Moreover, though the Commissioner has shown himself to be a poor reader of native customs and beliefs, lacking both the intellectual curiosity and the humility that are requisite to understanding another culture, he nonetheless passes as an African authority in the West. Achebe's narrative works to redress the reductive and distorted representation of traditional African cultures emblematized by the Commissioner's text.

The reference to the colonial text within the novel may be taken as an embedded reference to the extra-textual politics of representation in which the novel participates. Achebe reports that it was his anger at what he took to be the caricatures of Nigerians in Joyce Cary's novel *Mr. Johnson* that initially inspired him to write a counter-narrative, sympathetic to the indigenous perspective (Flowers 1989, 4). By the author's account, the novel is meant at once to "write back" to the Western canon,[3] correcting erroneous representations of Africa and Africans, and to restore to his people an awareness of the dignity and humanity of precolonial Africa—reminding them "what they lost" through colonization (Achebe 1973, 8). Published two years before Nigeria gained independence from Great Britain, *TFA* aims to wrest from the colonial metropole control over the representation of African lives, staking a claim to the right to self-representation.

While raising issues of authority and authorship, at the same time, the District Commissioner's indisputably alien perspective at the novel's end functions to reinforce the impression of the foregoing narrative's ostensible authenticity: as Neil ten Kortenaar perceptively argues, Achebe's "appeal to an obviously false authority deploys irony to establish Achebe's own credentials as a historian of Igboland" (2003, 124). Against the egregiously misinformed interpretation of an outsider, the rest of the novel is fashioned as a view "from the inside," as the author himself has described it (Flowers 1989, 4). With such remarks, Achebe has contributed to the aura of authenticity that surrounds his book, positioning himself as a kind of native anthropologist, who represents from within the life of the fictionalized Eastern Nigerian village, Umuofia (based on the author's native Ogidi).

Selling millions of copies and taught not only in literature classrooms, but in anthropology, comparative religion, and African Studies courses as well, *TFA* is widely appreciated for its richly detailed, "inside-perspective" of a traditional West African culture.[4] Indeed, the novel has frequently been deemed "ethnographic" for its vivid representation of the customs, ceremonies, and beliefs of the Igbo people. An early review captures this sense of confidence in the author's credentials as an ethnographic reporter: "No European ethnologist could so intimately present this medley of mores of the Ibo tribe, so detail the intricate formalities of the clan."[5] In 1980, critic David Carroll presents what by then is a received view, when he writes, "With great skill Achebe . . . combines the role of novelist and anthropologist, synthesizing a new kind of fiction. This is where his essential genius lies" (1980, 183). In 1991, the MLA's *Approaches to Teaching Achebe's* Things Fall Apart, based on a survey of several hundred teachers of African literature in the U.S., Africa, and Europe, lists among the principal reasons for teaching this novel the perception that it offers "an unusual opportunity to discover the foreign from within": "Readers everywhere may enter Achebe's Igbo worldview and see past and present African experiences from an indigenous perspective" (Lindfors 1991, 15, 2).[6] Finally, in another pedagogical volume, *Understanding* Things Fall Apart, Kalu Ogbaa informs teachers and students that Achebe's novel may be regarded as "an authentic information source on the nineteenth-century Igbo and their neighbors" (1999, xvii).

As a literary critic (in the American academy) and not an anthropologist, I have no intention of questioning the accuracy of Achebe's cultural portrait of the Igbo, which seems deserving of its reputation as authoritative.[7] What I do want to question is this persistent rhetoric of *authenticity, intimacy,* and (to coin a clumsy word) *insiderness* which pervades discussions of Achebe's text. Further, I want to challenge the pervasive ethnographic or anthropological mode of reading Achebe's novel, which I take as paradigmatic of a common approach to African literature, and to ethnic literatures more generally, at least in the West.[8]

As Keith Booker points out, "anthropological readings . . . have sometimes prevented African novels from receiving serious critical attention as literature rather than simply as documentation of cultural practices."[9] The naïve ethnographic or anthropological reading treats a novel like *TFA* as though it transparently represents the world of another culture, ignoring the aesthetic dimensions of the representation. Ato Quayson suggests that the tendency to read Achebe's novels as though they unproblematically represent historic and cultural reality is not limited to critics unfamiliar with the African context: West African critic Emmanuel Obiechina "duplicates this tendency from an insider's perspective," reading *TFA* "as reflective or mimetic of traditional beliefs and practices in an almost unmediated way" (Quayson 2003, 225).[10] (While I agree with the thrust of Quayson's critique, I will quarrel with his reification of the categories of insider and outsider shortly.) It is not merely that such readings give short shrift to the literary dimensions of this fiction, but in reading fiction like ethnography, some critics operate from the false assumption that ethnographic texts themselves are transparent.[11] In another context, Elizabeth Fernea defines the "ethnographic novel" as one "written by an artist from within the culture," which presents an "authentic" representation of that culture (1989, 154, 153). Leaving aside the objection that "auto-ethnographic" might be a more fitting term here, Fernea's definition highlights a common assumption of such readings: the writer's "insider" status rather circularly verifies the "authenticity" of the representation.

This article seeks to complicate the construction of postcolonial writers like Achebe as cultural insiders. My analysis demonstrates that neither the author nor the narrative voice of *TFA* can be aligned simply with a monological African (or even West African, Nigerian, or nineteenth-century Igbo) perspective, despite the persistent critical tendency to do so. Raised by Christian evangelists in a small village in Eastern Nigeria, Achebe has written eloquently about his childhood alienation from his family's ancestral traditions. I show that Achebe's perspective at the "cultural crossroads" (his phrase) is manifest in the narrative voice of *TFA*, which moves along a continuum of proximity and distance in relation to the culture it sympathetically describes. In this way, Achebe's position vis-à-vis the Igbo does exemplify many of the dilemmas of ethnographic observation—if we understand the relationship between the observer and the observed to be more complicated, and sometimes fraught, than most anthropological readings of the novel assume. To uncover the complexities in the narrative voice, I argue, we need to read the novel not naïvely as providing a clear window onto an alien culture—in contrast with the presumably distorted vision of colonial writers like Joyce Cary—but *meta-ethnographically*, in a way that attends to the complexity inherent in any ethnographic situation.[12] Such a reading restores Achebe's text to the realm of the literary, by encouraging subtle attention to the narrative's achievements as *fiction*, rather than as cultural documentation.

### A Voice from the Inside

Lauding Achebe's judicious and multifaceted representation of the Igbo in *TFA*, David Carroll writes, "It was an achievement of detachment, irony and fairness, demonstrating in the writing those qualities he admires in his own people" (1980, 29). But in what sense are the turn-of-the-century Igbo represented in the novel the author's "own people"? The formulation simplifies the writer's subject position, while ignoring the heterogeneity of the Igbo, as of all cultures. Achebe's divided identity as a colonial subject is emblematized by his christened name, Albert Chinualumogu, a tribute on the one hand to Queen Victoria's consort, Prince Albert, and on the other, to the writer's African heritage; at University, he dropped the former and cropped the latter name, refashioning his identity in a way that could be read as simultaneously indigenizing (by effacing the colonial marker) and modernizing (in his words, making the name "more businesslike") (Achebe

1975, 118). Achebe explains that he was born at the "crossroads of cultures": "On one arm of the cross, we sang hymns and read the Bible night and day. On the other, my father's brother and his family, blinded by heathen-ism, offered food to idols" (1975, 120). He attended a missionary school, not surprisingly, since his father was one of the first converts in the area (Ezenwa-Ohaeto 1997, 3), and, as a Christian, learned to look down on "heathens" and their pagan customs: Christians were regarded as "the people of the church," while heathens were "the people of nothing" (Achebe 1975, 115). Achebe has suggested that writing *TFA* was "an act of atonement" for this early repudiation of ancestral traditions, offered up by a "prodigal son" (120). At the same time, he recalls being fascinated by the traditional cus-toms and rituals taking place in the village, and even "partaking of heathen festival meals" unbeknownst to his parents. Thus Achebe's relationship to traditional Igbo ways is rooted in ambivalence.

Like many African writers of his generation, Achebe received a colo-nial education—meaning one calibrated to an English frame of reference—at both the prestigious secondary school he attended at Umahia and at the Uni-versity of Ibadan, where he became well acquainted with the English literary canon. In an oft-quoted passage, Achebe reflects on the psychological ramifi-cations of studying colonial fiction, for a young, black African man:

> When I had been younger, I had read these adventure books about the good white man, you know, wandering into the jungle or into danger, and the savages were after him. And I would instinctively be on the side of the white man. You see what fiction can do, it can put you on the wrong side if you are not developed enough. In the university I suddenly saw that these books had to be read in a different light. Reading *Heart of Darkness,* for instance, . . . I realized that I was one of those savages jumping up and down on the beach. Once that kind of enlightenment comes to you, you realize that someone has to write a different story. (Qtd. in Flowers 1989, 343)

This sudden shift in readerly identification is a kind of parable of the frac-turing of identity under colonization: Achebe is split between identifying with the white adventurer and with the savage, and though he consciously decides to take up the "savage's" cause, to tell "a different story," his experi-ence suggests that ultimately it is not as simple as choosing sides. Achebe remains a divided subject: "living between two worlds," he affirms, "is one of the central themes of my life and work" (Qtd. in Flowers 1989, 333).

The pervasive rhetoric of insiderness associated with this writer obscures the more apt trope of the artist situated at cultural crossroads. Achebe has referred to his position straddling cultures as one of the "major advantages" he has enjoyed as a writer (Okpewho 2003, 72): as Simon Gikandi notes, the Nigerian novelist learned to regard "the chasm between himself and the Igbo traditions" as a generative artistic space (1996, 15). Gikandi's word "chasm" denotes Achebe's alienation from indigenous customs. Yet I would stress that it is distance (a "chasm") in tension with *proximity* to traditional ways that is the enabling condition for Achebe's art. In this way, he resembles the figure of the modern fieldworker in the tradition of Bronislaw Malinowski, whose methodology of participant-observation involves shuttling back and forth between perspectives—adopting the native's point of view as a participant, and then pulling back, as an observer, to place customs and beliefs in context (Clifford 1988, 34). Exploring these affinities in greater detail will shed light on the intricacies of Achebe's narrative technique.

### A Participant-Observer

Mindful of the tendency to read Achebe's works in an ethnographic mode, one interviewer asked the author whether he regarded his novels as "a competent source of cultural information . . . about Igbo society"; Achebe concurred, explaining that he aimed to present "a total world and a total life as it is lived in that world," and adding, "If somebody else thinks, as some do, that this is sociology or anthropology, that's their own lookout" (Flowers 1989, 64). That Achebe is far from discouraging ethnographic readings of his fiction follows from his pedagogical view of art: to Achebe, the novelist is a teacher, and educating Africans and foreigners about a heritage that has been demeaned and eroded through colonization is a viable way of fulfilling an important social mission.[13]

The phrase Achebe uses to describe the purview of his novels ("a total world and a total life") resonates with the language of cultural holism employed by anthropologists like Malinowski to describe their object of study—typically, a tribal village prior to extensive contact with foreigners.[14] In another interview, Achebe states that while some African writers may object that Africans are "not tribal anymore," "My world—the one that interests me more than any other—is the world of the village" (Flowers 1989, 77). In its scope and orientation, *TFA* resembles the traditional village study of an anthropologist, except Achebe's "field" is both home and strange (or, rather, *estranged*). In aiming to capture what he perceives as a vanishing way of life (he speaks of observing "the remains" of village traditions in his youth [1975, 18]), Achebe also resembles the figure of the modern fieldworker, bent on what James Clifford has called a project of "ethnographic salvage."[15] In Achebe's case, the travel that is also a condition of conventional fieldwork is figurative: the village he "visits" and recreates in his historical fiction is one of the past, from which he is separated by time, education, and experience.

The fieldwork methods associated with British Social Anthropology and pioneered in the first decades of the twentieth century required the fieldworker to develop a close rapport with the natives and to take part in native customs and rituals, as well as to observe them. Referring to the fieldworker's oscillation between empathic identification and objective analysis, Clifford writes that participant-observation entails "a delicate management of distance and proximity" (1997, 72). The narrative voice of Achebe's first novels has been described in terms that resonate with these: Okpewho asserts that the "most striking quality" of *TFA* is "its empathic account of the Igbo society," a perspective inexplicably mitigated, in his characterization, by the "objective distance" of the narrative voice (25). Similarly Carroll lauds the opening of the sequel to *TFA*, *Arrow of God*, as "an extraordinary achievement of sympathy and detachment" (1980, 183). These critics fail to recognize—or at least to explore the ramifications of—the near paradox of this description, which makes the narrative voice of *TFA* more interesting than many acknowledge. Like the traditional anthropologist, this African novelist navigates between poles of empathy and objectivity, attitudes that are potentially at odds with one another. Achebe's account of his relationship to Igbo traditions illustrates this tension:

> I was brought up in a village where the old ways were still active and alive, so I could see the remains of our tradition actually operating. At the same time I brought a certain amount of detachment to it too, because my father was a Christian missionary, and we were not fully part of the "heathen" life of the village. (Achebe 1973, 18)

Achebe is at once the insider, speaking of "our tradition," and the outside observer, regarding village ways with a certain "detachment."

Rather than compromising his authority as a representative of Igbo culture, though, *distance* emerges in Achebe's account as the necessary condition for representation:

> I think it was easier for me to observe. Many of my contemporaries who went to school with me and came from heathen families ask me today: "How did you manage to know all these things?" You see, for them these old ways were just part of life. I could look at them from a certain distance, and I was struck by them. (Achebe 1973, 18)

Achebe implies that his "heathen contemporaries" can't see the cultural forest for the trees: too close to their own customs, they fail to see them clearly. Malinowski also insinuates that cultural insiders suffer a kind of conceptual myopia in relation to their own culture: in his words, "The natives obey the forces and commands of the tribal code, but they do not comprehend them" (1984, 11). Whereas Malinowski infantilizes the natives in this statement, implying they are incapable of comprehending abstraction, Achebe expresses a similar sentiment without condescension: his unique perspective, he implies, is a factor of an inherited position. In Achebe's assessment, the distance imposed between him and the old ways "by the accident" of his birth is an asset: "The distance becomes not a separation but a bringing together like the necessary backward step which a judicious viewer may take in order to see a canvas steadily and fully" (1975, 120).[16] The aesthetic analogy transforms Achebe into that "judicious viewer," able to comprehend the canvas of Igbo culture more fully than the participants whose proximity prevents them from making sense of the details. Achebe may overstate the fortuitousness of his position: the simile also reminds us that Achebe is an artist, as well as an intellectual, and, as such, is by (self-)training and inclination a self-conscious observer.

While Achebe freely acknowledges his partial disconnection from traditional ways, at the same time, he promotes an image of himself as an intimate observer, who has "largely picked up" his knowledge of indigenous culture through conversation and personal observation—that is, through firsthand experiences (Achebe qtd. by Wren, 16–17). This characterization is somewhat misleading: as Gikandi cautions, "however appealing" the temptation to read Achebe as "an authentic voice" of his people might be, "it must be resisted because it is not possible for the writer to appeal to an original notion of Igbo culture.... Igbo reality, insofar as it is available to Achebe, comes to him (and hence to the reader) mediated by the novelist's sources, both Igbo and colonial" (1991, 31). We know, for example, that Achebe studied West African religion with Geoffrey Parrinder at University (Ezenwa-Ohaeto 1997, 42–44), and that he read the works of P. Amaury Talbot, the administrator-anthropologist, and of G. T. Basden, the missionary-anthropologist on whom the character Mr. Brown is based; Robert Wren suggests that Achebe's fiction is informed by this reading (1980, 17–18). In effacing the textual sources that inform his understanding of native life, Achebe again resembles the self-mythologizing fieldworker of the early twentieth-century, who purportedly comes to know a culture through close identification and empirical observation, not through scholarly research (see Clifford 1997).

Finally, as an African novelist writing in English, Achebe, like the traditional anthropologist, confronts the challenge of rendering indigenous experience in a foreign tongue. The non-native reader of *TFA* is reminded of the act of translation that lies behind the entire work each time she stumbles over an untranslated Igbo word. In the Preface to *Argonauts of the Western Pacific*, Malinowski stipulates that ethnographers should incorporate native phrases into their texts as a means of establishing authority, by demonstrating their supposed mastery of the indigenous language (1984, 23). With shifted emphasis, Kortenaar observes of the Igbo words that pepper Achebe's narrative, "These foreign traces in an English text refer metonymically to a whole world that cannot be adequately translated, a world that Achebe implicitly shares with the characters he writes about. The non-Igbo reader, by implication, can only achieve a mediated knowledge of that world" (Kortenaar 2003, 127). I would suggest that, like all cultural knowledge, Achebe's is also *mediated* in ways I have mentioned, though certainly he possesses what might be called a "fluency" in Igbo culture, and thus—even as his "world" is not identical to theirs—shares a great deal with the characters he represents. In my reading, rather than functioning to reinforce an "us" vs. "you" divide for the non-Igbo reader, the native phrases woven into the largely English text of *TFA* serve to linguistically render the borderland from which Achebe writes.[17]

In an essay exploring the concept of anthropology as *cultural translation,* Talal Asad asserts that the skilled translator, whether of languages in a limited sense or of cultures more generally, "seeks to reproduce the structure of an alien discourse within the translator's own language" (1986, 156). For Achebe, the situation approximates the reverse: he has argued that "The African writer . . . should aim at fashioning an English which is at once universal and able to carry his peculiar experience" (1975, 100). As several critics have argued, Achebe *indigenizes* the English language, reproducing attributes of African oral tradition in a written text.[18] Reversing Asad's formula for traditional translation, one could say that Achebe "seeks to reproduce the structure of *native* discourse within an *alien* language"; yet for a writer who has described himself as "perfectly bilingual" (119) and who has written eloquently about his alienation from ancestral traditions, the native/alien binary does not quite hold.

Hence, though I have suggested that Achebe's position vis-à-vis the Igbo has much in common with that of a traditional anthropologist—similarities the insider/outsider dichotomy would obscure—important differences mark his position as well. Unlike Malinowski among the Trobriand Islanders, Achebe is not a stranger pitching his tent among natives; he is a native son, albeit a prodigal one. The stakes are also very different for Achebe than for the traditional anthropologist: he attempts to "salvage" a "vanishing" culture not out of disinterested intellectual curiosity or the necessity of establishing professional credentials (via the disciplinary rite-of-passage, fieldwork), but rather, as a cultural nationalist interested in recuperating a culture fragmented and maligned by colonization.

In many ways, then, a more apt analogy for this African novelist at cultural crossroads is the *native anthropologist,* who complicates the inside/outside binary that governs characterizations of conventional fieldwork. Like

the postcolonial writer, the native anthropologist is liable to be read uncritical-
ly as offering an "authentic perspective," a reading that has recently met with
criticism from within the discipline. Kirin Narayan, a fieldworker and scholar
who uncomfortably bears the label in question, rejects the native/non-native
binary, suggesting that, instead, we should "view each anthropologist in terms
of shifting identifications amid a field of interpenetrating communities and
power relations" (1993, 671). Considering such factors as "education, gender,
sexual orientation, class, race, or sheer duration of contact," she points out
that the "loci along which we are aligned with or set apart from those whom
we study are multiple and in flux." In this way, her work urges a rethinking
of the relationship between cultural observers and those they observe, casting
serious doubt on "the extent to which anyone is an authentic insider" (671).
Raised in Bombay by a German-American mother and Indian father, edu-
cated in a university in the United States, and conducting fieldwork in diverse
regions in India, Narayan's own situation amply demonstrates the multiple
and shifting identifications she describes.

Achebe's relationship to the Igbo parallels the complex positioning of
the native anthropologist vis-à-vis her native informants, which scholars such
as Narayan and Clifford suggest overlaps in significant ways with that of a
traditional anthropologist. As if with Achebe in mind, Clifford writes, "Going 'out' to the field now sometimes means going 'back,' the ethnography becoming a 'notebook of a return to the native land'" (1997, 80). Like Narayan,
Clifford stresses that "'native' researchers are complexly and multiply located
vis-à-vis their worksites and interlocutors," experiencing "different degrees
of affiliation and distance" (77). He also challenges the inside/outside binary,
pointing toward a continuum model, where cultural observers move fluidly
between poles of sympathetic identification and critical explication in relation to those they study: for "even when the ethnographer is positioned as
an insider, a 'native' in her or his community, some taking of distance and
translating differences will be part of the research, analysis, and writing" (86).
Clifford suggests that for the "native researcher" as well as the traditional anthropologist, distance and translation are preconditions of ethnographic representation. As the next section argues, the narrative voice of *TFA* manifests
the varying "degrees of affiliation and distance," which typify the dynamic
relationship of all cultural observers to the field, but which is intensified in
the case of the native anthropologist.

### *Things Fall Apart:* A Dialectic of Proximity and Distance

Part I of Achebe's first novel plunges the non-native reader into the world
of the Igbo, with detailed descriptions of the people's customs, beliefs, and
ceremonies. Seamlessly woven into the narrative fabric are accounts of the
Feast of the New Yam, the negotiation of bride price, the ceremony of the

*egwugwu* (ancestral spirits), the *nso-ani* (sacrilege) of committing violence during the Week of Peace, and so on; these details, together with the numerous proverbs embodying clan wisdom that punctuate the narrative,[19] function collectively to create a rich, vivid portrait of a traditional Nigerian culture. The narrator's intimate acquaintance with Igbo culture is signaled by the ability to closely document such beliefs and practices, to use the native tongue, and to omnisciently enter into Igbo characters' minds.

Not surprisingly, then, critics have interpreted the narrative voice as emanating "from the inside." In Carroll's estimation, "The voice is that of a wise and sympathetic elder of the tribe" (1980, 31). Innes also stresses the speaker's identification with the natives' point of view: "the narrative voice is primarily a recreation of the persona which is heard in tales, history, proverbs and poetry belonging to an oral tradition; it represents a collective voice through which the artist speaks *for* his society, not as an individual apart from it—he is the chorus rather than the hero" (1990, 32). Recently, Angela F. Miri has echoed these readings, asserting that *TFA*'s "storyteller undoubtedly represents the Igbo voice or the *vox populi*" (2004, 102). Whether the voice is individuated (a tribal elder) or collective (a communal chorus), critics persist in casting Achebe and the narrator in the role of native informant for the Western reader.

Yet assertions like Innes's that the narrator "speaks *for* his society, not as an individual apart from it" will not withstand close reading: the narrator frequently stands apart, becoming (in my terms) an observer, rather than an implied participant. We are told, for example, that "Darkness held a vague terror *for these people,* even the bravest among them. Children were warned not to whistle at night for fear of evil spirits" (Achebe 1996, 7; my emphasis). These remarks clearly install distance between the narrator—who presumably is not afraid of the dark, and likely does not believe in evil spirits—and "these people," who are cowed by their fear of the night. Here the narrator is aligned more closely with non-native readers than with the Igbo perspective, and, in this mediating role, is more ethnographic observer than native informant. The move is akin to what James Buzard has called the "self-interrupting style" of ethnographic narratives, whereby the ethnographer insists that however closely s/he may identify with the natives, s/he is not really one of them (2005, 34).

For the most part, pinning down the narrative perspective is not a case of discerning whether the narrator is inside or outside native culture, but, rather, of detecting the fluid movement between these vantage points. The slipperiness of the narrative voice is evident in a passage that begins, "Umuofia was feared by all its neighbours. It was powerful in war and in magic, and its priests and medicine-men were feared in all the surrounding country" (Achebe 1996, 8). That Umuofia is "powerful in magic" is presented in a declarative sentence that renders without question or judgment the native point of view. The narrator continues, "on one point there was general agreement—the active principle in that medicine had been an old woman with one leg. In fact, the medicine itself was called *agadi-nwayi,* or old woman" (8–9). This story of the origin of native belief is flagged as consistent with the clan world view: they agree that the old woman with one leg is the source of their reputation in magic. At the same time, the anecdote is consonant with anthropological accounts of primitive cultures that regard disability as a source of metaphysical power. Thus the narrator subtly provides an alternate frame of reference—a way of understanding Umuofia's reputation that accords with Western disbelief in magic. Rather than operating from a fixed viewpoint, the narrator moves freely between divergent perspectives.

Another passage that illustrates the narrative's liminal perspective—jockeying between inside and outside perspectives in ethnographic fashion—is the description of the Oracle, Agbala, in Chapter Three:

> No one had ever beheld Agbala, except his priestess. . . . It was said that when such a spirit appeared, the man saw it vaguely in the darkness, but never heard its voice. Some people even said that they had heard the spirits flying and flapping their wings against the roof of the cave. (Achebe 1996, 12)

The passage is respectful of the Oracle's sacredness to the Igbo: the narrator does not overtly proclaim disbelief. Yet the existence of Agbala is left in question: no one has seen it, except in dubious conditions ("vaguely in the darkness") and no one has "heard its voice." Indeed, what can be heard in the cave—the "flapping of wings"—above all conjures the image of bats, the probable denizens of a dark, dank place. Hence, again, the narrator subtly provides an alternative frame of reference, accommodating skepticism alongside Igbo belief.

The very few critics who avoid the reductive insider reading of *TFA* tend to equate the intermittent distance of the narrative to which I have been alluding with an anthropological perspective. For instance, Gikandi observes that the narrator at times "adopts distance and represents the Igbo as if they were an anthropological 'other'" (1996, 46). Similarly, Kortenaar notes that Achebe occasionally "lapses into the knowing tone of the anthropologist" (2003, 132), as in the glossary, when he defines several Igbo terms with "thoroughgoing disbelief."[20] While usefully complicating naïve ethnographic readings that fail to problematize the narrator's insiderness, these critics operate from an equally fallacious assumption that an anthropological perspective is inherently alienated. In doing so, they fail to realize that the anthropological perspective itself mediates between near and far, inside and outside, distance and proximity. They conflate distance and disbelief with the alien perspective of an anthropologist, rather than recognizing that the anthropological voice mediates between ostensible native and foreign perspectives—alternately *suspending* disbelief, to closely identify with a native perspective, and explicating belief, from an external vantage point.

This is more than a question of semantics. By reading the narration's often overlooked complexity as *ethnographic,* I hope not only to underscore the novel's artistry, but also to usefully complicate our understanding of ethnographic relationships themselves. When Achebe's best critics reverse the more common "naïve ethnographic reading" that I've been discussing by equating the novel's anthropological perspective with "a view from *outside,*" they unwittingly replicate the kind of dichotomous thinking Achebe himself so assiduously avoids in his nuanced narrative. On a stylistic level, the slippery narrative voice manifests the ongoing process of positioning and repositioning oneself at cultural crossroads.

Acknowledging inconsistencies in perspective that most Achebe critics ignore, Gikandi argues that the ambivalent narrative voice signals contradictions inherent within Igbo culture, contradictions highlighted by the character of Nwoye, who functions as an internal critic of such practices as the disposing of twins and the killing of Ikemefuna. For Gikandi, it is erroneous to read the narrator as either a representative insider or a unified, collective voice because a stable field of social values doesn't exist in the novel: precolonial Umuofia is represented as "a society with various voices and conflicting interests" (1996, 45). While taking Gikandi's point, I would stress that the fluctuations of the narrative voice also express the shifting affiliations of the author, who, like the native anthropologist, is pulled between the values and traditions of sometimes conflicting cultural frameworks.

Another notable exception to the reductive insider reading is that of Abdul JanMohamed, who interprets the novel's balancing act between sympathy and objective distance—or, in his terms, between "sacred" and "secular" perspectives—as narrative "double consciousness." JanMohamed conceives of this dualism as the author's creative solution to a dilemma he describes in this way: Achebe is "challenged with the unenviable task of ensuring that his characters do not seem foolish because they believe in the absence of [the] border [between the sacred and the secular], while he is obliged to acknowledge it for the same reason"; "double consciousness," then, is the simultaneous "awareness of the border and its deep repression" (1984, 32–33). Rather than serving to pander to a Western audience who will regard native belief with possible disdain (by regarding the characters as "foolish"), I have argued that the narrative tension between belief and skepticism registers the author's own shifting frame of reference, one akin to that of an ethnographic observer, continually navigating between indigenous and foreign viewpoints. Moreover, in its maneuverings among different Igbo as well as Western perspectives, the narrative consciousness that emerges is more than double; it has multiple, shifting permutations, as a final example will show.

Illustrating the narrative's ever-shifting vantage point is Chapter Ten's description of the trial, presided over by nine *egwugwu* (masked ancestral spirits) and their leader, the "Evil Forest."[21] To begin with, conjuring the momentousness of the ceremony, the *egwugwu* are deemed "the most powerful and the most secret cult in the clan" (Achebe 1996, 63); their voices are represented as "guttural and awesome" (62). The description continues, throwing the reader into the center of the action: "The *egwugwu* house was now a pandemonium of quavering voices: *Aru oyim de de de de dei!* Filled the air as the spirits of the ancestors, just emerged from the earth, greeted themselves in their esoteric language" (62–63). From the vantage point of the believer, the voices are presented as those of the ancestral spirits. The Igbo greeting remains untranslated, such that the narrator serves as the custodian of knowledge unshared with the reader. Yet the word "esoteric" signals that members of the clan also remain in the dark as to the significance of the utterance: "No woman ever asked questions" about the exclusively male cult (63). From a position of privileged omniscience, then, the narrator moves not only between an inside and an outside perspective, but also between the semi-opaque boundaries that divide the male and female spheres. This narrative flexibility resembles the shifting field relationships of the native anthropologist, as described by Narayan, with points of affiliation and disaffiliation that are "multiple and in flux" (Narayan 671).

It is only after building up a sense of the ceremony's significance from a point of view identified with the initiate that the narrator steps back from the event to give another perspective:

> Okonkwo's wives, and perhaps other women as well might have noticed that the second *egwugwu* had the springy walk of Okonkwo. And they might also have noticed that Okonkwo was not among the titled men and elders who sat behind the row of *egwugwu*. But if they thought these things they kept them within themselves. The *egwugwu* with the springy walk was one of the dead fathers of the clan. (Achebe 1996, 64)

The passage begins by subtly casting doubt on the native belief in ancestral spirits—*unmasking* the *egwugwu*, as it were—by intimating that one of them has "the springy walk of Okonkwo," and thus is a man, not a spirit. The narrative voice draws the female characters into complicity with its skeptical perspective, by tentatively attributing to them a glimmering awareness of Okonkwo's telltale walk; they "might have noticed" what the narrator knows for certain: there is a human being beneath the ceremonial disguise. If Wren is correct when he asserts that the Igbo perceive the *egwugwu* not as "mortals masked but [as] transcendent—even transubstantiate—beings, living presences of the dead fathers of the nine villages of Umuofia" (Achebe 1996, 35), then calling attention to Okonkwo's disguise represents a major breach with the insider's view. An episode toward the end of the novel lends support for this reading: when Enoch publicly unmasks an *egwugwu*, "reduc[ing] its immortal prestige in the eyes of the uninitiated," he is represented as "killing . . . an ancestral spirit," thereby throwing Umofia into a state of "confusion," and effectively presaging the "death" of the "soul of the tribe" (131–132). The language literalizes the belief that the *egwugwu* embody the spirits of the clan, as does the closing sentence of the passage quoted above, which rejoins the perspective of the devout believer, by affirming that the *egwugwu* in question actually "was one of the dead fathers of the clan." Thus the narrator inhabits shifting and sometimes contradictory perspectives, along a continuum that stretches from the most credulous believer to the skeptic or cultural outsider.

Through these maneuverings, the narrative voice replicates the dynamic positioning of the native anthropologist—at once part of Igbo culture and apart from it, a participant and a judicious observer, at turns closely identifying with various Igbo perspectives and "taking the distance" that is the precondition for ethnographic representation.

### Conclusion

It is tempting to read *TFA* as a voice from the inside for a number of reasons. The novel itself encourages this reading, with its detailed documentation of cultural practices, its fluid incorporation of native words and phrases, and its juxtaposition of the principal narrative perspective with the reductive and distorted view of outsiders like the District Commissioner. By construing his narrative as combating the misinformed representations of colonial writers, Achebe has contributed to the impression of the book's documentary realism.

Additionally, like other postcolonial literature, *TFA* has entered the Western canon as a kind of sequel to British Modernism, one that is perceived as providing a corrective to the ideological blind-spots of writers from the earlier historical period. Frequently partnered with Joseph Conrad's *Heart of Darkness* in introductory level courses and British literature surveys (including my own), *TFA* appears on the syllabus to show the "other side" of the colonial encounter. Too often this impulse leads critics and teachers to regard postcolonial writers as rendering the experience of colonized and pre-colonial societies in an unproblematic, unmediated way.

Yet this mode of reading oversimplifies the relationship between Achebe and traditional Igbo culture, threatening to fetishize the voice of the former colonial subject, while ignoring the complexity of the narrative voice, which is more dynamic than such readings acknowledge. Dubbing the novel ethnographic or anthropological is equally reductive, when these terms are understood to imply a kind of photographic realism, and when the author's indigenous status is assumed to vouch for an uncomplicated textual authenticity. The opposing, but still misguided, assumption that the novel's anthropological perspective is inherently *alienated* likewise simplifies the dynamic ethnographic relationship, which the novel subtly reproduces at the level of style.

Notwithstanding these cautions, I believe that literature is one of the most valuable tools we possess for imagining life in other cultures. Thus we should not stop reading ethnographically, but rather, by appreciating the complexity of the ethnographic project, especially when undertaken by a "native son," we can better appreciate the corresponding complexities of narratives that emerge from cultural crossroads.

## Notes

1. In *Morning Yet on Creation Day,* Achebe terms this voice the "sedate prose of the district-officer-government anthropologist" of the early twentieth-century (1975, 5).

2. In the sequel to *TFA, Arrow of God,* we learn that the Commissioner *has* profited from colonial anthropology, since his book has "become a colonial classic, a manual of empire-building," as Nahem Yousaf notes (2003, 39).

3. The phrase is not Achebe's, but rather an allusion to the well-known and seminal work of postcolonial criticism, *The Empire Writes Back* (1989).

4. According to Isidore Okpewho, as of 2003, the novel had been translated into nearly sixty languages and sold close to nine million copies. Charles Larson states that following Nigerian independence, *TFA* became required reading at the secondary level in Nigeria (Okpewho 2003, 27), but my focus in this essay is primarily the novel's critical reception in the U.S.

5. Hassoldt Davis, *Saturday Review,* 1959 (qtd in Larson 15-16).

6. Other respondents to the survey stated that they wanted to "give students a sense of African history and the effects of colonialism on Africa, as well as to dispel stereotypes about Africa," and many stressed that the novel provides an accessible, evocative introduction to African literature or to post-colonial literature more generally (Lindfors 1991, 15).

7. I employ "authoritative" as a relative, not an absolute, term, by which I mean "well informed." The authority I would ascribe to *TFA*—as to any well-founded historical and/or ethnographic representation—is that of what James Clifford calls a "partial construction" and what Donna Harraway calls "situated knowledge."

8. See, for example Eleni Coundouriotis, who has demonstrated that African novels frequently have been read (by Africans as well as Europeans and North Americans) as bearing ethnographic witness to their authors' cultures, such that

their historical specificity is muted or erased (1999, 4–5). Elizabeth Jane Harrison identifies a similar tendency in scholarship on the fiction of Zora Neale Hurston and Mary Hunter Austin whose "literary strategies" have been neglected "in favor of an analysis of the cultural context of their narratives" (1997, 44). Likewise, Henry Louis Gates complains that European and American critics too often appropriate African and African-American literature as "anthropological evidence" about these cultures (1984, 4).

9. Booker, *The African Novel in English* (1998, 65). As early as 1969, G. D. Killam makes an almost equivalent statement: "So much has been written about the anthropological and sociological significance of *Things Fall Apart* and *Arrow of God*—their evocation of traditional nineteenth- and earlier twentieth-century Ibo village life— . . . that the overall excellence of these books as pieces of fiction, as works of art, has been obscured" (Booker 1998, 1).

10. Pointing out that Achebe's fellow Nigerian writer, Wole Soyinka, has labeled Achebe a "chronicler" of the past, Nahem Yousaf similarly objects that Achebe's fiction has been assessed in too limiting terms, "according to its verisimilitude, its facility for reflecting external reality" (2003, 4).

11. Since the publication of James Clifford and George Marcus's *Writing Culture* (1986), there has been general acknowledgement within the field of anthropology that the classic genre associated with fieldwork, the ethnography, is a *text*—that the experience of fieldwork is mediated by language which shapes/constructs that experience.

12. I am using *meta* in the sense connoted by the term *metafiction*, meaning fiction that self-consciously alludes to its own artificiality or literariness, announcing, in effect, "I am fiction." To read *meta-ethnographically*, by extension, means to read in a way that is self-reflexive of ethnographic practice, attentive to the dynamism inherent in the ethnographic voice.

13. See "The Novelist as Teacher" (Achebe 1975, 67–73).

14. Cultural holism in British Social Anthropology has its roots in the discipline's first text book, E. B. Tylor's 1871 *Primitive Culture*, which defined culture as a "complex whole." Primitive villages, believed to be isolated from outside contact, organically integrated, and relatively simple in their organization, were regarded as ideal "laboratories" for studying culture (see for example Mead 2001, 6). However, the idea of the pristine native village has been critiqued in recent years as a romantic construct: for example, Arjun Appadurai writes, "Natives, people confined to and by the places to which they belong, groups unsullied by contact with a larger world, have probably never existed" (1988, 39). See also Clifford (1997).

15. Cf. Coundouriotos, who argues that "unlike the 'salvage ethnography' of European ethnographers who sought, as Clifford has explained, to preserve what was already lost, Achebe's authoethnography aims at affirming the contemporaneity of native cultures with those of the West" (1999, 38).

16. Ruth Benedict also employs an aesthetic metaphor in discussing the anthropologist's unique perspective: for Benedict, a kind of "gestalt" vision enables the cultural observer to make sense of a foreign culture, such that "hundreds of details fall into over-all patterns" (1946, 12). "Pattern" becomes an operative trope for Benedict, evident in the title of her 1934 anthropological classic, *Patterns of Culture*. For an analysis of the relationship between Benedict's concept of culture and the approach to art of literary studies' New Critics (both seeking organic unity and a complex whole in their objects of study), see Manganaro (2002, 151–174).

17. The allusion is to Gloria Andzaldua's innovative and powerful textualization of bi-lingual, bi-cultural experience in *Borderland/ La Frontiera,* which poetically theorizes the experience of literally and symbolically inhabiting the borderland between Mexico and Texas, from a Chicana perspective.

18. See JanMohammed (1984), Kortenaar (2003), Booker (1998).

19. By conjuring the effect of language in translation, the novel's proverbs evoke the semblance of cultural authenticity, yet ironically, it has been well established that these proverbs at best loosely approximate Igbo sayings, and in some cases are Achebe's pure invention. See Shelton (1969, 86–87).

20. See footnote 21.

21. Even the definition of *egwugwu* in the book's glossary reveals a shifting relationship to Igbo culture: prior to the 1996 edition, the term was glossed as "a masquerader who impersonates one of the ancestral spirits of the village" (Achebe 1996, 149)—a definition that reflects "thoroughgoing disbelief," as Kortenaar notes (2003, 130). The most recent edition of the text revises this definition to "the masked spirit, representing the ancestral spirits of the village" (liii)—wording that presumably more closely aligns with the Igbo perspective.

## Works Cited

Achebe, Chinua. 1996. *Things Fall Apart.* 1958. Reprint. Oxford: Heinemann.

———. 1973. "The Role of the Writer in a New Nation" (1964). In *African Writers on African Writing,* ed. G. D. Killam. Evanston: Northwestern University Press.

———. 1975. *Morning Yet on Creation Day.* Garden City, New York: Anchor Press.

Appadurai, Arjun. 1988. "Putting Hierarchy in its Place." *Cultural Anthropology,* 3.1: 36–49.

Asad, Talal. 1986. "The Concept of Cultural Translation in British Social Anthropology." In *Writing Culture: The Poetics and Politics of Ethnography,* ed. James Clifford and George E. Marcus. Berkeley: University of California Press.

Benedict, Ruth. 1946. *The Chrysanthemum and the Sword; Patterns of Japanese Culture.* Boston, Houghton Mifflin.

Booker, M. Keith. 1998. *The African Novel in English: An Introduction.* Portsmouth, NH: Heinemann.

Buzard, James. 2005. *Disorienting Fiction: the Authoethnographic Work of Victorian Fiction.* Princeton University Press.

Carroll, David. 1980. *Chinua Achebe.* London: Macmillan Press Ltd.

Clifford, James. 1988. *The Predicament of Culture: Twentieth-Century Ethnography, Literature, and Art.* Cambridge: Harvard University Press.

———. 1997. *Routes: Travel and Translation in the Late Twentieth Century.* Harvard University Press.

Clifford, James, and George Marcus, ed. 1986. *Writing Culture: The Poetics and Politics of Ethnography.* Berkeley: University of California Press.

Coundouriotis, Eleni. 1999. *Claiming History: Colonialism, Ethnography, and the Novel.* New York: Columbia University Press.

Ezenwa-Ohaeto. 1997. *Chinua Achebe: A Biography.* Oxford: James Currey Press.

Fernea, Elizabeth. 1989. "The Case of Sitt Marie Rose: An Ethnographic Novel from the Modern Middle East." In *Literature and Anthropology,* ed. Philip A. Dennis & Wendell Aycock. Lubbock: Texas Tech University Press.

Flowers, Betty Sue, ed. 1989. *Bill Moyers: A World of Ideas: Conversations with Thoughtful Men and Women about American Life today and the Ideas Shaping Our Future.* NY: Doubleday.

Gates, Henry Louis, Jr., ed. 1984. *Black Literature and Literary Theory.* New York: Methuen.

Gikandi, Simon. 1991. *Reading Chinua Achebe: Language and Ideology in Fiction.* 1991. London: James Currey Publishers.

———. 1996. "Chinua Achebe and the Invention of African Literature." Preface to *Things Fall Apart.* Oxford: Heinemann.

Griffiths, Gareth. 1978. "Language and Action in the Novels of Chinua Achebe." In *Critical Perspectives on Chinua Achebe,* ed. C. L. Innes and Bernth Lindfors. Washington, D. C.: Three Continents Press.

Harrison, Elizabeth Jane. 1997. "Zora Neale Hurston and Mary Hunter Austin's Ethnographic Fiction: New Modernist Narratives." In *Unmanning Modernism: Gendered Re-Readings,* ed. Elizabeth Jane Harrison and Shirley Peterson. Knoxville: University of Tennessee Press.

Huggan, Graham. 1994. "Anthropologists and Other Frauds." *Comparative Literature,* 46.2 (Spring): 113–128.

Innes, C. L. 1990. *Chinua Achebe.* Cambridge: Cambridge University Press.

JanMohamed, Abdul. 1984. "Sophisticated Primitivism: The Syncretism of Oral and Literate Modes in Achebe's *Things Fall Apart.*" *Ariel* 15: 4, 19–39.

Kalu, Anthonia C. 2002. "Achebe and Duality in Igbo Thought." In *Modern Critical Interpretations: Chinua Achebe's* Things Fall Apart, ed. Harold Bloom. Philadelphia: Chelsea House Press.

Killam, G. D. 1977. *The Novels of Chinua Achebe.* 1969. Reprint. London: Heinemann.

Kortenaar, Neil ten. 2003. "How the Center is Made to Hold in *Things Fall Apart.*" In *Chinua Achebe's* Things Fall Apart: *A Casebook,* ed. Isidore Okpewho. Oxford University Press.

Larson, Charles. 1971. *The Emergence of African Fiction.* Bloomington: Indiana University Press.

Lindfors, Bernth, ed. 1991. *Approaches to Teaching Achebe's* Things Fall Apart. New York: MLA.

———. 1997. *Conversations with Chinua Achebe.* Jackson: University Press of Mississippi.

Malinowski, Bronislaw. 1984. *Argonauts of the Western Pacific.* 1922. Reprint. Prospect Heights, Illinois: Waveland.

Manganaro, Marc. 2002. *Culture, 1922: The Emergence of a Concept.* Princeton: Princeton University Press.

Mead, Margaret. 2001. *Coming of Age in Samoa.* 1928. Reprint. New York: HarperCollins.

Miri, Angela F. 2004. "The Survival of Oral Speech Patterns in Modern African Literature: The Example of Chinua Achebe's Fiction." In *Emerging Perspectives on Chinua Achebe, Volume II: Iskinka, the Artistic Purpose: Chinua Achebe and the Theory of African Literature,* ed. Ernest N. Emenyonu and Iniobong I. Uko. Trenton, NJ: African World Press.

Narayan, Kirin. 1993. "How Native is a 'Native' Anthropologist?" *American Anthropologist, New Series.* 95.3 (September): 671–686.

Ogbaa, Kalu. 1999. *Understanding* Things Fall Apart: *A Student Casebook to Issues, Sources, and Historical Documents.* Westport, CT: Greenwood Press.

Okpewho, Isidore, ed. 2003. *Chinua Achebe's* Things Fall Apart: *A Casebook.* Oxford: Oxford University Press.

Quayson, Ato. 2003. "Realism, Criticism, and the Disguises of Both: A Reading of Chinua Achebe's *Things Fall Apart* with an Evaluation of the Criticism Relating to It." In *Chinua Achebe's* Things Fall Apart: *A Casebook,* ed. Isidore Okpewho. Oxford: Oxford University Press.

Rhoads, Diana Akers. 1993. "Culture in Chinua Achebe's *Things Fall Apart.*" *African Studies Review.* 36.2 (September): 61–72.

Rowell, Charles H. 2003. "An Interview with Chinua Achebe." In *Chinua Achebe's* Things Fall Apart: *A Casebook,* ed. Isidore Okpewho. Oxford: Oxford University Press.

Shelton, Austin J. 1969. "The 'Palm-Oil' of Language: Proverbs in Chinua Achebe's Novels." *Modern Language Quarterly.* 30: 86–111.

Stocking, Jr., George W. 1983. "The Ethnographer's Magic: Fieldwork in British Anthropology from Tylor to Malinowski." In *Observers Observed: Essays on Ethnographic Fieldwork.* Milwaukee: University Wisconsin Press.

Wren, Robert. 1980. *Achebe's World: The Historical and Cultural Context of the Novels of Chinua Achebe.* Washington, D.C.: Three Continents Press.

Yousaf, Nahem. 2003. *Chinua Achebe.* Devon: Northcote House Publishers Ltd.

# *Chronology*

1930      Born November 16 in the village of Ogidi in eastern Nigeria to Janet Hoegbunam Achebe and Isaiah Okafor Achebe, a catechist for the Church Missionary Society. The name Chinua is an abbreviation for Chinualumogu ("may God fight on my behalf"), in effect a prayer and a philosophical statement reflecting a belief in and desire for stability in life.

1935      The Achebe family returns to Ogidi. The storytelling tradition now exists side by side with book-reading sessions in Society's school. Later on, when looking back at his early days, Chinua remembers living in two worlds at once—the Christian world of hymns in church and the poetry of the litany, and the traditional religion of the Igbo culture, where masquerades and festival foods play an important role.

1936      Achebe begins school at St. Philip's Central School, Akpakaogwe Ogidi. The school itself was constructed of mud blocks in the shape of a *T* and surrounded by mango trees, which provided snacks for the children. After a week in religious class, the Reverend Nelson Ezekwesili sends him to a higher infant school because of his intelligence.

1938      Achebe learns English. He is in Standard Two when World War II begins.

| | |
|---|---|
| 1939–1943 | Chinua is taught by the inspirational S. N. C. Okonkwo from Standard Two upward. He excels in reading English and, among other things, earns Okonkwo's respect for his knowledge of the Igbo version of the Bible. Among the books Chinua reads during his primary-school days are *A Midsummer Night's Dream* and *Pilgrim's Progress.* |
| 1944 | Chinua enters Government College, Umuahia, one of the best schools in West Africa. The new principal, named Hicks, said to be a kind and gentle soul, carried on the tradition of Robert Fisher, emphasizing a careful selection of qualified boys for admission and academic excellence. The boys are expected to lead a very organized life, at times at the pace of a military school. In late 1944, William Simpson replaces Hicks as principal. Simpson, a Cambridge graduate who had spent about twenty-six years in the colonial service in Nigeria, was dedicated to improving the already high academic standards at Umuahia. During his tenure, Simpson introduces the "Textbook Act," which states certain times during which text book reading is not permissible, leaving sports, physical exercise, or time to become acquainted with the extensive college library as the only alternative. Chinua benefits from the Simpson "method," reading such books as *Up from Slavery, Gulliver's Travels, The Prisoner of Zenda, Oliver Twist, Tom Brown's Schooldays,* and *Treasure Island.* Among Chinua's professors are Adrian P. L. Slater, who teaches logic by emphasizing scientific methods of observation and experimentation, and inculcates the habits of writing correct English, and Charles Low, an Australian educated at Melbourne and Oxford universities, both a poet and playwright, and who had practically memorized *Paradise Lost.* |
| 1948–1953 | In 1948, Achebe enrolls at University College, Ibadan, as a member of the first class to attend this new school. Although his original intention is to study medicine, Achebe soon switches to English literary studies with a syllabus that is almost identical to the honors degree program at the University of London. Toward the end of his career at Ibadan, Chinua is greatly influenced by the lectures of Alex Rodgers on Thomas Hardy's *Far from the Madding Crowd.* |

1950        As a student in the Faculty of Arts, Chinua begins to express himself as a writer. He contributes stories, essays, and sketches to the *University Herald*. These stories are later published in 1972 in *Girls at War and Other Stories*.

1953        Achebe graduates from the University College, Ibadan. The degree examinations reflect the strict and rigid desire of the university to maintain the highest standards. By the time he graduates, his intellectual horizon and social understanding have been enhanced through his interaction with a variety of Nigerians and foreigners.

1954        Begins teaching English at the Merchants of Light School at Oba under the supervision of A. E. D. Mgbemena. As the school was in its infancy, the quarters for staff and students were inadequate. The dormitories were made of mud and coated with cement and there was at that time neither electricity nor piped water—the students had to fetch the water from either a neighboring village or a stream. His tenure at the Merchants of Light Secondary School is brief. About four months after his arrival, he receives a letter from the Nigerian Broadcasting Service inviting him for an interview, which is quickly followed by an offer of employment as senior broadcasting officer from around the middle of 1954.

1955        In the January issue of *Radio Times,* Chinua and Angela Beattie receive acknowledgment for their role in educating their listeners.

1956        Early in the year, Chinua Achebe and Bisi Onabanjo, editor of the *Radio Times,* are nominated by the NBS, Lagos to attend the BBC Staff School in London organized for participants from Africa, Australia, New Zealand, Canada, and Asia. The training was intended to emphasize "hands-on" experience within the UK broadcasting system.

1957        Goes to London to embark on a twelve-year career as producer for the British Broadcasting Corporation Staff School, where he meets the British novelist and literary critic Gilbert Phelps.

1958        *Things Fall Apart* published. The novel is published two years before Nigerian independence is gained in 1960.

| 1960 | Writes two short stories, one titled "Chike's School Days" which appears in the *Rotarian,* and "Macke," which is published in the anthology *Reflections,* edited by Frances Adeinola, who was working at the NBS in Lagos as head of Talks. Also publishes *No Longer at Ease.* |
|------|------|
| 1961 | Achebe appointed director of the Voice of Nigeria (external broadcasting) by the Nigerian Broadcasting Corporation. On December 10, he marries Christie Chinwe Okoli at Ibadan. |
| 1962 | Birth of his first child, a daughter named Chinelo, on July 11. *The Sacrificial Egg, and Other Short Stories* published. |
| 1964 | Birth of his second child, a boy named Ikechukwu. His name means "through the might of God." *Arrow of God* published. Publishes "The Role of the Writer in the New Nation," *Nigeria Magazine,* June 1964. In September, Chinua participates in the first Commonwealth Literature Conference to be held at the University of Leeds, where he presents a paper on "The Novelist as Teacher." |
| 1966 | *A Man of the People* published in January. Date of publication closely coincides with the first military coup d'état in Nigeria. Achebe resigns from his job with the Nigerian Broadcasting Corporation due to the increasing persecution of Nigerians and returns to his homeland. *Chike and the River* published. |
| 1967 | On May 24, his third child, a son named Chidi, is born. His name means "There is a God." The Eastern Region of Nigeria declares itself an independent state called Biafra following a thirty-month civil war. Achebe gives unwavering support for the young nation, so much so that he declines an offer by Northwestern University to teach in the Gwendolen M. Carter program of African Studies. |
| 1968 | Achebe declines a second offer, made by a letter dated January 9, from Gwendolen Carter. On August 25, he delivers paper on "The African Writer and the Biafran Cause" to a political-science seminar at Makere University College, Kampala. |
| 1969 | Serves as chairman of National Guidance Committee at Umuahia. In January, writes a poem titled "Air Raid," a requiem on a devastating air strike at Umuahia. |

1970        On March 7, his fourth child, Nwandois, born. Her name, which means "a child under which the parents would shelter," signifies their anticipation of a time after the war.

1971        *Beware, Soul Brother, and Other Poems* published. Republished as *Christmas in Biafra and Other Poems* in 1973. Publishes *The Insider: Stories of War and Peace from Nigeria.*

1972        Publishes *Girls at War and Other Stories.* Achebe receives D.Litt. degree from Dartmouth College.

1973        Achebe's impact in France is apparent with the publication of *Chinua Achebe et la tragedie de l'historie,* a critical study of his work, by Thomas Melone.

1974        Achebe lecturing at the University of Massachusetts, Amherst.

1975        Achebe publishes a volume of fifteen essays, *Morning Yet on Creation Day,* written between 1962 and 1973, on various literary and political subjects. Achebe decides to accept an appointment at the University of Connecticut in Storrs.

1976        Achebe leaves University of Connecticut to return to Nigeria. Among many responsibilities, he teaches a course in modern African fiction at the University of Nigeria, Nsukka.

1977        Publishes two children's books, *The Flute* and *The Drum,* based on Igboland folktales.

1978        Publishes a poem, "The American Youngster in Rags," in *Okike* and writes essay, "The Truth of Fiction," presented at the University of Ife.

1979        Delivers his essay, "Impediments to Dialogue Between North and South," at Berlin International Literature Festival held June 21 to July 15.

1980        In April, attends conference of the African Literature Association in Gainesville, Florida. Meets James Baldwin for the first time.

1982        Attends meetings and engages in discussions regarding general elections to be held in 1983. Joins People's Redemption Party (PRP) in late 1982.

1983        *The Trouble with Nigeria* published.

| | |
|---|---|
| 1984 | Achebe gives lecture at University of Port Harcourt, "Reflections on Nigeria's Political Culture." |
| 1985 | Heinemann publishes *Short Stories,* edited by Achebe and Lyn Innes. |
| 1986 | *The World of the Ogbanje* published. Achebe awarded the Nigerian National Merit Award for the second time. In his acceptance speech, Achebe notes the essential role played by literature in the comprehensive goal of a developing nation such as Nigeria. |
| 1987 | *Anthills of the Savannah* published. |
| 1988 | *The University and the Leadership Factor in Nigerian Politics* published. *Hopes and Impediments: Selected Essays, 1965–1987* published. |
| 1989 | *A Tribute to James Baldwin* published. Appointed a Distinguished Professor of English at City College of the City University of New York. Receives Callaloo Award for his contributions to World Literature. Publishes first issue of *African Commentary: A Journal for People of African Descent,* in America. |
| 1990 | Achebe birthday symposium held at the University of Nigeria, Nsukka, under the direction of Edith Ihekweazu. Achebe also accepts invitation to become Charles P. Stevenson Professor of Literature at Bard College. Many new critical works on Achebe are published. |
| 1993 | Achebe travels to University of Cambridge in January to deliver the annual Asby Lecture at Clare Hall on "The Education of a 'British Protected Child,'" which was subsequently published in the *Cambridge Review.* Toward the end of the year, the political situation in Nigeria has degenerated, with the military government canceling a scheduled election. In November, Achebe is awarded the Langston Hughes Medallion at a celebration sponsored by the City University of New York. |
| 2000 | Publishes *Home and Exile,* a collection of essays presented as the McMillan-Steward Lectures at Harvard University in 1998. |

2002          Awarded German Booksellers Peace Prize for promoting
              human understanding through literature.

2007          Awarded Man Booker International Prize for producing
              a body of work that has added significantly to world
              literature.

# *Contributors*

HAROLD BLOOM is Sterling Professor of the Humanities at Yale University. He is the author of 30 books, including *Shelley's Mythmaking* (1959), *The Visionary Company* (1961), *Blake's Apocalypse* (1963), *Yeats* (1970), *A Map of Misreading* (1975), *Kabbalah and Criticism* (1975), *Agon: Toward a Theory of Revisionism* (1982), *The American Religion* (1992), *The Western Canon* (1994), and *Omens of Millennium: The Gnosis of Angels, Dreams, and Resurrection* (1996). *The Anxiety of Influence* (1973) sets forth Professor Bloom's provocative theory of the literary relationships between the great writers and their predecessors. His most recent books include *Shakespeare: The Invention of the Human* (1998), a 1998 National Book Award finalist; *How to Read and Why* (2000); *Genius: A Mosaic of One Hundred Exemplary Creative Minds* (2002); *Hamlet: Poem Unlimited* (2003); *Where Shall Wisdom Be Found?* (2004); and *Jesus and Yahweh: The Names Divine* (2005). In 1999, Professor Bloom received the prestigious American Academy of Arts and Letters Gold Medal for Criticism. He has also received the International Prize of Catalonia, the Alfonso Reyes Prize of Mexico, and the Hans Christian Andersen Bicentennial Prize of Denmark.

KWADWO OSEI-NYAME is a lecturer in African literature at the School of African and Oriental Studies, University of London. His interests include African literature and nationalism and African cultural studies with reference to the Akan of Ghana and the Igbo of Nigeria. He has published actively on African literature.

D. N. MKHIZE is in the doctoral program in linguistics at the University of Illinois, Urbana-Champaign. Her scholarly interest is in which sociolinguistic theories can be applied to the analysis and understanding of the potential role that African languages, with a particular emphasis on Zulu, can play in the South African legal domain.

PATRICK C. NNOROMELE is associate professor/chaplain in the department of philosophy and religion at Eastern Kentucky University. He teaches courses in the African experience.

RAVIT REICHMAN is the Robert and Nancy Carney Assistant Professor of English at Brown University. She has published articles on Holocaust testimony, law and culture, legal character, Virginia Woolf and torts, colonial law, Albert Camus, and the Nuremberg trials.

JOSEPH R. SLAUGHTER is associate professor of English and comparative literature at Columbia University. He is author of *Human Rights, Inc.: The World Novel, Narrative Form, and International Law* (2007).

MAC FENWICK teaches at Trent University in Peterborough, Ontario. His 2002 dissertation at Queens University was "Perilous Adventures: Imagining the Eschatological Unity of Local and Global." He has written articles on postcolonial literature.

OLIVER LOVESEY is associate professor of English at the University of British Columbia, Okanagan. He wrote *The Clerical Character in George Eliot's Fiction* (1991) and *Ngũgĩwa Thiong'o* (2000).

FRANK SALAMONE is professor and chair in the department of sociology at Iona University. His books include *The Yanomami and Their Interpreters: Fierce People or Fierce Interpreters?* (1997) and *Encyclopedia of Religious Rites, Rituals, and Festivals* (2004), which he edited.

ANDREA POWELL WOLFE is an instructor in women's studies at Ball State University.

CAREY SNYDER is associate professor of English at Ohio University. She wrote *British Fiction and Cross-Cultural Encounters: Ethnographic Modernism from Wells to Woolf* (2008).

# Bibliography

Agetua, John, ed. *Critics on Chinua Achebe, 1970–1976*. Benin City, Nigeria: Agetua, 1977.

Beckham, Jack M. "Achebe's *Things Fall Apart.*" *Explicator* 60:4 (Summer 2002): 229–231.

Carroll, David. *Chinua Achebe*. New York: St. Martin's Press, 1980.

Counihan, Clare. "Reading the Figure of Woman in African Literature: Psychoanalysis, Difference, and Desire." *Research in African Literatures* 38:2 (Summer 2007): 161–180.

Egudu, Romanus N. "Achebe and the Igbo Narrative Tradition." *Research in African Literatures* 12 (1981): 43–54.

Ekpo, Denis. "Chinua Achebe's Early Anti-Imperialism in the Court of Postcolonial Theory." *Commonwealth Essays and Studies* 27:2 (Spring 2005), pp. 27–43.

Emenyonu, Ernest. *The Rise of the Igbo Novel*. Ibadan: Oxford University Press, 1978.

———, ed. *Emerging Perspectives on Chinua Achebe*. Volume 1. *Omenka the Master Artist: Critical Perspectives on Achebe's Fiction*. Trenton, NJ: Africa World, 2004.

Ezenwa-Ohaeto. *Chinua Achebe: A Biography*. Oxford: James Currey; Bloomington: Indiana University Press, 1997.

Fenwick, Mac. "Realising Irony's Post/Colonial Promise: Global Sense and Local Meaning in *Things Fall Apart* and 'Ruins of a Great House'." *Kunapipi: Journal of Postcolonial Writing* 28:1 (2006): 8–21.

Gagiano, Annie H. *Achebe, Head, Marechera: On Power and Change in Africa*. Boulder: Lynne Rienner Publishers, 2000.

Gates, Henry Louis, Jr., ed. *Black Literature and Literary Theory*. New York: Methuen, 1984.

Gikandi, Simon. *Reading Chinua Achebe: Language and Ideology in Fiction*. London, Portsmouth, New Hampshire, Nairobi: J. Currey; Heinemann; Heinemann Kenya, 1991.

Githae-Mugo, Micere. *Visions of Africa: The Fiction of Chinua Achebe, Margaret Laurence, Elspeth Huxley, and Ngugi wa Thiong'o*. Nairobi: Kenya Literature Bureau, 1978.

Greenberg, Jonathan. "Okonkwo and the Storyteller: Death, Accident, and Meaning in Chinua Achebe and Walter Benjamin." *Contemporary Literature* 48:3 (Fall 2007): 423–450.

Gunner, Elizabeth. *A Handbook for Teaching African Literature*. London: Heinemann Educational, 1984.

Herdeck, Donald E. *African Authors: A Companion to Black African Writing. Vol. 1: 1300–1973*. Washington: Black Orpheus, 1973.

Heywood, Christopher. *Chinua Achebe's* Things Fall Apart: *A Critical View*. London: Collins, 1985.

Innes, Catherine Lynette, and Bernth Lindfors, eds. *Critical Perspectives on Chinua Achebe*. Washington, D.C.: Three Continents Press, 1978.

Innes, Catherine Lynette. *Chinua Achebe*. New York: Cambridge University Press, 1990.

Irele, Abiola. *The African Experience in Literature and Ideology*. London: Heinemann, 1979.

Iyasere, Solomon O., ed. *Understanding* Things Fall Apart: *Selected Essays and Criticism*. Troy, New York: Whitston Publishing Company, 1998.

———. "Narrative Techniques in *Things Fall Apart*." *Obsidian* 13 (1975): 73–93.

Jabbi, Bu-Buakei. "Fire and Transition in *Things Fall Apart*." *Obsidian* 13 (1975): 22–36.

JanMohamed, Abdul R. "Sophisticated Primitivism: The Syncretism of Oral and Literate Modes in Achebe's *Things Fall Apart*." *Ariel* 15:4 (1984): 19–39.

Jeyifo, Biodun. *Contemporary Nigerian Literature: A Retrospective and Prospective Exploration*. Lagos: Nigeria Magazine, 1985.

Jones, Eldred. "Language and Theme in *Things Fall Apart*." *Review of English Literature* 5:4 (1964): 39–43.

Kemoli, Arthur, and Leteipa Ole Sunkuli. *Notes on Chinua Achebe's* Things Fall Apart. Nairobi: Heinemann Kenya, 1989.

Kronenfeld, J. Z. "The 'Communalistic' African and the 'Individualistic' Westerner: Some Comments on Misleading Generalizations in Western Criticism of Soyinka and Achebe." *Research in African Literatures* 6 (1975): 199–225.

Lindsfors, Bernth. *Conversations with Chinua Achebe*. Jackson: University Press of Mississippi, 1997.

———. "The Palm-Oil with Which Achebe's Words Are Eaten." *African Literature Today* 1 (1968): 3–18.

Lovesey, Oliver. "Making Use of the Past in *Things Fall Apart*." *Genre: Forms of Discourse and Culture* 39:2 (Summer 2006): 273–300.

Mbiti, John. *Introduction to African Religion*. London: Heinemann, 1975.

Morrell, Karen L., ed. *Person: Achebe, Awoonor, and Soyinka at the University of Washington*. Seattle: African Studies Program, Institute for Comparative and Foreign Area Studies, University of Washington, 1975.

Moses, Michael Valdez. *The Novel and the Globalization of Culture*. New York: Oxford University Press, 1995.

Mudimbe, V. Y. *The Invention of Africa: Gnosis, Philosophy, and the Order of Knowledge*. Bloomington: Indiana University Press, 1988.

Njoku, Benedict Chiaka. *The Four Novels of Chinua Achebe: A Critical Study*. New York: P. Lang, 1984.

Nnolim, Charles. "Achebe's *Things Fall Apart:* An Igbo National Epic." *Modern Black Literature*. New York: Black Academy, 1971: 55–60.

Obiechina, Emmanuel. "Structure and Significance in Achebe's *Things Fall Apart*." *English in Africa* 2:2 (1975): 39–44.

Ogbaa, Kalu. *Understanding* Things Fall Apart: *A Student Casebook to Issues, Sources and Historical Documents*. Westport, Conn.: Greenwood Press, 1999.

———. *Gods, Oracles and Divination: Folkways in Chinua Achebe's Novels*. Trenton, New Jersey: Africa World Press, 1992.

———. "A Cultural Note on Okonkwo's Suicide." *Kunapipi* 3:2 (1981): 126–134.

Ojinmah, Umelo. *Chinua Achebe: New Perspectives*. Ibadan: Spectrum Books Limited, 1991.

Okoye, Emmanuel Meziemadu. *The Traditional Religion and Its Encounter with Christianity in Achebe's Novels*. Bern & New York: Lang, 1987.

Okpala, Jude Chudi. "Igbo Metaphysics in Chinua Achebe's *Things Fall Apart*." *Callaloo: A Journal of African-American and African Arts and Letters* 25:2 (Spring 2002): 559–566.

Okpewho, Isidore. *Chinua Achebe's* Things Fall Apart: *A Casebook*. Oxford, England: Oxford University Press, 2003.

Olufunwa, Harry. "Achebe's Spatial Temporalities: Literary Chronotopes in *Things Fall Apart* and *Arrow of God*." *Critical Survey* 17:3 (2005): 49–65.

Omotso, Kole. *Achebe or Soyinka?: A Study in Contrasts*. London: Northvale, New Jersey: Hans Zell Publishers, 1996.

Ottenberg, Simon. "The Present State of Igbo Studies." *Journal of the Historical Society of Nigeria* 2:2 (1961): 211–230.

Owomoyela, Oyekan. "Chinua Achebe on the Individual in Society." *Journal of African Studies* 12 (1985): 53–65.

Parker, Michael, and Roger Starkey. *Postcolonial Literatures: Achebe, Ngugi, Desai, Walcott.* New York: St. Martin's Press, 1995.

Peters, Jonathan. *A Dance of Masks: Senghor, Achebe, Soyinka.* Washington, D.C.: Three Continents Press, 1978.

Petersen, Kirsten Holst, and Anna Rutherford, eds. *Chinua Achebe: A Celebration.* Oxford, England; Portsmouth, New Hampshire; Sydney, Australia: Heinemann, Dangeroo Press, 1990.

Podis, Leonard A., and Yakubu Saaka, eds. *Challenging Hierarchies: Issues and Themes in Colonial and Post-Colonial African Literature.* New York: P. Lang, 1998.

Robertson, P. J. M. "*Things Fall Apart* and *Heart of Darkness:* A Creative Dialogue." *International Fiction Review* 7 (1980): 106–111.

Salamone, Frank. "The Depiction of Masculinity in Classic Nigerian Literature." *JALA: Journal of the African Literature Association* 1:1 (Winter–Spring 2007): 202–213.

Scafe, Suzanne. "'Wherever Something Stands, Something Else Will Stand Beside It': Ambivalence in Achebe's *Things Fall Apart* and *Arrow of God.*" *Changing English: Studies in Reading and Culture* 9:2 (October 2002): 119–131.

Searle, Alison. "The Role of Missions in *Things Fall Apart* and *Nervous Condition.*" *Literature & Theology: An International Journal of Religion, Theory, and Culture* 21:1 (March 2007), pp. 49–65.

Shelton, Austin J. "'The Palm-Oil' of Language: Proverbs in Chinua Achebe's Novels." *Modern Language Quarterly* 30 (1969): 86–111.

Simola, Raisa. *World Views in Chinua Achebe's Works.* Frankfurt am Main; New York: P. Lang, 1995.

Stock, A. G. "Yeats and Achebe." *Journal of Commonwealth Literature* 5 (1968): 105–111.

Turkington, Kate. *Chinua Achebe:* Things Fall Apart. London: Arnold, 1977.

Ugah, Ada. *In the Beginning . . . : Chinua Achebe at Work.* Ibadan: Heinemann Educational, 1990.

Usongo, Kenneth. "The Tragedies of Shakespeare and Achebe: A Comparison of Morality in Superstition." *Journal of African Literature and Culture* (2006): 31–43.

Uwechie, Cele, and Moses Ugwoke, et al., eds. *Chinua Achebe: A Bio-Bibliography.* Nsukka: Faculty of Arts, University of Nigeria, 1990.

Weinstock, Donald J. "The Two Swarms of Locusts: Judgment by Indirection in *Things Fall Apart.*" *Studies in Black Literature* 2:1 (1972): 14–19.

Winters, Marjorie. "Morning Yet on Judgment Day: The Critics of Chinua Achebe." *Journal of the Literary Society of Nigeria* 1 (1981): 26–39.

Wren, Robert M. *Achebe's World: The Historical and Cultural Context of the Novels of Chinua Achebe.* Washington, D.C.: Three Continents Press, 1980.

Wynter, Sylvia. "History, Ideology and the Reinvention of the Past in Achebe's *Things Fall Apart* and Laye's *The Dark Child.*" *Minority Voices* 2:1 (1978): 43–61.

Yankson, Kofi E. *Chinua Achebe's Novels: A Sociolinguistic Perspective.* Uruowulu-Obosi, Nigeria: Pacific, 1990.

# Acknowledgments

Kwadwo Osei-Nyame. "Chinua Achebe Writing Culture: Representations of Gender and Tradition in *Things Fall Apart*," *Research in African Literatures,* Volume 30, Number 2 (Summer 1999): pp. 148–164. Copyright © 1999 The Indiana University Press. Reprinted by permission of the publisher.

D. N. Mkhize. "The Portrayal of Igbo Culture in Zulu: A Descriptive Analysis of the Translation of Achebe's *Things Fall Apart* into Zulu," *South African Journal of African Languages/Suid-Afrikaanse Tydskrif vir Afrikatale,* Volume 20, Number 2 (2000): pp. 194–204. Copyright © 2000 The University of Port Elizabeth Deaprtment of African Languages. Reprinted by permission of the publisher.

Patrick C. Nnoromele. "The Plight of a Hero in Achebe's *Things Fall Apart*," *College Literature,* Volume 27, Number 2 (Spring 2000): pp. 146–156. Copyright © 2000 Patrick C. Nnoromele. Reprinted by permission of the author.

Ravit Reichman. "Undignified Details: The Colonial Subject of Law." *ARIEL: A Review of International English Literature,* Volume 35, Numbers 1–2 (January–April 2004): pp. 81–100. Copyright © 2004 University of Calgary, Department of English. Reprinted by permission of the publisher.

Joseph R. Slaughter. "A Mouth with Which to Tell the Story": Silence, Violence and Speech in Chinua Achebe's *Things Fall Apart*." *Emerging*

*Perspectives on Chinua Achebe.* Volume 1. *Omenka the Master Artist: Critical Perspectives on Achebe's Fiction.* Ernest N. Emenyonu (ed.). (Trenton, NJ: Africa World, 2004): pp. 121–148. Copyright © 2004 Joseph R. Slaughter. Reprinted by permission of the author.

Mac Fenwick. "Realising Irony's Post/Colonial Promise: Global Sense and Local Meaning in *Things Fall Apart* and 'Ruins of a Great House'," *Kunapipi: Journal of Postcolonial Writing,* Volume 28, Number 1 (2006): pp. 8–21. Copyright © 2006 Mac Fenwick. Reprinted by permission of the author.

Oliver Lovesey. "Making Use of the Past in *Things Fall Apart*," *Genre: Forms of Discourse and Culture,* Volume 39, Number 2 (Summer 2006): pp. 273–299. Copyright © 2006 University of Oklahoma. Reprinted by permission of the publisher.

Frank Salamone. "The Depiction of Masculinity in Classic Nigerian Literature." *JALA: Journal of the African Literature Association,* Volume 1, Number 1 (Winter–Spring 2007): pp. 202–213. Copyright © 2007 Frank Salamone. Reprinted by permission of the author.

Andrea Powell Wolfe. "Problematizing Polygyny in the Historical Novels of Chinua Achebe: The Role of the Western Feminist Scholar," *Research in African Literatures,* Volume 39, Number 1 (Spring 2008): pp. 166–185. Copyright © 2008 The Indiana University Press. Reprinted by permission of the publisher.

Carey Snyder. "The Possibilities and Pitfalls of Ethnographic Readings: Narrative Complexity in *Things Fall Apart*," *College Literature,* Volume 35, Number 2 (Spring 2008): pp. 154–174. Copyright © 2008 West Chester University. Reprinted by permission of the publisher.

# Index